In the Forests of the Night

John Simpson is Foreign Affairs Editor of the BBC, where he has covered many of the most important events of the past twenty years. Following his coverage of the Gulf War he was made a CBE, named TV Journalist of the Year and given The Richard Dimbleby Award.

John Simpson is the author of *The Darkness Crumbles*, *From the House of War*, and *Dispatches From The Barricades*

IN THE FORESTS OF
THE NIGHT

Encounters in Peru with Terrorism,
Drug-Running and Military Oppression

John Simpson

ARROW

To those people we met in Peru who had the courage to speak out;

to my companions, who turned a difficult journey into something to be recalled with pleasure;

and to my daughter Julia, *la flor del rosal*.

Published by Arrow Books in 1994

1 3 5 7 9 10 8 6 4 2

© John Simpson 1993

First published in the United Kingdom by Hutchinson, in 1993

Arrow Books Limited
Random House UK Ltd, 20 Vauxhall Bridge Road, London SW1V 2SA

Random House Australia (Pty) Limited
20 Alfred Street, Milsons Point, Sydney,
New South Wales 2061, Australia

Random House New Zealand Limited
18 Poland Road, Glenfield
Auckland 10, New Zealand

Random House South Africa (Pty) Limited
PO Box 337, Bergvlei, South Africa

Random House UK Limited Reg. No. 954009

A CIP catalogue record for this book
is available from the British Library

ISBN 0 09 927181 8

Printed and bound in Great Britain by
Cox & Wyman Ltd, Reading, Berkshire

Contents

SONG OF DARKNESS

Secret darkness,
dark secret,
darkness that conceals.

    Felipe Guaman Poma de Ayala

SONG OF SUFFERING

Song, the song of sadness.
Queen, what evil enemy
Destroys us and controls us?

    Felipe Guaman Poma de Ayala

A Note on the Line-Drawings

The illustrations at the start of each section are taken from Felipe Guaman Poma de Ayala's book *New Chronicle and Good Government*, completed in 1613.

Page 1 ('Prologue'): Guaman Poma takes the road to Lima in the rain, to send the manuscript of his book to King Philip III in Spain. With him are his son Francisco, his horse Guiado, and his two dogs Amigo (left) and Lautaro, each thoughtfully labelled.

Page 9 ('To The Rainforest'): The indians of Antisuyu in the Amazonian rainforest make offerings to their gods, which include a large jaguar. The indians wear clothes similar to those of the Ashaninca today.

Page 57 ('Following The Shining Path'): The city of Lima, whose proper name is Los Reis de Lima. In the square in front of the cathedral stands a gallows.

Page 127 ('Valley of The Shadow'): A Spanish official takes a bribe.

Page 241 ('With The Real People'): The spirits of the river sing a song, accompanied on the flute by two indians on the cliff-top.

Page 263 ('Heart of Darkness'): A Spanish priest and a civilian attack two indians.

Page 295 ('Aftermath'): Guaman Poma has an imaginary conversation with King Philip III.

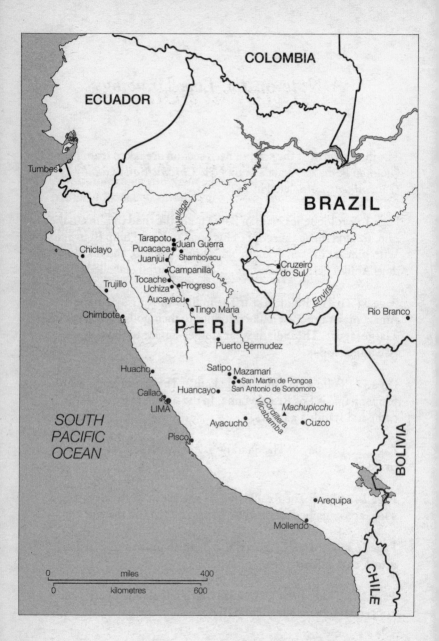

Introduction

This is the story of an expedition: not in the sense of a journey to an empty area on the map, but an exploration of the dark areas of a country where things have gone terribly wrong, and where serious and frightening crimes have been and are still being committed. Most people in the outside world know little about Peru, apart from its Inca past. Yet it impinges increasingly on almost all of us, because it is the place where most of the world's cocaine supplies originate. A growing proportion of the crimes that are committed in Britain, France, or the United States take place at the far end of a chain which starts in the vast coca plantations of Peru.

The country that has suffered most is Peru itself, a victim of the devastating effects of terrorism and the international drugs trade. In 1992, I travelled round it with a group of friends and colleagues, exploring a hinterland of violence and despair which few outsiders have penetrated.

This hinterland can be found in many places in Peru. Part of it lies in the Amazonian rainforest. Part of it is in the Huallaga Valley, in the north-east of the country, which produces more than 70 per cent of the raw material of the entire world's cocaine supply. Part is in the terrible, degrading shanty-towns on the edge of the capital, Lima. Part is in the underground structure of Shining Path, the Maoist guerrilla organisation which has rightly been described as the world's deadliest revolutionary force. And part is in the government of the country itself, which the Vice President of Peru described to us as being in the hands of a mafia tied up with drugs trafficking and murder.

The results of our expedition appeared in the television reports my colleagues and I produced in the autumn of 1992 for the BBC, ABC in the United States, CBC in Canada, ZDF in Germany, and

ABC in Australia; and in articles I wrote for the *Spectator*. In them we provided evidence of the deep involvement of sections of the Peruvian Army in the cocaine trade, as well as in serious abuses of human rights; and we showed the links between these things and the most powerful of the President's officials.

This book is about our experiences in the forests of the night, where terrorism and drugs-trafficking and the most appalling injustice have taken root. Some of these experiences were melodramatic, to say the least, but this is an area where melodrama comes naturally. They ranged from swimming a river infested with piranha and sampling the hallucinogenic drugs of Amazonian indians to encountering groups of terrorists and going to confront the military commanders responsible for the torture, rape and murder of hundreds of people. Yet our experiences were nothing compared with those of the people we met: the wives and parents of people who had been murdered, and the few brave characters who were prepared to come forward and describe what was really going on.

Because of people like them, this is by no means a story of unmitigated evil; and some of the heroes are unexpected ones. Peru is not necessarily the South America of popular Western imagination. It is a country which prides itself on its freedom and decency, so we should not be altogether surprised that the general in charge of one of Peru's secret police organisations emerges as a particularly strong defender of liberty and the rule of law.

In this account of our journey into the Peruvian hinterland I have not been tempted to polish up the facts or make them fit more neatly into a narrative structure: they happened to us in the way I have set out here. Nor was the dialogue reconstructed afterwards on the basis of a vague memory. Much of it has been transcribed from the original video tapes, and I jotted down the rest in my notebook as or immediately after it was spoken. My companions soon grew used to the idea that everything they said was being taken down and used; though not, I hope, against them.

They were a courageous and amusing group, and this book is intended partly as a tribute to them. Another companion was there only as a guiding spirit: an eccentric character who roamed Peru four hundred years before we did. Felipe Guaman Poma de Ayala was an Inca nobleman who wrote in 1613 about the conditions he had witnessed in thirty years of travel in its mountains and cities. The more I listened to people's stories in 1992, the closer some of them seemed to be to the abuses which Guaman Poma uncovered. I have used quotations from his *New Chronicle and Good Government* as an occasional device to take me through modern Peru, while his charming, idiosyncratic drawings appear at the head of each of the main sections of this book. The quotations, which appear at the start of each new section, are taken from the most recent English edition of his book, translated by Christopher Dilke and published under the title *Letter to a King* (Allen & Unwin, 1978).

One note of mild warning: at the risk of causing some irritation, I have spelled 'indian' with a lower case 'i' because it seems ludicrous that five hundred years after Christopher Columbus' classic error we should still refer to the original peoples of America as though they have something to do with the Indian subcontinent. Nevertheless, when I quote someone else I leave the word as they spell it. I rejected 'natives' as sounding too imperialistic, and 'indigenous inhabitants' as an unwieldy piece of political correctness.

A brief note on pronunciation: place-names like Huallaga and Huacho are indian words clad in Spanish orthography. These two should be pronounced, respectively, 'Wy-aga' and 'Watcho', since the Spanish transliterated the 'W' sounds of Quetchua by 'Hu'. Strictly speaking, I should have spelled Guaman Poma's name with an 'H' instead of a 'G', since this was an earlier form of the transliteration; but this was the way he spelled it himself.

I owe a debt of gratitude to many people. Some are named, and implicitly thanked, in the pages that follow. Others deserve special mention here: in particular, Simon Strong, Phil Gunson, William Fairbairne of the Canadian Church Committee on Human Rights, Peter Archard of Amnesty International, Rosemary Thorpe of St Anthony's College, Oxford, Nicholas Shakespeare, David Bradfield, Mike Goldwater, Alex Shankland, Clive Nettleton, Tim Bowyer and Pam Rumford of Health Unlimited, Anthony Daniels, Jonathan Kavanagh, Hernando de Soto, Carlos Ivan Degregori, Pilar Coll, Michel Azqueta, Nelson Manrique, Enrique

Zileri, Diana Zileri, Alejandro Diez Canseco, Jose Borneo, and Gustavo Gorriti. Keith and Toni Haskell and Russell Baker from the British embassy in Lima were most helpful and hospitable, yet bear no responsibility for anything I have said in this book. Noelle Britton worked hard on the early research. The people in the BBC News Stills Library were generous with their time. Sue Aldridge, my assistant in the Foreign Affairs Unit at the BBC, was tirelessly helpful, managing to keep in contact with me almost daily while I was in Peru and (as ever) finding all the things I needed when I returned; including Guaman Poma's book. Rosalind Bain, having endured the excitements of the trip, checked the manuscript to see whether I had got the facts right, and corrected my bad Spanish. Matt Leiper took the photographs in Peru. Thanks should also go to Maria McCarthy at the Chelsea Arts Club, and to Graham and Mary Bloomfield and the Fullers of the Lord Nelson Beach Hotel, Antigua, possibly the pleasantest small hotel in the world, where I began to write this. To Neil Belton, who first commissioned the book, and to Anthony Whittome who continued with it, I owe a debt of considerable gratitude; as I do to Tira Shubart, whose help and support were as unstinting as ever.

PART I

PROLOGUE

Felipe Guaman Poma de Ayala takes the road to Lima in the rain to send the manuscript of his book to King Philip III in Spain. With him are his son Francisco, his horse Guiado, and his two dogs Amigo and Lautaro, each thoughtfully labelled.

Rainforest

Antisuyu, which extends from Cuzco to the jungles of the
Amazon. . .

Felipe Guaman Poma de Ayala, 1613

There was a low, mechanical, industrial hum of insects:
the forest was producing and reproducing and decaying
and dying as actively and impersonally as a factory. There were
creeping, dripping sounds, and the descending note, pa-pa-peew,
of a bird in the forest canopy above me, and something that
sounded like the screeching of brakes, and a slithering noise
that came to a sudden stop. A leaf trembled with a regular
movement, its shadow flickering across the trunk of the tree
it sprang from. The dankness was hot and breathable; it filled
the throat with its nasty rich decay. Every leaf on every tree and
bush was shabby, mouldy, insect-chewed. Everything fed, and fed
on, everything else. Leaves the size of clock-faces hung on the
branches of trees, as though Dali had painted over a canvas by
Rousseau. One leaf, fifty feet up in the forest canopy, dropped
slowly towards the ground with a sound that sent vibrations
of nervousness and fear echoing through the entire area. It felt
increasingly disturbing to have to keep my back turned always
to one or other part of the forest. I could not see more than
five yards in any direction. In the darkness beyond that, there
seemed to be constant movement and noise and activity; yet
immediately in front of me everything was silent. A dead tree lay
across the path, forked like legs from buttocks, green with moss,
covered with brown and grey leaves. Large ants, blond in the
sunlight, marched purposefully along it waving irregularly shaped
pieces of green leaf like banners on a battlefield. A bird or a
monkey burst through the canopy somewhere overhead, and

the chatter of the insects suddenly went quiet. It was disturbing enough by day, I thought; what must it be like to be here at night?

Tocache

I decided that my intention was a rash one, and that, once started upon my story, I would never be able to complete it in the way in which a proper history ought to be written.

Felipe Guaman Poma de Ayala, 1613

In the rich, foul, thick atmosphere we sat and sweated, panting like dogs after a run. All we had done was unload our gear from the plane and carry it over to the open-air bar nearby, but this was a town in a place that had once been rainforest, low-lying and stiflingly damp. I went over and smiled at the tough-looking woman behind the counter. She showed me the gap in her front teeth, and reached into a rusting refrigerator for six bottles of distastefully-coloured yellow liquid: InkaCola, Peru's answer to American soft-drink imports.

'*Do*' *mil soles*,' she said.

I handed over the two thousand sols in furred notes and she went back to staring at the thick green jungle opposite. I carried the six bottles past a table where four men in uniform had been playing cards until we turned up. Their guns lay beside them on the ground. This was not a place where visitors were welcomed. Things were going on in Tocache which they preferred to keep to themselves: profitable, discreditable things. They looked at our television equipment, and they looked at us. We tried to avoid eye-contact with them, as you avoid a quarrelsome drunk.

A large blue Landcruiser drew up. Two nervous faces peered out at us through the windscreen. These were our contacts, the people who had said they would help us here. We were hoping they would put us in touch with a man we had come here to see. Our Peruvian fixer Cecilia, blonde and pretty, went over to talk to them, taking with her the stares of everyone at the bar. She gesticulated a little, and walked back towards us.

5

The Landcruiser started up harshly, and its wheels spun in the dust.

'Huancas,' she said dismissively, her face setting into its do-or-die look. 'They too fear to aid us.' If only her English matched her courage and determination, I thought. The Landcruiser disappeared down the dirt road in a little cloud of its own creation, and things were quiet again. The four men at the nearby table looked across at us. It could only be a matter of time before they came over and started giving us trouble. In the distant heat haze, there was a new sound, like an angry wasp attacking a fallen apple. From the direction in which the Landcruiser had disappeared there was another cloud, smaller and more insistent and somehow less apologetic. It grew, and turned into a man on an underpowered Japanese motorcycle. I looked at Cecilia.

'It is him,' she said.

We wouldn't need the two in the Landcruiser now. The man we had come to see, the man who was prepared to tell us in detail about the Peruvian Army's involvement in the cocaine trade and its habit of torturing and murdering anyone who questioned its activities, had come out to meet us himself. He parked carefully, as though this were Lima instead of a dusty open-air bar at an airstrip in coca-growing country. He was as small and compact as his motorcycle, a neat man with a carefully constructed moustache. The fact that he had come to meet us in full view of the uniformed men at the nearby table might in itself be enough to get him murdered. It was a risk he had decided to take, for reasons the men at the table would have difficulty in understanding. I shook his hand and looked down at him. It was a very firm handshake indeed.

We climbed into two taxis which looked as though they might have difficulty moving. He led the way on his motorcycle, sitting firm and upright in the saddle: a little man who wanted to clean up one of the nastiest towns in Peru, and who thought the best way to do it was to talk to us. The dust flowed around him and into the unclosable windows of our taxi like dry ice in a pantomime. The breeze was unbearably hot. Another car started up somewhere behind us, and followed us a little way down the road before stopping. I opened my notebook. My hand jerked with every rut in the unpaved road, leaving damp patches on the page where the ink would not take.

'If we get out of this, great story.' Even as I wrote it, I thought it was an absurdly trivial way to describe the situation.

PART II

TO THE RAINFOREST

The indians of Antisuyu in the Amazonian rainforest make offerings to their gods, which include a large jaguar. The indians wear clothes similar to those of the Ashaninca today.

Brazil

The Anti [Indians] still live in their mountains and forests beyond the rivers, among poisonous snakes, beasts of prey, monkeys and parrots, and are rich in gold and silver

Felipe Guaman Poma de Ayala, 1613

It had its origins, as so many things do, in guilt.

The worst kind of January London day was lashing the windows with sleet. From seven floors up, Shepherd's Bush looked like East Berlin. The standard-issue BBC curtains, long narrow vertical strips of some plasticated material the colour of porridge, whipped and shook where the wind leaked into the office. I was in a prefabricated box, fixed as an afterthought onto the flat roof of Television Centre: one of the ugliest buildings in London. In this wind, the box felt as if it might blow away.

A youngish man, thin and pale, sat at the desk in front of me. He had a bad cold. I, by contrast, had just come back from the Caribbean. That was one reason to feel guilty. The other was that I had let him down badly not long before. He was the editor of the current affairs programme 'Newsnight', and for a time I had been his stand-in presenter, contracted to appear in studio forty days a year. Whenever he asked me what would happen if one of my days of presenting clashed with some big news event I might want to cover, I would always say there would be no problem. I really meant it.

Then, on the day of the coup against Mikhail Gorbachev in Moscow on 19 August 1991, I came in to present 'Newsnight' as scheduled. All the regular presenters were on holiday. I was resigned to watching the events in Moscow from a distance, since there was no possibility of my getting a visa to go there. But someone noticed that an unused Soviet visa I had been given some months before was valid until midnight that night. An hour later I was boarding a plane, and the editor of 'Newsnight' was looking round for someone else to present his programme.

Now Tim Gardam looked across his desk at me speculatively, and blew his nose. I felt a considerable affection for him: he was a good ten years younger than I, and very bright. He was a fierce defender of his programme and its staff, and he had supported me at editorial meetings at various times in the past. His frame seemed almost too frail for his intellect, like that of a mediaeval theologian who had gone in for too much study and fasting. He appeared to regard me in a very different light: as a noisy early Victorian adventurer, perhaps, always impatient to go off and do a little empire-building.

I had come here to see him, not in the spirit of his notion about me but of mine about him: as a penitent, not an imperialist. Because I still felt badly about having let him down, I offered meekly to undertake any project he might have in mind. That in itself was a measure of my contrition: usually I like to have the ideas, and sell them to other people.

The wind whipped the curtains, the sleet hammered on the glass. Tim Gardam sneezed. I looked down at the brown backs of my hands.

'Have you ever thought about Peru?' he asked nasally, putting his handkerchief away. I couldn't say I had, very much: I had seen Anthony Shaffer's play *The Royal Hunt of the Sun*, and read Thornton Wilder's *The Bridge of San Luis Rey* and some books by Mario Vargas Llosa. Apart from a few news reports about the Shining Path guerrilla movement, that was the extent of it.

'Because it's exactly your sort of place: collapsing society, world's nastiest terrorists, Army out of control, that kind of thing. It would make a really splendid television essay: "I see the structure of civilisation crumbling around me". You'd love it.'

Why, I wondered, should anyone think I loved that kind of thing? But in the spirit of penitence I said, yes, it sounded tremendous; anyway, it was true that I had always wanted to visit the Inca ruins, so perhaps I could visit the ruins of Peru while I was at it. He smiled politely, then said 'Newsnight' would assemble a producer and a camera team for the project. He would raise the money by inviting a number of friendly television companies – Canadian, Australian, American, German, maybe one from Japan – to come in as investors. He sneezed again. I thought I had better leave, before he thought of somewhere worse for me to go.

I read a good deal about Peru over the next few months, and the more I read the more nervous I became. It was a seriously dangerous place. Journalists who dug too deeply into the activities either of the Shining Path guerrilla movement or the Peruvian Army frequently ended up dying by the roadside. More of them have died in Peru than in any of the wars which have taken place since Vietnam, the war in what was Yugoslavia included. Friends of mine who knew something of the country began to warn me against going. One of my fellow-contributors to the *Spectator* described in some medical detail the corpse he had found somewhere outside Lima: Shining Path had skinned the victim's head while he was still alive. A colleague told me that a woman journalist had been invited to the gaol where Shining Path prisoners were held, because they had an important message for the Western press. They seized her and pulled out her tongue: that was the message. It was hard, in London, to work out which of these stories were true and which fantasy; though the head was certainly true, since a photograph of it could be examined by those with a strong stomach.

Another friend told me how he had been walking down a street in an expensive section of Lima, and had been dragged into a passing truck. As it drove around, the men inside 'tried' him for being a Western capitalist, found him guilty, but failed to decide what to do with him. Eventually they threw him out as they drove through one of the roughest shantytowns on the outskirts of Lima. He was more worried than ever, he said; there was a persistent belief among many Peruvian indians that white men boiled them down to make oil, and some had taken to doing the same thing to white men first. Going to Peru was beginning to seem like a bad career move, as we say in the BBC.

Inevitably, though, other things pushed Peru into the background. I reported on John Major's victorious campaign in the British general election in March and April. There was the usual small change of my life as a specialist on foreign affairs: conferences, summits, European Council meetings, none of them the stuff of which memoirs are made. I became convinced, quite wrongly, that the most important event of 1992 would be the forthcoming meeting of presidents and prime ministers in Rio de Janeiro, to discuss the increasingly alarming state of the environment.

Yet all this time Peru was simmering away in my mind, and I read whatever I could about it. The subject touched on the general anxiety about the future of the planet and the state of the Third World, rather like a shantytown abuts onto a vast, poverty-stricken metropolis. Peru's concerns were those of the rest of the world, only wilder and more extreme: an example of what debt and political instability and a collapsing economy could do to a country. It lay, frightening and sick, on the outskirts of the world's awareness. It needed visiting.

Before the Rio conference began, I had decided to spend some time in the Amazonian jungle. I was lucky enough to be a patron of the small but highly effective medical charity, Health Unlimited, which operated in areas where people's lives had been wrecked by conflict of some kind: the areas where many of the bigger charities did not work. Health Unlimited had a couple of projects in the Brazilian rainforest. On Monday 11 May, a pleasant, golden spring evening in London, I caught a plane for Sao Paulo. I was going to visit Health Unlimited's man there and travel with him to the farthest reaches of his territory.

It was not a good morning to be in Sao Paulo. There was a bus strike, and everybody with a car drove to work, so the carbon monoxide level that day was 55 per cent higher than usual. We left the newly risen sun behind us and headed into the dark brown cloud which lay over the entire city. My taxi driver, a laconic man, took the less congested outer road at 75 miles an hour, twenty feet behind the car in front. Soon, though, we were becalmed in traffic and I could pay attention to the strange runic graffiti on the walls, the angry political slogans and the immense, extraordinary advertisements. The blank side of an apartment building was covered to a depth of five storeys by an enormous picture of a pair of women's panties. CALCINHAS HOPE 90, said the legend; the crotch alone covered an entire floor. How strange, I thought, to live on that floor.

In spite of the traffic I arrived too early to check into my hotel and too early to contact the man from Health Unlimited. I went to the Salao Phidias for a shave and a haircut. The abilities of the barber, a small energetic man called Jorge, were celebrated by dozens of certificates and statuettes, draped with patriotic yellow and green ribbons. Jorge shaved me with great panache and accuracy, letting his hand hang in the air after each stroke like a painter. Then, while a lesser employee raised my shoes to an unreasonably high oxblood gloss, my nose-hair, eyebrows and the sprouts from my ears were delicately scissored off and I was ready.

Alex Shankland of Health Unlimited proved to be a tall, fairhaired Englishman in his early twenties. In a previous decade he might have been a Collector or a District Commissioner in some distant imperial province; now, most of the Empire having largely evaporated, he administered various projects which meant the difference between disease and health for hundreds, perhaps thousands, of Amazonian indians. Among them were the indians of the Campa tribe. I had read about the Campa. At the time of the Spanish conquest of Peru they had sided with the Inca rebels.

'The Campa have come from Peru,' Alex said, not knowing the effect his words had on me. He was swinging in a hammock which he had set up in his flat, indian-style. 'They've been having a terrible time with Shining Path there. Shining Path. . .'

'I know who Shining Path are,' I said. 'It's the Campa I want to know more about.'

'You'll meet them in five days' time,' Alex said.

Five days later I was sitting in the bow of a long dugout canoe, on a river the colour and general temperature of the tea they serve in workmen's cafés in England. The river was the Envira, a tributary of a tributary of the Amazon. Even so it was one of the biggest rivers I had ever seen. Dark foliage ran down to the water's edge, and white birds like egrets floated elegantly along in front of us, pausing briefly at sandbanks or partly submerged trees which had fallen into the river and jammed there. We were a very long way indeed from any form of civilisation.

There were eight of us in the canoe: Alex and I, in the bows; an English photographer-cameraman, Mike Goldwater, whom I had met briefly once at Health Unlimited's office in London and had taken an immediate liking to; three indians who were being trained as health workers, but whose immediate job on the river was to fend off and tie up, and act as lookouts when the sun went down; a saturnine Brazilian of mostly African origin, who had great contempt for townies like me and possessed apparently telepathic powers which enabled him to steer the boat between the hazards of the river for fourteen hours or more, with scarcely a break; and the most important person on board, Dr Maria Bittencour.

Maria was in her late twenties, and could have lived the fashionable life of a doctor in the wealthy, comfortable cities of Brazil's Atlantic coast where she had been brought up. Instead she worked with the indians along the river. She was a farouche and beautiful young woman, but the life she led in the forest and on the river was already beginning to show its effects on her. Her delicate skin was becoming lined and the flesh on her arms and legs was shrinking. When I first met her, at the big houseboat which served as her mobile base, I thought for a moment that her feet and ankles, which were permanently bare, were finely tattooed: they were marked with hundreds of reddish dots. I soon realised what produced the dots: *pium*, tiny black flies which gathered round you in clouds and raised big welts with their bites, the worst affliction on the river. She must have suffered thousands of bites in the two years she had been working on the Envira, and each of them had left its scar.

I looked around me with keen pleasure, despite the *pium*. There was less wildlife than I might have expected – perhaps the noise of our outboard motor, like an old Harley-Davidson, had frightened it away – but small black and white birds with red legs strutted the sandbanks, and four macaws flew overhead two by two, stretching out their long green tails and screeching in excitement and companionable fear when they saw us. We kept in to the left bank; bamboo trees which were mostly secondary growth along the river's edge towered over us. I asked the name of a particularly grand and delicate tree with a silvery bark, whose tracery stretched out over the lesser growths.

'It is the *samauma* tree,' said the indian reflectively, 'and it is sacred to us because when our shamans die their spirits live in its branches.'

'Oh yes,' said one of the others, a noticeably plump indian who was training to be a health worker, 'and when it is in bloom, we call it fat-monkey season.' The others laughed in appreciation: monkeys are a considerable delicacy in the forest.

There was another tree, not so grand but more beautiful, with flame-like red flowers. It was, Maria said, the *mulugu*, the most beautiful tree in the forest. I saw from the river what I had observed earlier as we flew over the forest: that the *mulugu* trees, like all the other species in the forest, never grew together in a clump but were scattered at a distance of fifty or a hundred feet apart in the forest canopy. It was a natural defence against disease; the Brazilian government, in its attempts to replant the forest with eucalyptus, might have succeeded better if it had realised why the trees in the forest always spaced themselves out naturally.

The air along the river was distinctly cooler, maybe 45 degrees Centigrade, and the motion of the boat as it pushed its way up-current at a steady four miles per hour created a breeze which kept the *pium* and the mosquitoes away. Great tawny dragonflies buzzed around us like minuscule helicopters. In the earth-reddened waters of the river, thick and gritty, the fallen trees reared up like the skeletons of water-monsters. Sometimes their branches nodded ominously at us in the current. I looked across at the sandbanks on either side, white in the powerful sunlight, and at the thick forest wall behind. God help us, I thought, if our canoe sinks. The surface of the water lay only three inches below our heavy-laden gunwhale, and there was no saying what lived in the depths of the river.

We had made our first contact with indians the previous day, and had spent the night in their village. These were not from the Campa tribe; instead they were Kulina, who had mostly taken to wearing the ragged T-shirts and shorts of the rootless town indians. At first I had found the village, which was called Igarape do Anjo, an ugly, illusion-damaging place. Empty tortoise-shells lay around the approach to it, and a macaw which was to be eaten that night had been badly mutilated to stop it escaping. It screeched constantly in pain and terror. The corpse of a skinned monkey, its teeth bared and its fists clenched like a blackened embryo's, turned on a spit. The villagers were dirty, and some of them had unpleasant sores.

Gradually, though, I realised that it was my sentimentality which was affronted by Igarape: I wanted the indians of the forest not simply to be noble savages, untouched by the world, but also to be environmentally sound and photogenic and nature-loving in a strictly Western European, late twentieth-century sense. I resolved to watch them more carefully, and judge them according to their own terms, rather than mine.

When we arrived, there was an emergency in the village. A seven-year-old girl was in the last stages of meningitis, and lay on the floor in her parents' hut, her arms and body twitching convulsively. Maria knelt beside her and examined her, but she could see at once that there was little hope of saving her. Still, it would make a bad impression on the Kulina if she were simply to give up, so she announced that she would be taking the girl back down the river to her houseboat, and would ask for a plane to come in to the small airstrip and fly her to hospital from there. Within half an hour Maria and the girl were in the dugout, and the big Brazilian boatman was piloting them downstream. We watched them from the tops of the bluffs, their wake covering the whole broad river and glinting in the afternoon sunlight.

The village shaman, a sharp, clever man who had lost his right thumb in a hunting accident in the forest, announced that he would prepare *dime*, the hallucinogenic drink of the rainforest, so that the villagers could pray for the girl's recovery. He gathered branches of the *ayahuasca* vine and split them, then crushed them together with the leaves and berries of the *chacrona* plant and put them all into a large metal cauldron over a specially prepared fire. Each part of the operation was accompanied by an incantation. Soon the mixture, greenish-brown, was seething in the pot. The fierce heat of the day began to relent, and near the shaman a young boy lay in his hammock and played a tune on a little mouthbow which was so quiet and delicate that it was more for the player's enjoyment than for any audience.

Around us the dung beetles were working away on the available material, making an 'om' noise like the chanting of distant Buddhist monks. Mike, Alex and I put up our hammocks in the communal hut of the village and lay there, waiting for the events of the evening, talking quietly and relishing the gradual coolness. Enormous banks of cloud built up overhead in a sky which became a fiery orange, then crimson, then faded to a lapis lazuli blue. A moon the colour of an old English copper penny rose over the forest.

In the moonlight two small girls were sweeping the dancing area on the clifftop. The shaman, grunting, carried over the cauldron of still-warm *dime* and set it up in the middle. A man in a nearby hut lay in a hammock and taught his children by rote from a book in the golden light of a wick floating in some oil from the forest. The quiet, reflective sounds of a flute somewhere mingled with the children's voices as they chanted the responses: '*Make, maku, make, maparu, maboru, mabure.*' I could distinguish the delicate whisper of the mouthbow in the near-darkness nearby. It was as pleasing a scene as I had ever witnessed.

A small crowd of men and women had gathered round the cauldron. Alex, Mike and I had all decided to drink the *dime*, but Mike and I were hoping we could limit ourselves to a small amount of it. We had been told that it would rid us of devils; by which the indians seemed to mean that it would make us horribly, retchingly sick. Alex, who had drunk it several times in the past and was becoming increasingly expert in the ways of the indians, said they believed the *ayahuasca* vine opened the door to knowledge, while the berries and leaves of the *chacrona* made voices speak. I felt distinctly uncertain about it all. The shaman dipped a cup into the brew and blew into it with great intensity; he held it out to one of the older men, touching him first on the left shoulder, then on the right, then on the forehead. Then it was my turn. The cup touched me, and was put to my lips. Somehow my intention to drink a sip or two faded: I was expected to drain it, as everyone else had done. There was no point in delaying: I took one long gulp, looked over the cup at the shaman, and downed the rest, for better or worse. It was faintly warm and gritty, and had the bitterness of *maté*, the herbal drink of the South American pampas. The aftertaste lingered an unpleasantly long time, somewhere at the back of the throat.

Alex and Mike followed me in drinking from the cup. I looked at my watch and wondered how long it would be before I felt the effects. Alex sat down in the moonlight. Mike and I went over to film the twelve young girls, two of them with babies at their breasts, who were dancing an intricate little dance opposite five of the old men of the village, stepping towards them then away as the old men moved forwards, and singing an enchanting, wistful little song with a constant refrain:

Hendi peepu, hendi peepu, hendi peepu.

I stayed with Mike, shining a torch on to the group as he filmed: it was our only means of camera lighting. After half an hour, he put down the video camera and started shooting stills of the dancers. Since my torch was no longer needed, I wandered away and lay down not far from Alex. The *dime* was working on him: he sat with his head in his hands, exclaiming with pleasure. I assumed, with a mixture of disappointment and relief, that the drug's effects had passed me by. Still, my notebook was open beside me to record any experiences I might have; and within five minutes of sitting down, I began writing: 'Now at 9.20, beginning effect.' You have to think what you want to ask the drink, Alex had said earlier; so I looked up at the stars and thought, I want to see them. Immediately, shooting stars began flashing across the sky from right to left, blue, green and rose-red. My head seemed to leave my body and hover in the air a little way away, and I was conscious that I was making a fierce, or perhaps a wildly happy, grimace, my mouth stretched open as far as it would go. 'Red light,' I confided in my notebook, 'is coming from my pen as I write this.'

My writing was becoming much larger, and each word was an inch or more high. 'Now stars and colours,' I wrote with unimaginative vagueness. 'MY HANDS ARE VERY HEAVY.

I'M ALSO LAUGHING STUPIDLY. ALEX IS TALKING ABOUT PEOPLE BEING LIT UP WITH RADIUM.' By this time Mike had finished taking pictures and was lying down beside us, laughing in a low, reflective kind of way and saying things which at the time had a profound ring to them: 'The words are taking on all sorts of meanings, and more than merely sound.' In the background the girls were still dancing, and had taken up a new chant:

> *Anoyn, anoyn, anoynday,*
> *anoyn, a-a-a-a-anoyn, anoynday,*
> *anoynday.*

By now, I noted in huge straggling letters, I was finding it very hard to get the pen on to the paper: it seemed to want to write in the air, six inches or more above my notebook. A group of trees between two huts turned into the great gate of Babylon, which I had once seen in the archaeological museum in East Berlin. What was more, the two rampant lions on either side of the gate, reaching upwards as thin and as long as greyhounds, started talking to each other and arguing about the stars. Then the right-hand one turned to me. 'Don't you think I'm right?' he asked. I mumbled a reply and closed my eyes. My attention was taken by a goldfish of about my height – six feet, two inches tall – wearing a straw hat and dark glasses. He was standing on his tail, and put his fin round my shoulder. 'How's it going, man?' he asked. I assured him it was going just fine, and he disappeared. I opened my eyes again and noted this down; 'YET,' I added cautiously, in enormous letters, 'I CAN SPEAK PERFECTLY NORMALLY AND REMEMBER DIFFICULT WORDS.'

It was true, though expressed in pedestrian terms. This was not the near-incapacity engendered by alcohol, it was a heightened and fantastical awareness of sensation. Still, a six-foot goldfish and talking lions on the great gate of Babylon scarcely constituted a great mystical experience, and afterwards I was disappointed by the ludicrousness of it all; rather like Thomas Huxley, who awoke with impatience to read the secret of the universe which he had jotted down during the night, and found he had written 'Higamus hogamus, woman is monogamous; Hogamus higamus, man is polygamous.'

Mike exclaimed and pointed up at the moon. It seemed enormous and precise, like a painting on a ceiling twenty feet above my head. Yet as I examined the exactness of detail in the craters and plains on its surface, a mist covered it and sent it spinning backwards in space, so that it resumed something of its old size again. But not its colour: it was fading to gold, and turned silver only when the mist thickened.

Across the open space in the middle of the village the indians were sprawled around, laughing just as Mike and I were, or sitting solitarily like Alex, their eyes closed. The girls were still dancing, but they were convulsed with laughter at the older men, who were falling over themselves with the influence of the drug. Yet the pleasantest thing was that it never assumed total control. When I thought it was getting the better of me, I could always stop and resume my normal awareness; and when I wanted to see again the colours and visions which the dime brought, I had only to close my eyes and concentrate for them to come back. *Dime* is a drug for those who do not necessarily like drugs.

At 2.30, six hours after we had drunk from the cauldron, the influence was still as strongly upon us as ever. We decided to go to bed. As I lay in my hammock, under the linen sheet which kept out the *pium* better than any mosquito netting, I could still hear the high, gentle, sleepy voices of the girls as they danced:

> *Anoyn, anoyn, anoynday,*
> *anoyn, a-a-a-a-anoynday, anoynday.*

Afterwards, when I was back in London, I read an account by the sixteenth-century French explorer Jean de Lery, who had reached Brazil in 1557, about the singing of a group of indian women. It affected him much as I was affected now. In his *History of a Voyage to the Land of Brazil* he wrote:

> At the beginning of this witches' sabbath, when I was in the women's house, I had been somewhat afraid; now I received in recompense such joy, hearing the measured harmonies of such a multitude, and especially in the cadence and refrain of the song, when at every verse all of them would let their voices trail, saying 'Heu, heuare, heura, heuraure, heura, heura, oueh' – I stood

there transported with delight. Whenever I remember it, my heart trembles, and it seems their voices are still in my ears.

And in much the same way, as I write these words a full year afterwards, the gentle, drowsy, delicate words of the Kulina girls are still in my ears, too, and they fill the room with delight at the mere memory.

Simpatia

The inhabitants of the virgin forest itself did not have any developed system of worship, but this was replaced by the great fear which they felt at the prospect of being devoured or attacked by jaguars or snakes.

Felipe Guaman Poma de Ayala, 1613

Now our canoe left the stretch of river where the Kulina lived, and headed farther upstream into Campa territory. For me, this was the most important part of our visit. In the history of the conquest of Peru by Pizarro, the Campa played a small but noteworthy part; and as we threaded our way between the sandbanks and the sinister, whitened branches of half-submerged trees in the stream, I reflected on their loyalty to the defeated Incas and the fear they had inspired in the Spanish conquistadores.

The Campa lived in the dense forest in the east of Peru, close to the modern border with Brazil, and from early in the fifteenth century they had supplied their Inca overlords with tiny iridescent feathers from hummingbirds and other small birds of the forest. The Incas prized these greatly, and sewed them together to make shimmering garments for the nobility and the royal family. Pedro Pizarro, a cousin of Francisco Pizarro who led the conquest, wrote:

These were the feathers of small birds hardly bigger than cicadas, which are called 'pajaros comines' [hummingbirds] because they are so tiny. These birds grow the iridescent feathers only on their breasts, and each feather is little larger than a fingernail. Quantities of them were threaded together on fine thread. . .

In 1533 Manco Inca was crowned at Pizarro's instigation after Atahuallpa had been executed by the Spaniards. Three years later Manco rebelled and made his base in the area of Vilcabamba, in the Amazonian forest. The Campa were among the indians who gathered round him and acted as his guerrilla troops. The Spanish called them all 'Antis' because they came from the Antisuyo region of Peru. They believed, perhaps rightly, that they were cannibals. Certainly when Diego Rodriguez de Figueroa was sent to Vilcabamba to negotiate with the rebels in 1565, he received an alarming welcome from the Antis, as he later reported:

> About six or seven hundred Anti indians then marched up, all with bows and arrows, clubs and battle-axes. They advanced in good order, making reverence to the sun and to the Inca, and took up their positions. . . Then all those Antis made an offer to the Inca that, if he wished it, they would eat me raw.

Rodriguez appealed to the Inca to protect him, and the Inca did so. The next morning he told Rodriguez that it had all been in fun; and perhaps it had, though Rodriguez, who was a decent as well as a brave man, certainly didn't think so at the time.

Then, as later, the Campa indians did not go naked but wore a long garment which reminded the Spaniards irresistibly of the habits of their own friars: a long shift of coarse-woven cotton, which the Campa called a *kushma* and which was dyed brown with the bark of the mahogany tree.

'You can always tell the Campa,' Maria said as our canoe ploughed through the pale, thick waters of the Envira. 'Their robes give them a special dignity.'

She pointed out the trees from which they made their bows, and the other, lighter trees which provided them with their arrows; very long, she said, and flighted with parrot feathers. By now the Campa had taken on a mythic quality for me, and I found myself straining to look at every headland and clifftop along the river for the first sight of them.

The journey was long, and not always an uplifting experience: the indians on board hunted for caymans, small alligators, as we went along. They shone their electric torches on the sandbanks in the hope of seeing a cayman's red eyes gleaming in the darkness, and would then hack at it with machetes, laughing, until it died. The caymans were not large – only three or four feet long – and as each one was killed it was stowed under our seat, where it lay and stank.

At last, shortly before midnight, we came to the first Campa village, which had been given the congenial name of Simpatia by the Brazilians. The noise of our engine had preceded us in the silence of the river by a good forty minutes, and a little group of people stood like statues on the clifftop looking down at us. In the moonlight I could see they were wearing long, dark robes. The men were carrying bows and arrows as long as themselves: the ferocious weapons with which their ancestors had defended the Incas.

Stumbling with tiredness after fifteen hours in the open dugout, we carried our gear up the steep pathway to the village. By the time I reached the top, most of the indians had gone. A few open huts stood in the moonlit clearing, and we set up our hammocks in one of them, banging the wooden poles to knock the cockroaches and one particularly large, hairy, egg-carrying spider to the ground. I arranged my anti-*pium* sheet around me neatly, pinning it to the wooden floor of the hut with objects and books as a precaution against marauding insects, and lay stark naked in the fierce residual heat, my body at a slight angle to keep the hammock taut. It was, all things considered, surprisingly comfortable. More than that, I was drowsily excited: I had reached the Campa at last.

At six the next morning I woke up and extracted myself from the hammock. A cool mist hung over the river, and the entire world seemed drained of colour. Along the clifftop the Campa were sitting sleepily, painting their own and each others' faces with the brilliant red dye from the *urucum* seed, as thick and enduring as greasepaint. One or two of the men were already starting to whittle the wood for new arrows. All the men had long collars made of black seeds and decorated with green and scarlet parrot feathers, which they wore over one shoulder. They looked up politely and nodded as I walked over to greet them, as though they were used to seeing white men in the village; yet the chief was the only person in the village who had ever seen a European before, or a town of any kind.

These were the most primitive people I had ever come across, and their customs and methods were those of the Stone Age. I suppose I had subconsciously been expecting them to be little better than hominoids, crude and brutal figures in man-shapes. And yet they were as intelligent and sociable and swift in understanding as any other group of human beings, and gentler than most. Mike Goldwater had brought the transparencies of photographs he had taken at another Campa village some way away on an earlier trip, and the people at Simpatia knew many of the villagers there. When he showed them the transparencies they immediately recognised the faces of their friends and relatives, holding the pictures up to the sunlight to see them better, even though they had previously never had the slightest conception that it might be possible to capture someone's likeness in this way. Indeed, until Alex, Mike and I brought them mirrors to trade for the goods they wanted to sell us, there were some who had never seen their own faces.

Soon we came to recognise the characteristics that any human community throws up: the weak, easy-going man with an ambitious and competitive wife; the domestic tyrant whose mother and wives nervously watched his moods; the compulsive worker and hunter; the ne'er-do-well who existed on the charity of the village; the child whose dexterity and swiftness made him bored with village life at the age of ten, and who could have adapted within a few weeks to life at a school in London or Paris.

The Campa had come to western Brazil earlier in the century, as part of a general expansion and movement of tribes through the rainforest. But some of the people in Simpatia were much more recent arrivals from across the border in Peru, and had become refugees because of the campaign of terror and violence waged by the guerrillas of the Shining Path movement there. The tribe's old ferocity had not altogether deserted it, however: we heard stories of the way in which some of the Campa had used their skill with bows and arrows to chase out terrorist detachments. On one occasion they had surrounded a Peruvian Army base where a political adviser who worked with the Campa was about to be executed as a suspected terrorist. When the Peruvian commanding officer looked out and saw his perimeter fence circled by hundreds of grim little men in brown *kushmas*, carrying their outsized bows and arrows, the political adviser was allowed to go free at once.

Some days after we arrived the chief of Simpatia, a sturdy,

quiet, peaceable man, undertook to show us the forest. His name was Ira, and he wore an ancient green T-shirt and shorts rather than the *kushma* because they symbolized his contact with, and knowledge of, the white man. It was clear to him that he could do no hunting that day, because we were far too noisy and there was no possibility of disguising our unfamiliar smell. Instead, he guided us down one of the indistinguishable paths under the forest canopy, showing us along the way the trees and plants which the tribe valued. At first he seemed a mildly ludicrous figure in his wellington boots, which were badly split, and his baseball cap with 'Banco de Brasil' on it. Yet as he moved through the shadows of the forest with his elderly shotgun in one hand and his machete with raw latex tied around it, I began to see how formidable he was, and how deeply he understood the forest.

We climbed a steep hillside by a Campa hunting-path and edged along a fallen tree trunk, holding on to a thick liana. At last we came out on to a bald hilltop, and looked down on the canopy and the macaws and parakeets which fluttered, squawking, on a level with us. Ira strode across the clearing without stopping, and plunged back down into the forest again. The more we questioned him, the more impressive he became. He could speak four languages: Campa, Kulina (which he had learned from his wife), another indian tongue, and Portuguese. He knew the names of four thousand different species of plant in the forest.

'This is the *santisimikatsi* tree, which the white man calls *burani*. It is used for making boats, and we use the seeds for our necklaces. This is the *metok* plant, which the tapirs and tortoises like; so we come here in the early morning if we want to catch them. This bush is called *kotsima*; the animals of the forest do not eat it for food, but when they have gorged on other things they come here and eat its fruit as a purgative.'

He pointed out the trees and plants with far greater rapidity than I, sweating behind him, could note down. I stared at the trees and their root systems, some like the fins of rockets, some lying shallow on the ground, some reaching up in the air like legs, some guying up the trunk as though the tree were a tent pole, growing dead straight for a hundred feet into the canopy itself. Ira stopped at an unremarkable branch of a tree that hung down and scraped the bark. He opened his hand to show us the greyish dust from it, then smeared it on his face: it gave good luck in hunting, he said, because it disguised your smell from the animals.

'There are men who can walk all day and find no game. We call them *panema*. But we call a man who is a lucky hunter *mariapiara*.'

He whistled into his hand: a curious, haunting sound which seemed to come from much farther away, like a ventriloquist's voice.

'The men who cannot find big game like tapir and deer have to hunt *imbara*: small game, like monkeys and birds. They make calls like this.' He whistled into his hand again. 'When you call the birds like this, they come to you. But the monkeys answer when you call, and then you can go and find them.'

He showed us the bush where the *amexixitse* bird laid its eggs, and pointed out the tiny *kanneh* ants which swarmed all over the nest like little specks of fly-dirt. Their stings were worse than those of hornets, he said, but the *amexixitse* was immune to them and took advantage of them to protect its eggs.

'*Kiratarixi*,' Ira said, pointing out a small green plant with pink lines on its leaves. 'If you have inflammation or swelling on your legs, you boil it and put it on. It is good even for septic wounds, even for a tumour. If your leg or arm is broken, you make a poultice from the *txaringaxe* plant and bind up the limb for two months, with a splint from a vine. It will be healed.'

I looked down at his legs: they were cabled with sturdy veins like the vines which grew up the trees and could be turned into splints for broken limbs. Ira was of the forest himself.

'You hear the *mari* bird?' The sound was a sad chirrup from somewhere in the forest nearby. 'That tells you that you will kill some game today.' Not, I thought, while we are with you, frightening off the wild life with our smell and our noise.

At last he sat down under a kapok tree, whose red blossoms lay everywhere on the ground.

'We are the Ashaninca, which means "the real people". We came down from the high mountains. We do not like the expression "Campa"; we have our own name for ourselves.'

I determined never again to use the word 'Campa'.

It was, nevertheless, frustratingly difficult to know what Ira was saying: Alex, who was acting as translator, often became so interested that he would forget to tell us altogether, or would simply sum up five minutes' talk in a single sentence. It was impossible to ask Ira specific questions, because the subject would long have passed. I took down what I could of the conversation.

'The first of our people to come here was Mixikoiri, whose father was Xangyentse. This was not many years ago: perhaps fifty. When my father came here from Peru I was eight years old. In the past, time was never broken up like this; you were born when you were born, that was all. But now we have learned to count as you do.

'Our people are wanderers, and Kuxari, who was our chief for ten years, would sit in a place for some time and then feel bored, so he would leave, and because he was the chief everyone would have to go with him. But at last the village did not want to move, and Kuxari's brother, who was next in line to be chief, took over. And when he left, I became chief. At first when you are chief there is a period of waiting, to see if you are any good. Then perhaps a woman will come with a complaint: someone has done something. It is for the chief to sort it out. If he has courage, he will do it and so prove himself. It is the women who provoke the men to fight. It happens everywhere. My own younger wife came to visit, then said she would move in. My old wife was angry, and I am now trying to redress the balance between them.' He laughed, awkward and embarrassed.

'Strength and the ability to manage people make one particular family dominant in the village. My people don't steal anything, because the others in the village wouldn't like it, and I wouldn't stand for it. I suppose if I caught someone stealing something I would make them give it back. But there are no such things as punishments in our village. My job is to keep the tribe united and at peace. I am *antare ashaninke*: the head of the tribe.'

It was true about the village's honesty: day after day when we were out travelling we would leave out for inspection the mirrors, knives and packets of beads which we had brought to trade for the Ashanincas' marvellous collars of seeds and parrot feathers.

Not so much as a bead disappeared, although the villagers prized them highly, and played with them and looked at them every day.

I steered him towards a more difficult subject, that of religion. He became more reticent.

'When we came down from the mountains where our god created us, Páwa was our mother and we drank the hallucinogenic vine, which we call *nana kamembi*, because it shows us the way to our father.'

The Ashaninca, who served Manco Inca at his forest base until his murder in 1545, have a haunting belief in a creative spirit whom they call Inca. Inca taught them the arts of hunting and warfare, including the use of the bow and arrow; but at last he was captured by the white men, who forced him to give them the secrets of his knowledge. This explains why the white men know so much, and have conquered the entire territory. The Ashaninca believe that one day there will be a great flood, which will wash Inca back to them. Then he will teach them everything he taught the white men, including the manufacture of guns, and they will be able to get rid of the whites once and for all.

Like other indians, the Ashaninca call the white man Viracocha, which was one name for their supreme deity, whose face was white. It was the whiteness of their faces that earned this name for the Spaniards, though the belief is widespread that the indians of Peru regarded them as gods because of their technological superiority.

An enormous yellow dragonfly with four wings and markings like an aircraft flew across the clearing in the forest where Ira sat explaining these things to us. Did he, I asked, think that life was going from bad to worse for the Ashaninca?

'When the Viracochas arrived there was no conversation, no negotiation. They just took things. But I don't feel they will take this away from us now, because the land has been demarcated as ours. The game is coming back to the forest. Why is there any need to be bitter?'

I was glad, looking at his sturdy frame and his machete, that he felt there was no need to be bitter; and I remembered what Diego Rodriguez de Figueroa had written in 1565: 'Some of these people were small, but they were very fierce; and their arrows put our men in great fear of their lives.'

On our way back, an ant fell on to my neck and bit me on the shoulder. It was as long as my thumb-nail, and very black. By the time we were back in the village my whole arm was numb. I showed the bite to Ira. It was, he said, the work of a *tocanderro* ant. The best thing, he said, would be to rub on the juice of the *uaritongroxe* plant, but they had none in the village and it was getting too dark for anyone to go and gather some. He looked up at the sky, and asked when the ant had bitten me. I told him.

'The pain will go in four hours' time,' he said.

Later that night my arm began to feel better, and sensation returned to it. I looked at my watch: it was 10.20. Ira was twenty minutes out.

The Envira River

These Indians are often resourceful and clever... Sometimes it is almost impossible to reach their territories because the rivers are swarming with poisonous snakes...

Felipe Guaman Poma de Ayala, 1613

Everyone on board our canoe knew that a single misjudgement could capsize us. But the young and inexperienced Claudio, who had taken over for the day from the saturnine boatman, was keen to show that he could do just as well. The rainforest lay dark and impenetrable on either side of the river, its noises drowned by our outboard motor.

Zezinho, another indian who had come up the river with us, was entrusted with the job of sitting in the bows and shining his torch on the submerged trees and sandbanks which lay in our path. But he was a town indian, who worked in Rio Branco for the organisation which represented the interests of the indigenous people. He was as useless as his organisation; all he wanted to do was find the caymans which lay on the wide sandy shores of the river.

With these two in charge of us, and night coming on, Mike Goldwater and I had guessed that something might go wrong. We had already made our dispositions: he would take care of his stills camera and the rolls of film he had shot, I would look after the video camera and the cassettes. We clutched them to us in their watertight bags, and looked unfavourably at Claudio in the darkness. He was speeding up now, and occasionally broke into song. Time and again we narrowly missed sandbanks which neither he nor Zezinho had spotted.

We reached a particularly wide bend in the river. The walls of jungle lay dark on either side, the sand glimmered palely in the moonless dark. Claudio's small, unimpressive figure stood out against the sky. He was taking the bend too fast. The boat veered across to the right, almost out of control. Claudio stopped singing, and clutched the rudder with both hands. All I could do was hold my waterproof bag and watch. We left the clear channel of water, and were on our own in the dark. The torch in Zezinho's hand waved wildly at the water and the sky. Two large submerged trees lay in the water ahead of us. We missed the first by a fraction. With a despairing shout Claudio took us right into the second. Our canoe reared up to the right and stopped, its bows jammed in the branches. The stern began to fill up with water.

At first no one did or said anything. The canoe had taken in as much water as the stern would hold, and the bows were stuck fast enough to ensure that we would not take in any more yet. But we were alone in the darkness, in one of the least populated areas on earth, and the nearest small town was seven days' journey away. As for the forest, it was not welcoming at night. Mike and I sat on the upper rim of the canoe, still gripping our bags like passengers on the *Titanic*. Things began to slip into the water: some carved animals for which I had just traded a shirt, a knife, and a BBC pen; my boots, which I managed to save; Alex's expensive camera, which he didn't; and a small tortoise which he had been given at the last village.

Everyone behaved remarkably well. Maria was as matter-of-fact as if this had often happened to her, though it had not. Alex and Mike and I spoke in the clipped dialogue of a British war film of the 1950s; Claudio and Zezinho, who made up the rest of the crew, were too abashed by their part in the disaster to speak at all. We decided, if there were time before the boat sank, to tie the important things to the uppermost part of the tree we had come to grief on. This was the season when the river was at its lowest, so there was no danger that the water-level would rise and swamp them. Our strategy then would be to scramble or swim to the other fallen tree, which we had narrowly missed and which the feeble beam of our torch had picked out, and from there perhaps make it to the white sandbank of the shore. It lay only thirty yards or so away; but it was a long thirty yards.

One by one we edged along the canoe and into the submerged

stern. A little splashing, and we made contact with the branches of the tree, which were under the water. Soon we were perched on it like grotesque versions of the elegant snowy egrets we had so often seen in the daytime. Frogs croaked at us from the shore, and an occasional vampire bat swooped past low in the night air. Moths which fluttered down the torch-beam struck the protective glass in front of the bulb with as little warning as we had struck the tree. The torch battery was starting to fail. Round our feet the water was dark and swirled alarmingly.

It seemed possible that our combined weight would dislodge the tree we were in, so as the heaviest I felt obliged to ease myself into the water. I was worried about this, but the current was so strong that it pinned me against the branches of the tree, without my needing to hold on. I could just touch the bottom with my bare feet, and the sand melted away unpleasantly beneath my toes. The one good thing was the water's warmth: after the fierce heat of the day it cooled far more slowly than the air, and was probably still in the nineties Fahrenheit.

As for the animal life in the water, my journeys up and down the river in the canoe had taught me to worry less about that. The piranha which infested the river were no danger unless one of us was bleeding, or unless (as happened with one of our health-workers, Gilberto, who had a large triangular scar between thumb and forefinger to show for it) it was caught in a net and handled carelessly. As for the distasteful *candiou*, famous from travellers' tales for its habit of swimming up a stream of urine into its victim's body and refusing to be dislodged, Maria had extracted several of them and assured us that they were not as dangerous as they had been represented. It was not, for instance, true (as we had read) that a man would have to amputate his penis or his bladder would explode. Still, Maria admitted that she had never been asked to take one out of a man, so the doubts lingered; and as I stood in the warm water I decided not to do anything rash.

There were also stingrays which could lay the flesh of your leg open to the bone, and electric eels which could shock you from fifty yards away and kill you by stages. The only positive thing that could be done about them was to hope they weren't around.

We knew by now what we had to do, but no one wanted to be the first to do it; and then Claudio, in an access of remorse and bravery, flung himself suddenly into the water and struck out towards the shore. Zezinho threw himself despairingly into the water after him in the darkness. By the increasingly feeble light of the torch we could watch as the current caught them, once their first impetus flagged. They were forced downstream, splashing and panicking. For a moment I thought they were lost, but they found a foothold at last and stood up, spluttering and triumphant. Maria crossed herself and dived in next, but she was a weak swimmer and almost failed to catch their outstretched hands. Then she, too, was standing up and shouting.

It was inescapably my turn now, and since I was already in the water I would not have the initial advantage of a dive from the tree like the others. I thought I would probably drown. I looked up at the clear stars and thought of saying something, then changed my mind. I launched out, my clothes constricting me, feeling the current fighting for control, hearing vaguely the shouts of encouragement, and then I was crashing into Claudio's legs and finding my feet. It was a good moment; and when the others joined us and we stumbled up on to the sandbank there was a general shout of relief. The only one who hadn't made it was the tortoise.

We were shipwrecked, and all our necessities were tied to the tree in the middle of the river. But Alex had brought his cigarette lighter, and Claudio continued his atonement by drying it out and producing a flame from some dried leaves.

'An appreciative letter to Mr Bic might well be in order,' said Alex, though no one afterwards remembered to write one.

We were all congratulating ourselves on our escape when Maria said she thought it was likely to be more dangerous on the bank of the river than it had been in the water. And indeed as I was collecting wood for a bonfire and began to pull a log from the bushes in the darkness there was a harsh, dry susurrus which Alex and the others judged to be the warning sound of a fer-de-lance, the second most deadly snake in the forest. It contented itself with an irritable warning. Wild pig and other animals lived close by, and might come down to the water to drink. We gathered closely round our bonfire and slept fitfully.

There was the faintest hint of light in the sky. I could bear the harshness of the sand and the incessant whine and bite of the insects no longer, and stood up. Mike, who had not slept properly either, suggested a walk, and we headed down towards the river. In the gloom we could just make out our belongings hanging from the stranded tree in the water, like fruit. On the white sand in front of us I noticed a line of footmarks as large as my own: animal tracks. We followed them apprehensively from the forest's edge, down to the river, then back up the slope of the beach to within twenty yards of our bonfire. The animal that had made them had obviously decided to come and take a look at us. As it grew lighter, Mike and I realised from its footprints what it was: a very large jaguar. Maria had already told us how a female jaguar, six and a half feet long, had swum across the path of the canoe not long before. It had also run into a nearby village, seized an unfortunate pig weighing a hundred pounds or more, slung it over its shoulder, and run off into the forest. From its place at the top of the forest's food chain the jaguar had no need to worry about us, though our fire would have kept it away. We wondered idly what would have happened if one of us had gone for a stroll along the bank.

The light grew stronger, and we could make out the shape of the canoe in the middle of the river. Throughout our trip I had been immune from insect bites, which had annoyed my companions, but now I was covered with the night-work of mosquitoes and sand fleas, and with the vicious little ticks which burrow up inside the flesh of your legs and come out at the backs of your knees and at your waist. Mike was in as bad a state as I was, and we stared out, itching, at the river, wondering what on earth we were going to do now. We could be here for days, I thought.

Yet most such experiences end in anticlimax. When Claudio and Zezinho woke up, an hour or so later, they realised we were stranded only an hour's walk from a small Kulina village on the river-bank. By 6.30 the beach was occupied by pleasant, wondering indians, and our goods were being off-loaded into another and more stable canoe. We shook hands with our rescuers solemnly, and I counted the bites on my face and neck: there were eighty-eight of them.

A new boatman took us off in the direction of the rising sun.

Shepherd's Bush

Everything has been conscientiously set down in this book, and now I am able to proceed further and tell what I have personally observed and experienced.

Felipe Guaman Poma de Ayala, 1613

The red light showed that one of the hourly news summaries was on the air. A woman's cool, pleasant, rational voice came faintly across the newsroom: 'There are reports of renewed shelling in Sarajevo. . .' It was my first day back at work after my return from Brazil, and as always after a trip I was wandering around the newsroom, picking up gossip and reminding people of my existence.

I headed towards the foreign desk. Once, I thought, they used to write the news in a newsroom, and broadcast it from a studio; now they did their broadcasting from the newsroom. It was the sourness of the ancient villager wandering round the newly built suburb.

In the fourteen years I had worked there the newsroom had changed and grown with the speed of a new dormitory town. It had doubled in size as the news bulletins had grown longer and more demanding. Walls I had once leant my chair against had been torn down to allow the newsroom to expand. Entire time-zones in the morning and afternoon which had once been empty of broadcasting were now colonised by news programmes. Formerly, messengers had delivered armfuls of evil-smelling, smudgy wire-copy from the Reuter's or Press Association machines, and subeditors had wielded real power by selecting who should and should not see it; now each of the eager, efficient-looking young people at the desks could tap into his or her computer terminal and find out everything that was happening in the world without

39

the need of a middleman. I looked at these faces with annoyance: I didn't know most of them, and most of them didn't know me. What did they know or care that a short time before I had been swimming for my life in a tributary of the Amazon?

'Glad to see your ducking in Brazil didn't do you any harm,' one of the young, efficient-looking people said as she passed. My gloom evaporated in an instant.

A burst of purposive music over by the television cameras showed that the brief summary had come to an end.

'Off air,' said a voice loudly.

I reached the foreign desk. Under the blackboard where they listed the names and telephone numbers of everyone who was abroad on assignment stood a familiar figure: not particularly big, yet somehow bearlike; a face which could once have been rather cherubic but now looked distinctly tough; thinning curly hair. Eamonn Matthews had worked with me as a producer in Afghanistan, and in Baghdad before and during the Gulf War. I knew him to be ferocious in pursuit of a good story; and behind his pleasant, self-deprecating manner he was, as far as I could tell, entirely without fear.

Fortiter in re, suaviter in modo: tough in purpose, smooth in manner; the motto fitted Eamonn perfectly. I pointed my finger at him like a gun, and he fired one back at me: Tim Gardam of 'Newsnight' had selected him to work with me in Peru. He had an air of suppressed excitement, and we went over to the tiny glass cubicle, like a separate cage at a zoo, which served the news editor as an office. I looked inside: Richard Sambrook, a man in his mid-thirties whose style of humour I enjoyed and who, unlike most managers, was capable of a sometimes disconcerting bluntness, was looking unenthusiastically at a computer terminal. Beside him was a photograph of a recent baby.

'I don't think we should tell anyone else this,' Eamonn began. Richard nodded. Eamonn went back over everything he and I had talked about: how we were hoping to arrange the first television interview with the leader of the world's most ferocious terrorist organisation, Shining Path; how we wanted to investigate the appalling human rights abuses being carried out by both Shining Path and by the Peruvian Army; and finally, and most difficult of all, how we would try to find out who was behind the cocaine trade. Richard sat back in his chair.

'That all sounds easy enough,' he said; 'what will you do for the rest of the week?'

It was true that we were setting ourselves a very considerable undertaking. Eamonn remained serious. He explained that while I had been away in Brazil he had met a key figure in the Shining Path movement. Within minutes, he said, it had become clear that this was the man who some months before had arranged for a television team to visit areas controlled by Shining Path. When the resulting documentary was shown on the independent Channel 4 in Britain, it turned out to be shamefully uncritical of Shining Path's methods. There were many complaints that Channel 4 should have broadcast something as slanted as this without at least indicating that it was the view of one side in a bitter guerrilla war.

Eamonn believed that the makers of the documentary, who were from Colombia, wanted to ingratiate themselves with Shining Path in order to get a television interview with its leader, Abimael Guzman; but having spoken to the Shining Path emissary he believed we were in with a better chance.

'They liked the Channel 4 film,' he said, 'but they knew perfectly well it was one-sided. What they want now is to present Guzman to a world audience, and to do that they need an outfit which is respected to come and interview him.'

'And what happens if this respected outfit goes there and gets caught?' Richard Sambrook asked.

Eamonn smiled and made as if to slit his throat with a forefinger.

'Just another part of the BBC staff cuts,' I said. 'Think of it as a new form of early retirement.'

But Richard was clearly worried. I started a rearguard action by saying that the Peruvians would never want to run into problems with an organisation like the BBC, and that if we were caught we would just be put on a plane with a warning not to do it again; it might be humiliating, but it wouldn't be dangerous. I didn't altogether believe it, and neither did Eamonn: but we knew that if there were sufficient anxiety about it among the BBC's managers, our Peru trip would be aborted altogether. We had to persuade everyone that it was tricky but not really dangerous: that was our only chance.

'There's another thing,' Richard said. 'I appreciate that it'd be a great exclusive to get this Guzman, but wouldn't you be glorifying him, and showing up the authorities as incompetent and so on? Isn't it like French television coming here and interviewing the head of the IRA?'

I had thought this through with some care in the previous weeks.

'What always counts in these things is the tone of your reporting. If the viewers get the impression you think it's exciting and wonderful to interview someone like Guzman, and you're full of self-congratulation, they will feel, quite rightly, that the whole thing is morally questionable. But if your tone is serious and balanced, and you make it clear what kind of outfit Shining Path really is – and if you do an attacking interview, which this would have to be – then I don't think the problem will arise.'

Richard nodded. Eamonn moved the subject on a little.

'The people who made the Channel 4 documentary told me they'd made contact with Shining Path in Bolivia. I think they said that just to put us off the scent. I think they made their arrangements in Europe, and I'm sure I'm talking to the right people. They seem pretty keen.'

Like a door-to-door salesman faced with a reluctant buyer, Eamonn was showing Richard Sambrook the bargain that could be his, if he took this once-in-a-lifetime opportunity. Richard knew the technique perfectly well; when he was a producer, he had done the same thing. He also knew that Eamonn was telling the truth: we had a good chance of achieving an exclusive which would make headlines all over the world. But he had a natural reluctance about sending other people out to do something dangerous.

He looked at us both speculatively.

'There are times when I really don't like this job,' he said after a moment. 'I'll have to have words higher up, and come back to you.'

'But in the meantime we'll press on,' I said. It wasn't a question. It is always difficult to explain why one should deliberately set out to thrust both hands into a hornet's nest like Peru. At the age of 47 I could have made a perfectly good living from covering international conferences and interviewing presidents and prime ministers; Eamonn, twelve years younger, could have produced documentaries on subjects that were entirely safe. Perhaps it was that each of us knew that the more difficult subjects tended to produce better pictures and therefore received more attention; and if you are ambitious, attention is one of the chief requisites to doing well in broadcasting.

There were other, worthier motives; I felt strongly that it was important to open up to public attention areas of the world which, like South America in general and Peru in particular, tended to be ignored in the West. There was a moral element too: people were being mistreated on a large scale in Peru, and to direct international attention to that fact might do something to help the situation. Yet the reason that underlay all the others was far simpler: once the idea had been suggested, we both found it much too interesting to turn down.

'They aren't going to stop us,' I said to Eamonn as we walked out of Richard Sambrook's office.

'In that case we can go ahead with fixing up a lunch with Shining Path.'

I found the idea of lunching with Maoist guerrillas irresistible.

'We can invite them to the Chelsea Arts Club,' I said. 'No one will even spot them there. The members are all barking mad.'

'We can get Rosalind Bain along too,' Eamonn said. He had hired her to do the translating and setting up for us, but I still hadn't met her. 'She's a tremendous hard worker, and she's serious.'

I knew Eamonn's habits of mind well enough by now to realise that 'serious' was one of his highest terms of praise. His first career had been as a nuclear scientist, and when he switched to television he brought to the business of current affairs a rigorously empirical approach that set him apart from most of the arts graduates he worked with. He had also been brought up a Catholic, and I could easily imagine him as a priest. There was a powerful moral consciousness about him which I would not have liked to offend; flippancy, weakness, infirmity of purpose were, you felt, character faults he would not easily forgive. In his eyes, to be serious was to be the kind of person he approved of.

Chelsea

Both the men and the women are fierce by nature... They prefer death to conquest.

Felipe Guaman Poma de Ayala, 1613

A BBC car drove me through Shepherd's Bush to the round-about at the foot of Holland Park Road: I always thought of it as the Green Line, because it was the final divide between Kensington and the western suburbs. From there we headed up to Notting Hill Gate, then cut down towards Chelsea.

'Meeting anyone interesting?' asked the driver.

'A couple of Maoist guerrillas from Peru.'

'Better watch their table manners, then.'

We turned right off Fulham Road into Old Church Street. It was the first time I had seen the Chelsea Arts Club in two months, and I peered out at it affectionately. I have never found a pleasanter place to eat or simply hang out in, anywhere in the world, and the long, low, unremarkable white façade seemed remarkably welcoming.

As we arrived, a taxi drew up and a woman in her late twenties or early thirties got out. She was attractive in a distinctly hispanic way, with long dark hair tied up in a mid-Victorian chignon. She disappeared through the front door while I was still arranging with the driver when he should pick me up. I found her waiting in the cramped, low-ceilinged hallway, reading the notices about members who had failed to pay their subscriptions, or died, or both.

'You're John Simpson, aren't you? My name's Rosalind Bain.'

She shook my hand firmly. There was a straightness and directness about her. For the time being she was just helping Eamonn to set up the trip from London, but he was already

45

starting to suggest that we might take her to Peru with us. The child of an English father and a Belgian mother, Rosalind was a natural rebel and had not fitted in at her convent school. Time and again on our trip to Peru and afterwards I noticed a restlessness which could amount to irritation when she thought someone was trying to sell her a line which was phoney. She was indefatigably cheerful and friendly, but she insisted on saying what she thought. There was another quality I liked about her, too: although she had clear opinions about politics, she never allowed them to get in the way of things as she found them.

We walked into the bar of the Chelsea Arts Club. A desultory game was going on at the members' snooker table in the middle of the room. Other people read the papers or wandered out to the garden. Unlike most of the grander London clubs, there is no barrier to women there, and the Chelsea Arts Club is much pleasanter as a result. Eamonn arrived, and I went over to buy the drinks. I ordered three orange juices.

'I need my wits about me this lunchtime,' I explained.

The door to the bar opened, and two people came in. They scarcely stood out in a place like this, as I had anticipated. If Eamonn had not murmured something I might not have recognised who they were. Only Bridie, who knew everyone, looked up sharply at them from behind the bar, and then across at me. The man came towards us smiling, his hand outstretched. He was an inch or so taller than I, which made him around six foot three. He wore a loose green sweater, jeans, and open sandals. His grey hair and curly grey beard gave him a vaguely Roman look, like a coin-portrait of one of the more self-indulgent emperors. He would often turn up at public meetings about Peru and interrupt them with slogans and points of argument in Shining Path's favour. He was obviously a Shining Path sympathiser, but the precise nature of his links with the movement were unclear.

He was in his late forties: the little round gold-framed glasses he wore, 1960s-style, seemed to confirm that. I felt I could tell a lot from his appearance: well-to-do family of European rather than indian descent, radical chic, a break with the past, a deeper and deeper descent into revolutionary politics. The small, slightly built woman who followed close behind him was his complete opposite: dark where he was silver-haired, typically indian where he was typically European, silent and watchful where he was relaxed and bonhomous.

The contrast extended to their clothes. If he was dressed like an artist, she was dressed for a demonstration, in white jeans and a leather jerkin with a brooch in the shape of a scorpion. But it was her feet which gave her the truly military look: she was wearing a pair of heavy black army boots. With her sharp, observant dark eyes she was, I thought, extremely handsome, but she made me feel uneasy.

The dining room was dark and cool. James McNeill Whistler, one of the Club's founders, looked out at us through a monocle from his portrait on the wall above us. We sat and offered each other the bread and read through the menu, but each side was covertly examining the other. We all knew that an interview with Abimael Guzman was a possibility, and we hoped to hear over lunch whether an answer had come to our request. I rehearsed the phrases with which I would edge us towards the subject.

We ordered. The woman chose frugally, the man in a way that showed he knew what good food was. That done, we all relaxed a little. She continued to sit there, watchful and silent, but the man was witty and confident, and although his pronunciation was not always perfect, his grasp of English idiom and vocabulary was superb. 'The Boadicea of our times', he called Margaret Thatcher, in a way that was not unadmiring. At one point he said, 'All these intellectuals and their lucubrations – it's all so pointless.'

I had read English at university, but although I had come across the word 'lucubration' once or twice in Victorian novels, I had never in my life heard anyone use it in conversation: let alone a Maoist sympathiser from South America. In spite of my instinctive dislike of people who justify terrorism, I was impressed by the man's grasp of a language that was not his own. No doubt he intended that I should be.

He had finished his penne in fennel sauce and was starting on the fillets of John Dory when I felt we should get down to business. I caught Eamonn's eye, and was about to speak. The grey-haired Lucullan figure across the table, perhaps sensing that the moment had come, got in first. He talked in general terms about the importance of Shining Path in Peru; beside him, the woman listened approvingly. The important moment came as the plates were removed and we sat back in our chairs to wait for coffee.

'I am glad to be able to tell you,' he began in his precisely turned, accented English, 'that the people I have spoken to believe you may get an interview with the Chairman. He would like to do it: they have told me that much. The time is right, and the conditions are right. Apparently he wants to speak to the world.' His benevolent smile embraced us all. 'What better way than to do so through the BBC?'

I acknowledged the point without smiling back.

'The movement regards the recent Channel 4 documentary,' he went on, 'as a goal for its side. Now the game is coming to an end, and it wants the referee to give his decision. You, the BBC, are the referee: you will come and visit Peru, you will see the Party's achievements, you will interview the Chairman, and you will give your verdict. That is all.'

He beamed; the girl cracked a faint smile; I did not respond. For one thing, he seemed to be presenting himself as nothing more than an intermediary. For another, Eamonn and I had agreed that we would never deal with Shining Path, or anyone else in Peru, under false colours. Now was the time to test that out, even if it meant aborting the whole project.

'We would have to keep total control over the way the interview was done, and the way it was broadcast.'

He went silent. That's it, I thought: he'll say his friends won't like that. By making that identical point I had lost the chance of interviewing Saddam Hussein in Baghdad three months before the Gulf War started. I was very sorry both at the time and afterwards that I did not interview him, but I had not the slightest regret about making it clear that we could not lend ourselves to someone else's propaganda purposes.

'Would you allow a member of the organisation to translate it into English?' he asked, eventually.

My hopes rose again: it looked as though Shining Path's only worry was that the revolutionary terminology should be exactly right. As far as I was concerned, the points of fine theological concern were up to them; they were more likely to translate Guzman's ideology with total accuracy than we were. Nevertheless, I felt I had to establish the main point once and for all.

'You do understand,' I said, 'that we would have to edit the interview ourselves. Our news programmes are not long, as you know – the whole thing lasts only half an hour, and each individual news report is between two and three minutes long. . .'

Saddam Hussein had refused to be interviewed by us because we would not guarantee him an hour's air time; how long, I wondered, would a Maoist guerrilla leader who had never spoken in public before insist on going on for?

'It's your interview,' the relaxed, grey-bearded figure opposite me said. He took off his glasses and put them away, carefully, in the pocket of his shirt. 'You have your requirements; you must do what you have to do, in order to satisfy them.'

Shepherd's Bush

I, the author of this work, went out into the world ... to strengthen my position as a writer who wanted to see and hear as much as possible...

Felipe Guaman Poma de Ayala, 1613

From now on the preparations for our trip to Peru went ahead at full speed. We had decided that Rosalind should come with us to Peru; it seemed preferable to bring someone from London to be our interpreter and make the arrangements, and we were both impressed by her energy and involvement. Between them, she and Eamonn spoke to most of the authorities on Peru who were based in Britain. Books, articles, photostats of speeches, theses and position papers were continually landing on my desk.

The picture which emerged from it all was a grim one. Someone told us we should change our hotel every night, to avoid the danger from Army death squads. Someone else said Shining Path's campaign of bombing in the more expensive areas of Lima meant that we should stay in some small, cheap hotel in one of the city's outer suburbs, or maybe rent a flat. We were told we would need to hire armed guards to travel with us to the shantytowns on the edge of Lima, since violent crime was endemic there and anything as valuable as television equipment would be at risk.

As for travelling in the coca-producing area of Peru, the Huallaga Valley, most people tried to persuade us strongly against the idea. We were told again and again about the number of journalists, Peruvian and foreign, who had been murdered there. Indeed, travelling anywhere in the areas where the Shining Path was active seemed extremely dangerous; time and again people likened them to the Khmer Rouge in Cambodia, who killed most of the journalists who were foolhardy enough to make contact with them.

I listened to all this as carefully as I could, and read most of the literature Eamonn and Rosalind gave me; but I had a department to run and a good deal of broadcasting to do on other topics. It was a busy time: the European Community was in trouble, there was open civil war in Yugoslavia, and changes were coming in the Middle East. I relegated Peru to the late evenings, when I got home. Eamonn, by contrast, lived and breathed Peru and made himself an expert on it. Slowly, too, he planned out the details of the films we would make, and the subjects they would cover.

That was his speciality. Over the years different approaches had arisen within the BBC between the people who worked for current affairs programmes like 'Panorama' and those who worked for the news programmes. In current affairs the producer was the boss: he or she planned out the documentary to be made, and was in charge of the filming and later of the editing. The reporter who narrated the film would generally travel with the producer and camera team, but there was no question who had control.

In the news department, things had always been very different. There, the correspondent was in charge. He or she gave the camera crew its instructions, worked out the day's schedule, took all the decisions, oversaw the editing of the report. The job of the producer in news was to make the arrangements, organise the logistics and be the quartermaster, the comptroller-general, and a defensive screen between the correspondent and the editors in London. Now, though, the news and current affairs departments had merged, and the differentiation was fading; but the question of who had ultimate control always needed settling.

We had to find ourselves a camera crew. Eamonn had worked with a cameraman called Steve Morris under dangerous circumstances in Afghanistan not long before, and had the highest praise for him. I had often worked with Steve myself: he and his wife had travelled to Rumania with my companion, the television producer Tira Shubart, and me in the spring of 1989 — only seven months before the revolution which overthrew Nicolae Ceausescu. We had pretended to be tourists but were caught by the Securitate, Ceausescu's secret police, and harassed everywhere we went. Thanks to the quality of Steve's camerawork we made a very satisfying film out of it, in spite of all the difficulties. He was quick-witted and very funny.

'If you're serious that Steve wants to come,' I said to Eamonn, 'I think we've got the perfect combination.'

'That's what he says.'

'What about his sound-man?'

'Someone called Matt – Lyper, is it? They've only recently teamed up.'

'Matt Leiper,' I said. 'Rhymes with Grim Reaper. Probably very suitable.'

I was pleased about Matt too. He was a Scotsman, and commuted from Aberdeen at the start of his shifts in London. I had worked with him during the run-up to the Gulf War. Once, in the claustrophobic circumstances of Baghdad and fired up by single malt whisky, we had fitted up an outsized watermelon with cardboard fins and dropped it from the eleventh floor of the Al-Rasheed hotel. When the hotel staff heard it land, they thought the war had started early. Matt lived an adventurous life, and was a mountain-climber and a certified scuba-diver. He and Steve sparked each other off well.

We explained to each of them separately the nature of the stories we were going to cover, and the strategy we had been working out. We looked endlessly at maps of the country, trying to work out how to move around, and whether we should enter from Bolivia or Brazil. At one stage I even wondered if we should try to slip across the border in the company of the Ashaninca indians I had met earlier.

The question that both Steve and Matt raised was that of protection: if things were as dangerous and as out of control in Peru as we had been told, might we need armed minders when we filmed? Neither Eamonn nor I had any clear idea about this, and told them so. But there seemed to be a worse problem: how could we protect ourselves when we finished filming with the Army in the Huallaga Valley and moved across to meet the Shining Path guerrillas?

We talked it over and over in the office we shared. I had offered Eamonn a desk there when he had ceased to be a deputy editor on 'Newsnight' and had gone back to the more congenial business of producing and directing documentaries. Now we sat side by side, leaning back in the springy seats, propelling the chairs to and fro on their castors whenever there was a point to be checked in the mountain of literature we had accumulated on our desks. Eamonn had an answer of sorts for the problem of the switch-over.

'There's a town in the Huallaga called Aucayacu,' he began. 'I went back to the map and tracked it down.' Throughout the project, from first to last, he persisted in pronouncing it 'Acu-yacu'. 'It's a kind of interface between the Army and Shining Path. The Army's in the town, they're in the countryside just across the river. There are some Canadian priests there who we can make contact with, and maybe they can help us. All we need to do is to slip across from one to the other.'

'Oh well, if that's all,' I said. He gave the grin that always made him look like a cross between Socrates and a satyr from a frieze in the British Museum.

Steve said much the same thing when we told him: 'Oh, fine, no problem then.'

'It'll sort itself out,' I said vaguely. 'It always does.'

The other thing Eamonn and I discussed obsessively was how we were going to get our video tapes out of Peru.

'What do you think about the British embassy? Maybe they could get them out for us in the diplomatic bag.'

'Forget it,' I answered. 'I've never found an embassy yet that was willing to help like that. They always say it's against the rules, and you know how snotty civil servants can be.'

We sat back in our chairs and thought about it.

'If we had some dubs made,' I began. Dubs are copies of video tapes.

'Dubbing the rushes would take hours of editing time; and anyway whoever we hired to do the editing would know exactly what we'd got, and we'd never know if we could trust them.'

'Maybe we could take our own gear and bring someone with us to do the editing?'

But I already knew that was an impossibility. This was going to be a well-funded trip, given that several television organisations were prepared to buy into it; but an extra person, plus a large amount of extra equipment, would quickly use up the money. It wouldn't be worth it, just as a safety device. We would have to look after ourselves and our tapes as best we could.

'There's one thing we mustn't forget,' I said. 'I've worked in lots of places in Latin America. Even in Chile and Argentina, when they were military dictatorships and there were spooks everywhere, it wasn't anything like working in Eastern Europe or the Soviet Union. They're Latins, for one thing – they aren't that organised. And the other thing is, even in dictatorships they don't have the same instincts about state control. They're all basically free enterprise societies. And Peru isn't a dictatorship anyway. Maybe we'll be all right if we can just keep one step ahead.'

Eamonn nodded. It was another version of the doctrine that things always work out; but neither of us had a better idea about what to do.

I took three weeks off to go trekking in the Himalayas with Tira, and celebrated my birthday with a bottle of champagne; one of our friends had brought it, on the principle that there will always be something to celebrate. (The champagne was chilled in ice which he and another friend chipped out of a glacier.) I could never entirely forget the Peru trip. It seemed to me that of all the things I had done, this was the most questionable; and I seriously doubted whether it would end happily.

Back in London I had several meetings with senior people in the BBC who wanted to be certain that none of us felt we were under any pressure to go, and that the risks we would be taking were justified. I had checked out the first, and had nothing much to say about the second; if we all came back safely then it would be worthwhile, and if things went badly wrong it would seem to have been a foolish and unjustifiable escapade. I said each time that it was obviously worth it, and the risks were negligible. No one believed me.

The telephone rang beside the bed.

'Your wake-up call, sir,' said the operator.

I had been waiting for it for a good hour, and now I turned

off all the other alarm clocks and watches I had set for 6 am just in case I overslept. There was not the faintest chance that I would; I had slept uneasily and had woken several times. Yet it was something of a relief that the day had finally arrived. I finished packing, and waited rather awkwardly for the car which would take me to the airport.

I drank a second cup of Keemun tea, standing at the ground-floor window looking out at the quiet, grey morning. The car arrived. I picked up the suitcases, and took a last, filial look at my family portraits hanging in the hall. They looked distinctly gloomy, I thought.

I climbed into the car. Tira stood at the open window, and said something I couldn't catch. I smiled back enthusiastically, to give the impression I had no qualms about leaving. But as I looked at her, and at the familiar collection of objects on the wall behind her, garnered from dozens of trips which were less dangerous than this seemed likely to be, I felt a great deal less happy than I pretended.

PART III

FOLLOWING THE SHINING PATH

The city of Lima, whose proper name is 'Los Reis de Lima'. In the square in front of the cathedral is a gallows.

Peru

You should consider that in the time of the Incas . . . people had much faith in God and were loyal, and very charitable and humble, and they raised their sons and daughters with discipline and teaching. . . In the time of the Incas there was none of this greed for gold and silver. But now there are many thieves: Indians, Negroes, and most of all the Spaniards, who flay the poor Indians and rob them. And not only that, for they take their wives and daughters, especially the priests. . .

Felipe Guaman Poma de Ayala, 1613

We were travelling to a country of great natural and political extremes: one of the world's poorer nations, yet by far the greatest source of coca, the raw material for one of the most profitable of all products: cocaine. One of the few middling things about Peru is its population: 22.3 million in 1990. Its geography is extraordinary. A long, dreary, arid coastal plain stretches along the Pacific, a desert in sight of the sea. Sixty miles or so inland, the mountains begin: a great spinal column from top to bottom of the country, thickening as it heads southwards and eastwards.

The tallest mountain in the Andean range, Huascarán, is 22,205 feet or 6,768 metres high. Those who fly directly from the coastal plain to one of the Andean cities – Cuzco, say – must beware of the effects of the sudden leap in altitude; though people of Inca origin have the advantage of especially enlarged lungs, which thousands of years of adaptation to the mountain environment have given them.

If you fly from the developed west of the country to its empty quarter in the east, it takes no more than half an hour to cross the immense Andean range. Then you are over the same kind of country I visited in Brazil: rainforest which stretches as far as the eye can see in every direction, and muddy rivers which wind their way down from Brazil or Bolivia. On the land reclaimed by cutting down the rainforest, the fields of coca proliferate.

The ancestors of the tribes there had once travelled across the Bering Strait from eastern Asia and made their way down through what is now Alaska, the west coast of Canada and the United States and so into Central and South America. Over thousands of years they adapted themselves to the life of the rainforest. They have always kept a faint sense of kinship with the indians of the mountains, who developed rather differently. When the Chinese came to Peru in the nineteenth century to work for the big mining and railway groups, and were followed by smaller numbers of Japanese in the first half of the twentieth century, it became obvious simply from comparing their physical appearance that the indians of the forest and the mountains were of roughly the same original stock as the newcomers: short, delicate, with high cheekbones, slanted eyes and a golden skin.

The indigenous people of the Peruvian region have never entirely recovered from the moment, towards the end of 1526, when the first contact was made between Europe and the Inca empire. Two small Spanish vessels commanded by Bartolome Ruiz, who was working for Francisco Pizarro, sighted an ocean-going balsa raft on a trading mission for the Inca empire. It was equipped with large quantities of artefacts in gold and silver, clearly the products of a highly developed society. At that instant the notion of Peru as a vast source of easy riches became fixed in the Spanish consciousness: it was there to be robbed.

The Inca empire's name for itself was Tahuantinsuyu, meaning the Four Provinces of the World. Like the Chinese, the Incas were largely uninterested in what lay beyond their extensive borders. The northerly quarter stretched up to what is now Ecuador. The westerly one included much of modern Peru. Antisuyu, to the east, reached into the Amazonian jungle and part of what is now Bolivia. The southern quarter took in half of Chile and the north-western part of Argentina. The imperial capital, Cuzco, which lies in the Andes to the south-east of Lima, was roughly in the empire's centre; its name in Quechua, the main language of the Inca empire, means 'navel'.

Tahuantinsuyu was a relatively recent creation. The empire proper began in 1438 with the accession to the throne of Pachacuti Inca Yupanqui, the ninth Inca, who captured Chile. It lasted less than a hundred years in its fullest form, and owed its sudden rise to the extraordinary energy and organising power of the Incas, who took over the various smaller powers in the region and laid down roads, bridged abysses, built vast storerooms and warehouses, and extended the irrigation of the soil. It was said that an insect could be picked off a leaf in the farthest north of the empire and be placed in the Inca's hand in Cuzco, still alive.

A population of at least six million – the precise figure is disputed, and has sometimes been put as high as thirty million – was fed, clothed and marshalled with great effectiveness. More land was under irrigation in 1525 than at any later time until around 1965; nowadays the agricultural output of Peru is lower than it was under the Incas. Society in Tahuantinsuyu was highly stratified, but moderately benevolent. Like the Anglo-Saxons before the Norman Conquest, the people of the Four Provinces lived a settled and orderly existence which was to seem all the more harmonious after the catastrophe in which their ruler was killed and their entire national life destroyed.

The daring and courage of Peru's conquerors is beyond doubt; but so is the brutal treachery with which the conquest was achieved. It was an act of piracy on a national scale. The men involved were rough characters: Francisco Pizarro was illegitimate, started life as a swineherd in Spain, and probably never learned to read or write. His original partner in the exploit, Diego de Almagro, was a foundling who escaped from Castile to the New World to avoid arrest for violent crime. The conquistadores of Peru were there for the sole purpose of making themselves rich.

The series of disasters which brought the Four Provinces of the World to destruction began with the smallpox epidemic which followed the Spanish across the Atlantic. The disease took the route the ancestors of the autochthonous tribes had once taken: southwards along the littoral of Central and South America in the 1520s, then inland to Cuzco. One of its thousands of victims there was the powerful and respected Inca ruler Huayna Capac. Francisco Pizarro arrived in Peru at the precise moment when Huayna Capac's two sons, the half-brothers Huascar and Atahuallpa, were fighting a bitter civil war for the succession. 'The Spaniards were able to walk in as if by an open door,' Felipe Guaman Poma de Ayala wrote, 'because our Indians in their confusion and disunity failed to defend themselves. . . '

Atahuallpa made the serious mistake of underestimating the threat which the 170 or so Spaniards posed to him and his country. What finally destroyed him and the country was his decision to go to the main square of Cajamarca to meet the Spaniards in the late afternoon of Saturday 16 November 1532. He judged that his escort of 6,000 men was so vast they would have no need of weapons. The Spanish opened fire on them without warning and charged them on horseback. Several thousand Inca warriors and courtiers were killed. The only injury on the Spanish side was a cut to Pizarro's hand when he protected Atahuallpa from a Spanish sword.

Pizarro did not save him out of humanity: he wanted Atahuallpa alive. The following year, in spite of his solemn promise that he would ransom the Inca for a roomful of gold, which was duly provided, Pizarro yielded reluctantly to the urgent pressure of his partner Almagro and had Atahuallpa condemned to death for treason. It was a panicky decision, taken because Almagro and the others thought an attempt was underway to rescue the Inca. By agreeing to be baptised a Christian, Atahuallpa saved himself from being burned alive and was garrotted instead. The execution took place at nightfall on Saturday 26 July 1533, in the square in Cajamarca where he had been captured with so much slaughter eight months earlier.

The conquerors quickly fell out over the spoils. A bitter and violent dispute over the control of Cuzco cost both of them their lives. In 1538 Almagro was taken prisoner by Pizarro's brother Hernando, tried, and garrotted in his turn. Three years later, in June 1541, twenty of Almagro's supporters in full armour broke into Pizarro's palace in Lima and attacked him. He put up a good fight for a man of sixty-three, but he was wounded more than twenty times and eventually collapsed and died.

The self-defeating cruelty of the Spaniards in Cuzco itself had forced the puppet ruler, Manco Inca, to cease collaborating with them. They had chained him up, urinated in his face, and raped his wives in front of him. Before he escaped he gathered his advisers together. 'Soon,' he told them, 'we shall wipe them out, until none remains. Then we can awake from this nightmare, and start rejoicing.' He slipped out of Cuzco and took refuge in the rainforest around Vilcabamba. There he established an Inca state which survived for nearly forty years with the help of tribes like the Ashaninca.

In 1545 Manco himself was murdered by a group of seven Spaniards, whose lives he had spared when they sought refuge in Vilcabamba. He enjoyed their company, and used to play horseshoe quoits with them. One day, as he was making a throw, one of them stepped forward and stabbed him. There were no guards present, and the only witness was his son, Titu Cusi. They left Manco Inca and turned to deal with Titu Cusi. He was wounded, but managed to escape into the surrounding forest.

After a period of regency he succeeded his father as ruler of the free Inca state, and tried to keep a line of communication open to the Spanish. He died in 1571. His successor, Tupac Amaru, suspecting that he had been poisoned, ordered the death of a Spanish missionary on suspicion of having murdered him. The Spanish viceroy, Francisco de Toledo, decided it was a good pretext for wiping out the small Inca enclave. The following year, 1572, the Spanish made their final assault on Vilcabamba. Tupac Amaru was captured, paraded with a chain of gold, tried hastily, and (despite the strongest protests of many Spanish officials and clergy) beheaded in the city of Cuzco.

By this time the population of Peru had fallen catastrophically. In 1570 it was estimated at 1.3 million. At least five million people, and possibly many more, had fallen victim to the new diseases brought from Europe, the collapse of agriculture and of the complicated system of food distribution, the frequent civil wars between the indians as well as the Spaniards, and the constant depredations of greedy colonists.

The *encomienda* system introduced to Peru from Mexico was

usually little more than a system of slave, or at best forced, labour. Hundreds of thousands of indians died in the mercury mines of Huancavelica, the gold mine at Carabaya, and the great silver mining complex at Potosi: 'these infernal pits', one horrified Spanish visitor described them. The Spanish Crown had declared that work in the mines should be voluntary and well paid, and believed that these conditions were being followed.

Above all, the indians had suffered a devastating blow to the spirit. At a stroke, the elaborate economic and social system which sustained the old empire of Tahuantinsuyu had collapsed. Based on the clan or extended family, it had ensured that there were sufficient people to cultivate the land in a properly organised way and maintain the all-important irrigation systems. The difficult terrain of upland Peru needed intensive labour over long periods of time to keep it productive; and the various scourges which followed the Spanish Conquest made that much harder to ensure.

Spanish critics of the way Peru was being run, and there were many of them, spoke out with increasing frequency. Some, like Bartolome de las Casas, tended to exaggerate the cruelties of Spanish rule; but the continual sense of moral unease resulted in the New Laws issued in 1542 by Charles V, whose intention was to protect the indian population. They had little effect.

Felipe Guaman Poma de Ayala produced an impressive body of anecdotal evidence about the disaster in his native country. Guaman Poma (which means Falcon Puma in Quechua) was born soon after the Conquest, perhaps as early as 1535, the son of a senior Inca nobleman and an Inca mother. His adopted brother was half-Spanish; Guaman Poma took the name de Ayala from him. He began assembling the materials for his master-work, *The First New Chronicle and Good Government*, in the 1570s. It was finished on 1 January 1613. Two years later, by now almost eighty, he travelled to Lima in order to send it to King Philip III in Spain.

The King probably never saw it, but it certainly reached the Spanish court. Some forty years later it was bought by the Danish ambassador to Spain, Cornelius Pedersen Lerche, who took it back to Copenhagen with him when his tour of duty finished.

It ended up in the Royal Library in Christiansborg Castle, and came to light only in 1908. Its black ink now a reddish-brown, it can be seen there still: 1,179 pages of text, including the four hundred or so skilful, idiosyncratic drawings which he put in, he said modestly, 'to alleviate the dullness and annoyance' of reading the text.

Guaman Poma was an eccentric, and inclined to pursue his own relatively slight grudges with the same anger he applied to more serious crimes against the indians he travelled among. But it is only necessary to read a paragraph or two to realise that we are in the presence of someone who thinks and responds recognisably as we ourselves do:

> My readers should not be annoyed by my accusations, but reflect that I have found some honest officials and some kindly priests serving in parishes. Good people will take no offence. It is the evil ones who will be angry and want to kill me. But surely everyone can remember a brother who has loved him and been able to relieve him of his care and sadness. My book should be read, word by word, in the same way. Tears will come, but the good will be separated from the evil.

He travelled round the country, often living with the poor and going without decent food and clothing. One of his most charming drawings (see p. 1) shows him walking to Lima to deliver his book for shipping to Spain. It is raining heavily and he is accompanied by his son Francisco de Ayala, his horse Guiado and his two dogs Lautaro and Amigo. Little labels, as in a cartoon, identify them for us. He has labelled himself 'author'. He wears a broad-brimmed Andean panama hat, an indian cloak and Spanish doublet and hose. His hair is cut in Inca fashion, and although he is in his eighties, he has drawn himself as being in the prime of life. Perhaps he was being vain. He carries a staff in one hand, and a rosary in the other to show that he is a faithful Christian; though some of the things he writes cast doubt on that.

The first part of his book is a history of the Incas and the kingdom of Tahuantinsuyu, together with a description of the systems of administration and justice, the different months of the year, and the festivals and songs of ordinary people:

> There is also a happy song called the cachiva, the words of which run: 'I am waiting, my Chanca girl. Come from wherever you are hiding and join me... Put on your ribbon and sash and let us be together. I shall carry you, carry you everywhere and hide you away, my gentle maid. When your linnet sings, you will come to me. When my linnet sings, linnet, linnet, you will be with child.'

'There is no cause for any criticism or censure of these entertainments of the people,' he writes. 'It is simply a case of the poor mitigating their hard work by singing and dancing among themselves.'

The second part of the book deals with the Conquest, and runs through the terrible events which Guaman Poma's father had lived through and often witnessed. There are some remarkable flashes of eccentric insight:

> But the people with the most influence in the Christian world are often light in body, thin and narrow-chested. These are the ones who become learned doctors or men of great wealth and position, because of their energy.

It is in the third part of his book, gloomily entitled 'There Is No Remedy', in which this element of personal observation is strongest. He describes his journeys around Peru, his meetings with ordinary indians and their oppressors. His methods are those of the journalist:

> In my work I have always tried to obtain the most truthful accounts, accepting those which seemed to be substantial and which were confirmed from several sources. I have only reported those facts which several people have agreed upon as being true.

Above all, he describes what he saw himself as he moved around the country:

> Whilst I was in this region a disturbance occurred in Huachos. It seems that a priest demanded Indians to work for him and especially girls for weaving cloth. The local chief, a certain Don Pedro, refused. Out of spite, the priest accused him and his people of idolatry and proceeded to manufacture evidence that they had been worshipping rocks and stones. He did this by hanging

up Don Pedro, some old people of both sexes and some children one by one, torturing them until in their agony they admitted the offence and produced stones which they said were their idols. Then a hundred Indians were taken to Castrovirreyna, stripped, cruelly flogged in the presence of the judge and kept in prison until eighty of them, including Don Pedro, had died. The priest and his friends then appropriated all the ornaments, silverware, scarf-pins, feathers and garments of coloured wool, which are worn by our Indians at their celebrations, from the houses of the dead and those nearby. These priests even took the bedspreads.

It is the last sentence that gives the ring of truth to the entire story: this is precisely what happens on such occasions, as we were to find ourselves when we travelled around Peru.

Guaman Poma explains that because of his advanced age he cannot travel to Spain to speak to the King in person. Instead he imagines a dialogue between himself and the King, who turns out to be chatty and (of course) greatly interested in what Guaman Poma tells him:

> Tell me, author, what is wrong nowadays? Why is the population declining and why are the Indians getting poorer and poorer?

To which Guaman Poma has plenty to say. He describes how the indians who have flooded into the cities can be encouraged back to their villages. He advocates a return to the old clan system whereby the fields can be tilled and irrigated. Not liking priests, he thinks they should be kept under much greater control, and prevented from debauching the wives and daughters of the indians. He wants a Visitor-General appointed, who will ensure that the King's instructions will be properly obeyed.

By writing his book, with its strange judgements and observations, its eccentric conversation with the King, its quirky drawings and descriptions of the way things had changed, Guaman Poma was trying to reintroduce order into the chaos and disaster which he saw all around him as a result of the Conquest. 'It was,' he said, 'as if the world were turned upside down.'

Miami

All Spaniards travelling on honest business ought to carry passports, showing their rank and social standing. If they fail to produce these credentials on demand, they should be liable to confiscation of their belongings.

Felipe Guaman Poma de Ayala, 1613

For no very clear reason, you cannot transit through most American airports. Even if you are only there to catch a plane to another country in an hour's time, you have to fill in all the forms about your parents and your diseases and your hopes for a better future as though you are planning to stay in the United States for the rest of your life. This process can be a nuisance.

A sour immigration official, irritated by a long line of people from Colombia whose plane had landed at the same time as ours, disliked the visas from Iran and Iraq in my passport. Was I an arms dealer? A government agent of some kind? An illicit trader, operating in contravention of United Nations sanctions? He was disappointed to find the answer was nothing more than journalism.

Steve Morris and Matt Leiper had not been on our plane. We had decided that Eamonn, Rosalind and I should go ahead by a week, in order to prepare the way and be ready to start filming when the other two arrived. The three of us had flown over from London on the same plane, but Rosalind and Eamonn shared my preference for sitting separately. I listened to my CDs of Bartok and Django Reinhardt, and read my files on Peru. On the movie screen above, like some new Pizarro, Mel Gibson was killing more and more people in a variety of painful ways. Whenever I glanced across at Eamonn in the darkness of the plane, his overhead light was on and he was going through his notes, just as I was. Hunched over them, he looked like St Jerome in his study.

By the time we reached Gate D-7 at Miami airport, it felt like Peru already. Even the American Airlines staff were Latinos, and the passengers had either indian features or mediterranean ones. Half a dozen nuns chattered away in Spanish. No one kept to any order: if you could push your way on first, you did so. It was very friendly, but very competitive. On this plane we sat together, and were no longer in business class. We talked fitfully about our plans for the trip, trying not to say the key names too loudly. After twenty hours' non-stop travelling, we began to descend.

I noticed a strange absence of nerves on my part. Usually, the worst moment of any difficult assignment is when the plane lands and there is no longer any chance of backing out. Perhaps it was the length of the journey which made it easier; perhaps it was merely that after so many months of preparation the scope for anxiety was much smaller. Reluctantly I switched off the Bartok. Our navigation lights flashed red and white on the low cloud cover. A few streetlamps showed on the ground. At 11.21 pm we made a clumsy landing.

We had gone in a single day from an English summer to a southern hemisphere winter. The air was damp and chilly, and I put on the Barbour I had bought at the Harrods shop at Heathrow. In the elderly airport building, drab and run-down, the solemn line of people arriving ran parallel to the excited line of people catching the same plane to Miami. Some of the people in our queue were well-to-do and showed it, but most had dressed down for the moment of arrival. There had been stories of taxi drivers picking up customers at the airport and robbing or even killing them on the way into town.

We were shuffling apathetically forward towards the front of the passport queue when a small, extremely pretty, bouncy woman in her twenties pushed her way through, smiling broadly and calling out to us. Rosalind threw her arms round her and kissed her.

'This is Cecilia Valenzuela,' she said.

Rosalind and Eamonn had talked a good deal about Cecilia in the previous few weeks, but I had never expected her to look like this. She had been a famous television news reporter in Peru, and had covered the most difficult stories about politics, drugs and human rights. Then the government had put serious pressure on the television channel which employed her. The programme was axed, her contract was withdrawn.

I had not been looking forward to working with Cecilia: I was anticipating a television star's massive ego and an unwillingness to do the humbler tasks of a locally hired fixer. I could see at once that I had been wrong. Cecilia was full of enthusiasm for every aspect of the job, small or great. Her English was only rudimentary, not even as good as my Spanish, yet it was easy enough to understand roughly what she meant.

Now she rattled out an account of the things that had happened in Lima that day: a university professor's body found on the beach, riddled with bullets; an Army officer kidnapped and reported murdered; a car bomb here, an ambush there. It came tumbling out from her, and she was strangely jolly about it all, as though it were just part of a highly enjoyable game. She was by no means, I found later, lacking in compassion, but she seemed to find the details of the daily situation in Peru so fascinating that she could not restrain her enthusiasm for all of it. I asked her lamely how she had been able to get into the arrivals' hall; she laughed and produced a plastic card marked '*Prensa*' – Press. The number was 0001. We were to find constant examples of her ability to use her charm, and her television fame, to get past the most hostile of officials.

Outside in the dark and chill of the evening two other people were waiting for us: Sally Bowen, the BBC correspondent in Lima, and her son Rory. Sally was quieter and cooler, a delicate blonde woman. When I was at Cambridge and she at Oxford, I remembered hearing of her as a famous undergraduate beauty, and we had various friends in common. She had come to Peru in the late 1980s after the break-up of her marriage, and became a journalist for the BBC and the *Financial Times*, never having done anything of the kind in her life before.

Sally had already given us a good deal of help and advice, and we were hoping she would be able to travel with us occasionally as a fixer and translator. But we were careful never to tell her, or

Cecilia, about our contacts with the Shining Path, nor about our hopes for an interview with Guzman. They would have to work in Lima long after we had gone back to the safety of England, and it was important that they should be able to say with complete honesty that they had known nothing of our plans.

We met the last member of our new team in the car park: our driver, a pleasant-featured, laid-back character who had taken the nickname Johnny and came from a powerful and wealthy Peruvian family. He had trained as a psychologist, and had studied the behaviourist theories of Skinner. Skinner's best known experiment dealt with the difference in reaction of female monkeys when they were handed either their own offspring or a doll after giving birth. Skinner is not a name often heard now, but in the 1960s, when he became involved in a bitter controversy with the American political and linguistic philosopher Noam Chomsky, he was a significant (though scarcely attractive) thinker.

Johnny's family, the Salaverrys, were very grand. Later, as we drove round Lima, we would find streets named after them, or vast mansions where they had lived. Johnny's great-great-grandfather had been one of the leading generals in the war against Chile, and another member of the family, Carlos Augusto Salaverry, was one of Peru's greatest poets. Johnny had set aside his Skinnerism and his family tradition, and found life more interesting and profitable driving foreign television teams around Peru. He was excellent at the job, but it was dangerous to tell him we were in a hurry. A hurry, to Johnny, meant an excuse to force a way through gaps in the traffic that no minibus was designed to penetrate, or – when we were really pushed for time – getting round the obstacles by driving down the pavement and frightening pedestrians into doorways. There was no hint of this as we met him, though. We loaded up our gear into the back of the minibus and settled down for the drive into Lima.

The streets were mostly dark and empty. We did not see any of the fires which we had been told burned at roadblocks set up by the Army or – according to another version – Shining Path. Even at this stage, it seemed that some of the things we had heard about Peru were exaggerated. Still, there was no electricity in large parts of the city as we passed through it, and when Johnny came to a Marine base he had to swerve across the roadway and drive the wrong way down a one-way street; there was, he explained, the danger of car bombs there. The roads were terrible, but we bumped along in good humour, as Sally joked about the difficulties of life in Lima, translating for Cecilia's benefit as she went.

There was no electricity or water on alternate days, she said, and the country seemed to be falling apart; but at least you could get a decent meal in a restaurant still. Johnny laughed and nodded, as he swerved to avoid some outsized pothole. At last we reached the expensive and fashionable district of Miraflores, by the ocean. Our hotel, the Las Americas, was large, modern, and unremarkable except for the fact that it had been built at a time when the economy was in serious trouble and no visitors were coming to Lima. That seemed very strange. When that happens in other places, rumours start about the laundering of drugs money.

Many of its windows were still unmended after the biggest of the car bombs in Miraflores, three months before. I didn't care: it was pleasant enough, the rooms were of a decent size, and there was a minibar big enough to climb into. I unpacked and, like an old soldier, set out all my things methodically: radio, compact disc player, speakers, books, clothes.

Just before I got into bed I went over to the window and pulled the curtains aside. Miraflores was without power that night. Then a car nosed its way through the darkness and silence. Its headlights were full on and yellowish, and they briefly played on a figure standing in the doorway of the bank opposite. It was a man dressed entirely in black, with a balaclava over his face. He was cradling a pump-action shotgun, like a priest carrying a cross in a procession. The badge on his beret glittered faintly, and showed that he was a security guard. As the car passed, its rear lights shed an ominous red aura on him. Then that faded, and the street was entirely black again. I let the curtain drop, and went to bed.

Revolutions

The royal administrators and the other Spaniards lord it over the Indians with absolute power. They can commit crimes with impunity because of the support which they count on from higher authority. All complaint against them is stifled by fear of the consequences.

Felipe Guaman Poma de Ayala, 1613

It took a hundred and fifty years for Peru to achieve a kind of balance after the savage destruction of its political structure and its economy. A settler, creole culture prospered, and Lima became the seat of the Spanish Viceroy and the centre of government for much of South America.

In the small provincial town of Tinta to the south of Cuzco in the middle of the eighteenth century, a local indian cacique, Jose Gabriel Condorcanqui, took up the study of the Inca classics and his imagination was fired. He was a wealthy, cultured man who did what he could to protect his tenants and subordinates from the cruelties of the system; and he was the great-great-great-grandson of the last Inca, Tupac Amaru, beheaded in 1572.

His confrontations with the Spanish authorities became fiercer, until in November 1780 he assumed the name Tupac Amaru II and came out in open rebellion. By the following year there were risings in support of him in many parts of the old Inca empire, and tens of thousands died. Yet in the end Tupac Amaru II was defeated in battle, betrayed and captured. On 18 May 1781, in the square in Cuzco where his ancestor had been beheaded, he was forced to witness the mutilation and execution of his wife and eldest son before being put to death himself with mediaeval barbarity.

Forty years later, the rebellions which led to the independence of Latin America began in earnest. In Peru, the leaders were Jose de San Martin from what was to become Argentina, and Antonio Jose de Sucre and Simon Bolivar from Venezuela. After the Viceroy had been deposed, San Martin entered Lima in July 1821 and declared Peru's independence. Bolivar defeated the royalists at Junin in 1824, and Sucre finished them off, with British help, at Ayacucho in December that year.

Peru became a backwater. Britain, having been heavily involved in the war of independence through men like Admiral Lord Cochrane and General William Miller, now became the new country's biggest overseas trade partner. Words such as *huatchiman* (watchman), *gasfitero* (gas-fitter) and *eswiche* (switch) were adopted by the Peruvians. So was the dish called *airistu*, which appeared on the menus of restaurants along the railway lines. Irish stew had reached Peru.

The nineteenth-century liberal tradition by which Peru was governed, with strong British encouragement, did not favour the indians, any more than Spanish rule had. Economic orthodoxy regarded them as an underclass. A dispute over access to the profitable nitrates in southern Peru led to war with Chile in 1879; by 1883 Peru and its ally Bolivia were beaten. Peru's decline continued.

After the First World War new forces and new ideas seemed to be called for. Victor Raul Haya de la Torre created APRA, the Popular Revolutionary American Alliance, as a nationalist movement for indians and creoles to defend the economic and social interests of Latin America against foreign capitalism. By contrast, the frail left-wing political philosopher Jose Carlos Mariategui turned back to Tahuantinsuyu, seeing it as the forerunner of the Marxist state. In 1929 he founded a political party which joined the Communist International. Mariategui wanted to redistribute land to the indians whose ancestors had lost it at the time of the Spanish Conquest; he believed that the peasants of the highlands and the coastal plain were the class on which to base a truly revolutionary movement.

After the defeat of Tupac Amaru II there had been dozens of rebellions with Inca overtones. One as late as 1923 even assumed the name 'Tahuantinsuyu'. Conditions remained as bad as anything Guaman Poma had witnessed: slave labour, women raped, men hanged or shot for petty theft. Even by the 1960s nothing had seriously changed.

On 3 October 1968 Juan Velasco Alvarado – that unusual phenomenon, a radical general – seized power, ousting an old-fashioned and weak liberal, President Fernando Belaunde Terry, who had to leave the presidential palace in his pyjamas. The new regime set out to offer a third way, neither capitalist nor communist. It soon found itself in trouble with the United States, and turned to the Soviet Union for its military agreements.

General Velasco was a reformer who understood the terrible divide which still existed between conquerors and conquered. He had the support of many junior officers, who had been appalled by the treatment of indians which they had witnessed during their service in the highlands. The new president began a programme of land reform, intended to follow the old *ayllu*, or collective, system of the Incas. He quoted Tupac Amaru II approvingly ('The land-lord will no longer feast on your poverty') and made Quechua an official language to be taught in schools.

Most of his reforms failed utterly. Expectations were raised among the indians, yet resentful landowners made it totally impossible to satisfy them. Other legislation passed by the regime had a different tendency altogether: in March 1969 Decree 006 cut back heavily on the provision of free secondary-school education. The demonstrations which followed were violent, and the police and Army opened fire on angry crowds with machine guns.

Velasco was overthrown in 1975, and a more traditional military dictatorship was introduced. The Peruvian economy was in serious trouble. Industrial growth dropped by 8 per cent between 1973 and 1975; during Velasco's period in office real wages fell by 11 per cent, while the cost of living went up by 139 per cent. Altogether, the years between 1968 and 1975 had been a deeply unsettling time for Peru: some of the basic assumptions of its society had been challenged in a hasty, unthought-out way. Velasco had introduced a profound process of destabilisation, which continued under Belaunde Terry, the man who had left the presidential palace in 1968 in his pyjamas. He was re-elected in 1980 after the military relinquished power, but by now he was sick and elderly.

In 1985 Belaunde left office and was replaced by the young and charming Alan Garcia Perez, the candidate of the nationalist APRA, which won power for the first time. There was huge public enthusiasm for him. After the gloomy last years of Belaunde, when the Army had begun a dirty war against Shining Path and the violence on both sides had reached frightening proportions, Garcia seemed to have the right answers: respect for human rights, control over the Army, social policies to improve the condition of the peasants and the working class and so undermine Shining Path. Nothing came of any of it: the economy continued to decline, and the condition of Peru's working class grew worse. His announcement that he would use only 10 per cent of Peru's gross domestic product to pay off the country's international debt was made without consulting either the World Bank or the International Monetary Fund. As a result, they cut off all credit and loan facilities to Peru. His attempts to nationalise the country's banks failed, and he was forced to make a humiliating retreat.

Within the Army, death squads began to spring up. In June 1986 Shining Path prisoners in three gaols in Peru staged coordinated mutinies, and the armed forces wiped them out. In Lurigancho, every one of the 124 Shining Path prisoners died, at least a hundred of them after surrendering. Alan Garcia was embarrassed by the international reaction, yet in the end only thirty soldiers were confined to barracks for a few weeks. By the time his five years in power ended, he was completely discredited. Shining Path, meanwhile, seemed to be closer than ever to overthrowing the government.

The movement was the personal achievement of one man: a philosophy lecturer at Ayacucho University with a powerful intellect and a remarkable flair for leadership. Abimael Guzman Reynoso was born near the port of Mollendo in southern Peru on 3 December 1934, the illegitimate son of a wealthy wholesaler. He was five when his mother died, and went to live with his father, whom he disliked. As a student and then a lecturer he was quiet and impressive, and soon had a big personal following among his students. He joined the Communist Party, having seen for himself the terrible conditions of the poor after the 1960 earthquake in Peru.

He moved to Ayacucho, the capital of one of the country's poorest, most backward departments. The faculty of the University of San Cristobal de Huamanga, which appointed him to a teaching post, was dominated by Marxists. The Peruvian Communist Party, founded on the base created by Jose Carlos Mariategui, was riven by disputes, and Guzman began to move closer to the Maoist faction. In 1965 he visited China.

He returned, greatly impressed, and joined Bandera Roja (Red Flag), the pro-Peking faction of the PCP, turning it into the organisation whose full name would eventually become The Communist Party of Peru by the Shining Path of Jose Carlos Mariategui and Marxism, Leninism, Maoism and the Thought of Chairman Gonzalo. Soon Shining Path dominated the political activities at a number of universities and colleges throughout Peru. 'Liberated zones', where all government representatives were forced out by popular vote, were being established. In 1979 the Party prepared to start 'the People's War'. The date chosen was 17 May 1980: the day of the election which brought the return of Belaunde Terry.

Few people noticed at the time: the Lima press took days to print a paragraph which reported that five men had burned the ballot boxes in the obscure village of Chuschi, south of Ayacucho. The war had started, all the same; and the quiet, polite, intense academic was turning into 'Puka Inti', the Red Sun: beacon of world revolution and the Fourth Sword of Marxism, after Marx, Lenin and Mao.

On 19 April 1980 Guzman told some of the leading figures in his new Army:

> The people are rearing up, arming themselves and rising up in rebellion, putting nooses around the neck of imperialism and the reactionaries, taking them by the throat, squeezing them, and, by necessity, they will strangle them. Reactionary flesh will be stripped and shredded and those black scraps of offal will be buried in the mire; what is left will be burned and the ashes scattered to the ends of the earth.

Some of this was to come about, literally and in detail. The usual estimate is that in the period between the start of 'the People's War' and Guzman's arrest in September 1992, $15 billion of damage was done to the Peruvian economy and something like 25,000 people died.

Following the principles of China's Cultural Revolution, Shining Path adopted the notion of a constantly self-cleansing, self-recreating power, based on the overriding authority of a supreme directing leadership. For those outside its ranks, the distinguishing feature of Shining Path is its policy of exemplary terror, in which entire families have been wiped out in order to show the movement's ruthlessness and determination. It will not accept competition on what it regards as its home ground from anyone who sets up any alternative system.

The policy was announced in 1990; by May of the following year four women, four children and a man had been murdered for helping to distribute milk to the young. The next month, six members of a mining union, the head of a local Catholic charity and two foreign aid workers died. In July, four agricultural experts and two peasants working in alpaca husbandry were murdered, together with four Japanese horticulturalists. The most famous case occurred in the shantytown of Villa El Salvador, on the outskirts of Lima, where the deputy mayor, Maria Elena Moyano, helped to found an organisation which provided soup kitchens and advice centres. She had campaigned strongly against Shining Path, and was active in a number of feminist and left-wing causes.

On 14 February 1992 she had led a protest against the Shining Path's call for an 'armed strike'. Shining Path had a policy of killing people who ignored the call. Maria Elena told those who had turned up, 'We do not support those who undermine the people's organisations, and who want to instal themselves with force and brutality.' The following day, at a fund-raising occasion in a school, a group of Shining Path enforcers shot her at close range in front of everyone. They dragged her body into the school playground, and blew it up with dynamite.

Shining Path's rigorous system of internal discipline ensured its growing success. Each new candidate for membership must submit entirely to the Party's authority, writing out the fullest possible self-criticism and waiting humbly for the Party's judgement on it. Again and again I was to notice a certain look about Shining Path's true believers: a calmness, a total certainty which came from the complete relinquishment of personal ideas, ambitions and feelings, and a wholehearted acceptance of Gonzalo Thought. They reminded me of Scientology's 'Clears', or the followers of Ayatollah Khomeini, or religious fundamentalists in the United States.

The only way to combat Shining Path effectively was to capture its prophet; and yet he seemed so much cleverer and more resourceful than his enemies that it was hard to think such a thing would ever happen. And even if it did, the deaths of Atahuallpa, Manco Inca, Tupac Amaru and the others had shown that it would not necessarily bring the movement to its knees.

Lima

In the City of Kings, or Lima ... money is sent abroad
for safe keeping or dissipated in wild living. Some people
go naked and others, the fortunate ones, are richly dressed.
Some weep and others sing.

Felipe Guaman Poma de Ayala, 1613

The morning was leaden, and the distant ocean was indistinguishable from the sky: the colour of fog, of dirty linen, of
uncleaned windows. I put my passport and credit cards into a
linen wallet like a holster under my shirt, and ventured out.
The excitable wail of an ambulance briefly overrode the noise
of the traffic. Everywhere there were men in uniform: some
were policemen, but most were from private security firms. Like
the solitary figure I had seen the previous night, they carried
big pump-action shotguns of the kind that could clear a street
in a single burst, and kill everyone within thirty yards. Their
expressions seemed entirely dead: big, impassive indian faces,
whose eyes registered you as middle class and unthreatening and
then flicked to the next passer-by.

There was a constant racket of motor-horns and the shouting of young conductors who reached out from the minibuses
which had recently been permitted to ply for hire, exhorting or
if necessary grabbing people to get them on board. I walked
along, looking at the once-expensive shops, some with windows
still unrepaired from the recent wave of car bombs in Miraflores.
The shops seemed empty, dreary and dark because of the morning power cut, and there was the continual hum of generators.
Beggars, most of them indian women wrapped in blankets, lay
apathetically against the walls, with scarcely the energy or the
expectation to reach their hands out for money. Street traders

thrust lottery tickets, packets of cigarettes, chocolates, batteries in my face. Others waved calculators, not to sell but to show that they were in the currency business.

'You want change dollar?'

'*Cambio – dolares.*'

'Best price here.'

'I got dollar, soles, an't'in' you wan'.'

But Peru was looking-glass land, and the rate they were offering for the American dollar was actually less good, by some 15 per cent, than the rate I could have obtained merely by walking into one of the nearby banks. It was the exact reverse of the arrangement in almost every other closed economy in the world. The moneychangers were not looking for tourists or foreign visitors; that supply had long since dried up. They were looking for people up from the country who had sold their coca leaves or their basic paste to the big cocaine dealers for large amounts of dollars, and wanted to change them quickly into Peruvian soles with no questions asked. Unlike the banks, the dealers on the streets did not demand to look at your identity document nor ask you to sign a currency exchange form. Later, we were unable to find a bank which would change more than $250 in traveller's cheques, and had to rely on the perfectly legal but slightly anxious services of a man called Percy, who would come to the hotel with huge wads of soles.

Round the corner from the Las Americas hotel was a vast twenty-four-hour supermarket, with as good a range of food and household goods as the Sainsbury's in South Kensington or the Prisunic in the Champs Elysées. Armed men stood beside the entrance and checked your bag as you left, to make sure that you had paid for everything you were taking out. Each trolley was fitted with an electronic calculator. By the time we arrived, in September 1992, inflation was down to 57 per cent a year and the calculators were merely useful accessories. When they were installed, two years earlier, inflation was 7,650 per cent and prices in the supermarket were going up every half hour.

I went back to the Las Americas, and settled down for coffee in Eamonn's room. Cecilia and Rosalind were there, talking seriously together, while Eamonn flicked through his notebook looking for points to raise. We had decided not to hold our meetings downstairs in the lobby for fear of being overheard. Now there was a knock at the door: a waiter brought in coffee and orange juice. Ten minutes afterwards another brought in a big basket of fruit, the gift of the hotel manager whose name was English. On both occasions the waiters were inclined to hang around, adjusting things and watching us, until Cecilia told them sharply to go. Maybe it was just our imagination, but in those first days we felt very much under observation.

For the first time since we arrived, I felt the chill of nervousness I had missed at the airport. This was a society where people at the very top had things to hide: things which it would be our job to make public. We were going to offend some of the most powerful people in the country by what we did here. The discussion switched to tactics. There was a long discussion in Spanish. Rosalind nodded sharply, and translated.

'Cecilia says we will have to keep moving around all the time, and – what's the English expression? – play all the ends against the middle. It's the only way to do it here.'

Cecilia nodded brightly, and smiled: she loved this kind of thing, the conspiracy to make things public, the secret search which would end in disclosure.

'It's going to be interesting all right,' Eamonn said, and laughed harshly: he obviously felt the same way I did. He stood in front of the window swinging his hands backwards and forwards in unison, so that his left fist struck the palm of his right hand each time. It was a habit I remembered from the time when I had worked with him in Afghanistan, three years before. He looked out at the empty building site opposite, at the long lines of washing, the only bright colours in view, at the blocks of flats with their flaking paint, their water-stains, their dark windows, their dreary, dirty concrete façades. Anxiety settled on us both for a moment, as debilitating as the grey atmosphere which hung over Lima. Then Rosalind laughed.

'Cecilia says you should see your faces! You both look really glum, she says.'

Johnny drove us out of Miraflores, towards the equally expensive suburb of San Felipe. A soldier looked at us incuriously from the back of his Army patrol vehicle, his rifle hanging loosely in his arms. Outside the studios of the television station Channel 2 a couple of armoured personnel carriers were parked, and the road was partly blocked. Three months earlier there had been a huge car bomb here. The houses opposite were as badly wrecked as if they were in Beirut or Sarajevo; huge chunks of concrete, thrown up by the explosion, had smashed through their roofs and broken down their walls. Heavy artillery could not have done a more destructive job. To be here was like being in a war zone. Perhaps it was a war zone.

We headed on towards the city centre, past the Sheraton Hotel, big and well defended and featureless; we had decided not to stay here, because it was too dangerous to walk around in this part of town at night. In front of us lay the old city, founded by Pizarro, the city of La Perichola and the Viceroys. Now it was tawdry and decaying, and many of the windows in the grandest buildings were boarded up. A palace of the viceregal period, converted in the nineteenth century into an hotel, stood empty and vandalised, its ground floor taken over by Kentucky Fried Chicken.

The splendid, charming, overdecorated palaces of princes, archbishops and presidents rose on the edges of seedy plazas like cliffs out of a dirty sea. The mistresses of the powerful had once peered through the delicately carved wooden balconies which jutted out of the house-fronts, to see which of their lovers might be coming down the narrow streets. The red and yellow ochre with which the grander buildings were painted flaked off as though from a kind of permanent skin disorder.

Small shops, gloomy from the power cuts and unchanged in decoration since the 1930s, sold old-fashioned items: hats, walking canes, outmoded furniture, pipes, clothes of an unstylish cut. Larger shops sold the cheap mass-produced Japanese goods made by companies unheard of in the rich countries of the world. Everywhere in the delightful squares and narrow streets of this viceregal Lima, young men looked you over with a professional eye.

'Here is always, any hour, night-time, day-time, getting

mugged,' said Cecilia gaily; she pronounced 'mugged' in Chaucerian fashion, so that it had two syllables.

We paid a courtesy visit on the Foreign Ministry in a grand building of viceregal date. After walking down long corridors and questioning apathetic secretaries we found the man we had come to see: short and neat and gloomy, he sat behind a very large desk. In front of him lay a long telex marked 'Secret'. It had been sent by the Peruvian embassy in London, and parts of it had been obsessively underlined. 'Peru is the heart of darkness,' the neat figure behind the desk read out slowly. The words were mine, and the telex contained the text of an article which had appeared in a London newspaper the day before. My interviewer had asked me about my Peruvian trip, and I had told her a little, but not much. I had, however, let myself go about the condition of the country.

The official and I had a discussion about what I had said, and it seemed to me that he did not altogether disagree. A day or so later I saw a former government minister, who went further. 'In a few months' time,' he said impressively, 'this country will have no government. It will have collapsed. And then Shining Path will be the only force capable of governing. It will be like Year Zero in Cambodia.' Most government officials and middle-class people were profoundly depressed by the state of the country, and a disturbing number seemed to agree that Shining Path was close to victory in its war against the government.

It was a relief to leave the gloom of the ministry, where people seemed to be going through the motions of working while waiting for something worse to happen. Outside, the streets seethed with people selling things, squatting in the gutters, begging, sleeping.

'Coca,' said Johnny, and drew up beside a man who sat on the kerb with a blanket spread out in front of him. On it were little piles of half-dried green leaves that reminded me slightly of privet. It is not illegal to chew coca leaves in Peru: that is one of the legacies of the Inca period. Beside the leaves was a little pile of whitish substance. I might have taken it to be cocaine, but it was calcium, which you have to take when you chew, in order to neutralise the burns which the coca would otherwise inflict on throat and tongue.

'*Oje*,' Johnny called to the man when I said I would like to buy some coca leaves. He took no notice, his chin resting on his chest, his eyes half-closed.

'Too estoned,' Johnny said, with the characteristic Hispanic difficulty of pronouncing an initial 's' followed by a 't'. He rammed his minibus into first gear and barged his way into the traffic.

At the corner of Jiron Ocona and Calle de Serrano a big crowd had gathered. Men and women were waving pieces of paper in the air, pushing and shoving each other and occasionally looking down to consult newspapers. It looked like an auction.

'They fixing dollars price. Drugs.' This, not the finance ministry or the stock exchange, was where the rate for the Peruvian sol was fixed each day. The US dollar, most often in the form of hundred-dollar bills, was the real currency of the country. The big cocaine dealers from Colombia, who sold to the United States and Europe, paid and were paid in dollars, and dollars followed the line of the coca plant back to its source. The areas where coca was grown had, indeed, been effectively annexed by the Colombian drugs mafia. Peru was triply colonised: by the Spanish Conquest, by the American dollar, and by the drugs trade.

We drove on. In a park, beneath the pompous busts of generals who had never won a war, homeless children as young as six were putting bags over their heads and sniffing glue. Two policemen, their uniforms unbuttoned, cigarettes in their mouths, wandered through the park. They took no notice of the glue-sniffing. The children for them were merely the effluvia of Peruvian society. In four or five years they would be selling coca or the heroin which was starting to be produced in the north-east of the country, trading for dollars, robbing, killing or being killed.

The city dragged out in front of us: inner suburbs where the roads were lined with factories and the mean single-storeyed houses of the people who worked there, outer suburbs where the houses became briefly larger and grander. They were protected by electrified wire fences and by guardrooms with tinted and armoured windows. The entertainment of the householders was provided by vast satellite dishes which could draw in programmes from the United States and every Spanish-speaking country in the hemisphere. Beyond that the city took on a new phase, unplanned and unfinished, with the incompleted foundations and partly built walls of buildings for which the money had long ago run out. The road evaporated and turned from a six-lane highway into an unsurfaced, rutted track, the big vehicles rocking up and down over the holes and folds in the ground.

We had reached the Lima of the poor, though not yet that of the dispossessed. Little unplanned patches of shantytown spread over the hillsides like fungus, following the pattern of the ridges and folds. Here the houses were mostly of unfaced, dusty grey brick like the surrounding earth, though some people, more confident in their possession and more individualistic than the rest, had painted their house-fronts in the Nile greens, candyfloss pinks and swimming-pool blues of 1950s American automobiles.

Shining Path had passed by here: the walls proclaimed '*SOCIA-LISMO O MUERTE*', '*VIVA EL PRESIDENTE GONZALO*', or '*PARO ARMADO*': Socialism Or Death, Long Live President Gonzalo, Armed Strike. Yet it hardly seemed possible that Maoists occupied these tidy, petty-bourgeois homes, where people fought bravely to maintain appearances and went dutifully to the lean-to churches crowning every rise. Maybe the slogans were to frighten rather than recruit them. At a small open-air market chickens hung, alive or dead, by their necks, and a man was slicing a big watermelon with a machete. Soldiers hung around watching, their arms resting on their rifles, black baseball caps on their heads. They were there to enforce a new law which prohibited the sale of ammonia and other chemicals which could be used by the Shining Path for making bombs. A stream flowed over rocks and discarded bones and shreds of plastic; women laboured home from the open market we had passed two miles back, laden down with the vegetables which were all they had to live on.

Yet even this wasn't the worst of it. The worst were the miserable huts of plaited straw, with no other floor but the clogging, insistent sand of the desert and no decoration but pictures cut from ancient newspapers. These were the places which were degrading even to look at: the rows of hundreds upon hundreds of identical straw boxes where people struggled to retain an approximation of humanity. The government had abandoned them to utter despair. There were no services of any kind: no water, no electricity, no schools, no telephones, no police, no church, no local government structures, no doctors, no shops, no one to bring you into the world and no one to bury you.

The government of Alberto Fujimori, in seeking to put life into the Peruvian economy, had followed almost to the letter the classic economic liberalism which had been fashionable throughout the 1980s. The so-called 'Fujishock', which had removed subsidies from food and opened up the economy unmercifully to the full blast of external competition, had devastated the lives of people like this. Since they lacked even the minimal rights of squatters and their houses were an eyesore, the authorities would move in from time to time to bulldoze the feeble shacks to the ground and disperse the weeping, miserable, unprotected population. Sometimes, with an affecting naïveté, the squatters would name their settlements after members of the President's family, in the hope that this might act as a talisman against the bulldozers of a state which seemed to care nothing about where or how they might live.

In the shantytown of San Juan de Lurigancho that Sunday morning we met a man marked out for violent death. Michel Azqueta had received many threats from Shining Path: he represented an alternative form of leadership, and Shining Path was not prepared to brook a rival. His friend and colleague Maria Elena Moyano, the charismatic activist for women's rights, had been murdered by Shining Path seven months earlier after a number of similar threats. Everyone expected Azqueta to be next, and they looked at him as one would look at someone sentenced to execution.

Azqueta was a Basque by birth: balding, pudgy, short-sighted, wearing a brown sports jacket. He seemed tired and utterly resigned; as though he would merely turn his head, slowly and unsurprised and perhaps even with a sense of relief, if someone burst into the room to shoot him.

'Shining Path is the fruit of frustration and desperation,' he said patiently to us. 'The government has done nothing in the last two years for the people: nothing, nothing, nothing.'

He was the reverse of a publicity-seeker, we found; irritatingly so. He was unwilling to agree to let us film anything except the briefest of interviews, and even then tried to get out of it until the last minute. It was not simply an ingrained instinct for his own security; he had a genuine dislike of the things most grassroots politicians find satisfying: the attention of the cameras, the questions of journalists.

We followed him on a march to an open-air theatre which the police, for reasons that were obscure, wished to take over. For Azqueta this was a useful opportunity to show that he was not a stooge of the government, as Shining Path claimed. He walked down the street, along a previously announced route, and it was noticeable that most people tended to stay clear of him. Any car that passed, any overlooking window, might have contained a Shining Path assassin. Six police bodyguards walked with him, but he asked them not to stay too close. They were armed with shotguns or machine pistols; yet they seemed poorly trained and careless, given that Shining Path had murdered a thousand mayors and councillors during the twelve years of its campaign.

Nothing happened. On the stage of the little open-air theatre he introduced a number of local stars: including The Deep One, who was a stout elderly woman with a famously low range which she demonstrated to great applause, and El Elegante, who wore a black and white checked jacket of quite startling appearance, and said that while he didn't want to knock salsa, we had to support our own folkloric music; some of which he proceeded to sing. Azqueta received the greatest applause. To turn up for this occasion, as The Deep One and El Elegante and the crowd of a hundred or so people had, was an act of considerable political courage; now they were here they presumably felt there was no point in holding back.

I looked around at the dark indian faces surrounding me. Among them there would have been several Shining Path agents, whose job was to note who was there and if necessary to punish them later. The police bodyguards stood in the wings, and by the entrance a tough-looking character in black held a pump-action shotgun at the ready. When Maria Elena Moyano was murdered, her bodyguard had been off duty. The government might dislike Michel Azqueta deeply, but it did not want any more of the criticism it had received for not protecting Maria Elena properly.

Azqueto made a brief, unimpassioned, tired speech about the need to keep the theatre open and working for the people. It was the kind of thing you could hear in Lambeth town hall in London, or anywhere else where a traditional socialist might be expected to talk about the need for civic action and the value of the arts in the lives of ordinary people. No one paid much attention to what he said: it was the fact that he had come out in public to say it that was important. He stopped speaking. People applauded enthusiastically, clapping their hands over their heads and whistling. He looked a little embarrassed, and walked offstage. The bodyguards, who probably disliked him, gathered round him again and led him to his car. There would be no walk back down the road this time. He had made his point: Shining Path had not stopped him talking, and had not stopped other people coming out to listen to him. I caught a glimpse of his face as his car drove away. He looked suddenly relieved and at ease, and was talking with a new animation. That Sunday, at least, Michel Azqueta was not going to die.

Miraflores

Tell me more, author, about these fugitives.

Felipe Guaman Poma de Ayala, 1613

I sat near the window of Eamonn's room, drinking an after-dinner glass of Laphroaig. We were relaxed, and things seemed relatively pleasant. Steve and Matt would be with us in three days. Above all, our links with Shining Path seemed to be going well. It was Tuesday night; we had been told that someone of significance within Shining Path would make contact with us the following day. Outside the window, above the noise of the traffic, I thought I heard a couple of gunshots.

The following morning I stayed at the hotel, waiting for someone from the Shining Path to appear. The others went out to the shantytown of Villa El Salvador, checking on reports that there had been a big Army sweep there and elsewhere. I established myself in the hotel lobby and ordered a large pot of coffee; this would be a long wait, and I had supplied myself with reading-matter and a radio set accordingly. I opened *El Comercio*, the most conservative of the Lima newspapers, which always seemed to underplay the threat which Shining Path presented to the government and social structures of Peru; the previous day, when a large bomb had gone off on the outskirts of the city, killing several people and doing huge damage, *El Comercio* reported it on page 17. Its front page was largely taken up with a natural disaster in the Philippines.

Now I checked through it with some care: a policeman had been killed outside our hotel the previous night. Those were the shots I had heard; while I sipped my whisky and chatted lightly to the others, some unfortunate man had been bleeding to death in the gutter. No one would have gone out to see what had happened:

the enormous bomb in Miraflores three months before, whose effects were still obvious, had been preceded by several shots, and as people looked out of their windows the bomb had gone off. Nowadays a shot was treated as a signal to keep your head down.

I finished *El Comercio* and put it aside. Every time the telephone rang in the lobby I would listen for my name to be called, but nothing happened. I ran over in my mind the four things we wanted from Shining Path: the arrangements for our interview with Guzman, help with filming Shining Path activities in Lima, contact with their organisation in the Huallaga Valley, and – hardest of all – some kind of safe conduct pass which would help us if we were picked up by Shining Path guerrillas in the countryside. It was coming up to ten o'clock: I switched on my radio set and listened to the BBC World Service news.

'A spokesman in Washington said some sixty thousand Iraqi troops had been assembled, and that there had been further artillery attacks on Shi'ite villages in the southern exclusion zone.' It was not, I reflected, a good time to be in Peru. If only we could get our interview with Guzman quickly, I might be able to get out of the country with it and be back in London for whatever was going to happen in Iraq.

'*Senor Ramela, por favor.*'

An American businessman walked across to a Peruvian sitting not far from me, and pumped his hand. He began to address him like a public meeting about the up-turn in business in the United States. The Peruvian smiled self-deprecatingly, politely:

'Here in Peru things are worse. Awful.'

'*Senor Seemson, por favor.*'

I forced myself to walk slowly and coolly across to the telephone. A well-dressed security man was standing nearby: near enough, I thought, to hear what was said.

'Yes?'

It was not Shining Path. It was the British embassy, inviting us to a party on Saturday for the British Home Secretary who, unlikely though it seemed, was visiting Peru and Colombia to offer help with the battle against drugs. I tried not to sound disappointed, and went back to my seat and my books. From outside, over the noise of the muzak and the American businessman, I could hear the street sounds of Peru: hooting, the grinding of old vehicles, the sharper sound of microbuses and their conductors plying for hire. I stared hard at everyone who came into the hotel: a man in his fifties in a grey rollnecked sweater, a young girl whose gleaming black hair was strained back in a ponytail, a man of around thirty in a grimy anorak. Any of them could have been the messenger from Shining Path. I turned back to the book I was reading: E. M. Forster's *Howards End*:

> Actual life is full of false clues and signposts that lead nowhere. With infinite effort we nerve ourselves for a crisis that never comes.

It was a depressing thought: sitting in Lima, waiting for a crisis which might never come, while the world's attention was fixed on Iraq.

The lights went out: it was the morning power cut. I sat and waited in the blackness, listening to the little sounds of annoyance and distress. Then came the sudden crash and hum of a generator, and power was restored. Everyone in the lobby looked at each other, blinking in the light and smiling. But the electricity supply was no longer quite as stable, and for the rest of the day the light was inclined to fade and the muzak would drop several tones at random. I continued to wait, while the businessmen met around me, the coffee tray was removed and replaced by others, the security guard in his almost well-cut suit clicked his teeth and shot his cuffs and looked at the attractive women who came in, and I worked steadily through my supply of reading matter.

The others returned from Villa El Salvador. Cecilia, who had been with them, had not been told why I had stayed behind. I was depressed at having waited so long for no purpose. I went back to my room and settled down to read some notes. The telephone rang.

'Senor Simpson?'

There was a nervous edge to the voice. Our contact had arrived at last. He was downstairs in the lobby, and I asked him to come up and meet me on the eighth floor. I knocked hurriedly on Rosalind's door, almost opposite the lift.

'He's here. This is it.'

The lift doors opened. A serious-looking man in early middle age stepped out.

'I had a message to come here,' he said. It was clear the whole affair was a disturbing mystery to him; yet it was equally clear that he had been selected as our point of contact. I whispered the list of our requirements, making sure he understood each one. He nodded, without looking at me. He would, he said, pass the message on. Someone from room service came through a door at the end of the corridor. Our contact pressed the button for the lift. There were a few moments of awkward silence while the lift made its way slowly up, then the doors closed on him. He had not said another word to us. He was a cut-out man, and we would never see him again.

The contact had been made, though; and that evening, in a house in a genteel part of Lima whose owner we never saw, Rosalind and I met another figure in the chain. It was a woman, stern-looking but well dressed and well educated. The only two people whom we so far knew to be members of the Shining Path organisation in Lima were as unlike the usual notion of the revolutionary as it would be possible to imagine. The woman who came to lunch at the Chelsea Arts Club had looked and dressed like an urban guerrilla; this one wore high heels and make-up.

She was bright and open-seeming, and shook my outstretched hand firmly. I wanted to be sure, first, that she was genuinely working for the Shining Path, so I asked her some questions just to hear her talk.

'Why have the car bombs come to an end?'

'The Party feels that this tactic is one to be used sparingly,' she answered without hesitation. I was reassured; the reply itself was meaningless, but the assurance with which she said it, the hint of jargon, and the sense of total obedience all gave me confidence.

As with the man by the lift, I went through the list of what we wanted: an interview with Guzman, the opportunity to film Shining Path activities in Lima and later on in the Huallaga Valley, and a safe-conduct document of some kind. She pursed her lips and put her hands together, like a headmistress.

'Some of these things are easier to arrange than others,' she said. 'You must understand that the Party is highly disciplined, and its structure is vertical. Some messages I can pass on directly. Others will take longer.'

I realised which of them would take longer, and why: it was the filming in the Huallaga Valley, because this woman worked for the organisation in Lima rather than for the national leadership. The Huallaga could only be dealt with by people she knew nothing of and had no contact with. And the interview with Guzman?

'I shall pass the request on. They will know about you. Someone will contact you.'

For no reason that I could be precise about, I suddenly had the impression that Guzman was in Lima. Until that moment I had been inclined to think that he must be in one of the areas which the Shining Path called its 'liberated zones'. She smiled a little coldly.

'It would be best if you signed your list of requirements and gave it to me.'

I grinned back at her across the neat table: twenty years of dealing with difficult governments and groups of insurgents had made me unwilling to give any hostages to fortune.

'You must understand that I work for a disciplined and vertical organisation too. I have no authority to sign any documents.'

We all laughed. The meeting was over.

Defence Ministry

The[se] people are loyal to the Crown, and know how to deal with the English.

Felipe Guaman Poma de Ayala, 1613

'Roach hotel,' said Eamonn in an American accent; 'they check in but they don't check out.' It was a quotation from an advertisement for an anti-cockroach device he had seen in the United States, and he was looking at a rack which contained the identification cards of visitors to the building. Our identification cards, and our passports, were being examined by two military policemen in dark, formal uniforms and plenty of white plastic garnish on the edges. They seemed to be having difficulty with the longer words. We were visiting the Ministry of Defence, and the general in charge of public relations was waiting to greet us.

In all our contacts, whether with the government, or Shining Path, or the people involved in the drugs trade or in the torture and murder of civilians, we had to be very careful. If the government or the Army guessed our real plans, we would have serious problems. In Peru, our area of operation was a strange moral and political no-man's-land, and we would find ourselves crossing the lines between government officials and terrorists many times during our time there.

The general proved to be energetic, businesslike and a little overpowering, as though he had been on too many public relations courses. His big, crumpled brown face wore a slightly injured expression at first; apparently he had been expecting us four days earlier, although we had made no such arrangement. His injuries were salved when I started running through the names of the government ministers we had been seeing, and expected to see.

'The General' – perhaps he meant the defence minister – 'has given strict instructions that you are to be helped,' he said.

I inclined my head in acknowledgement, but took this to mean the General had given strict instructions that we were to be embraced totally and prevented from doing what we really wanted. We had always recognised that this might prove a problem.

He led us with fresh enthusiasm and energy along a rucked and wrinkled carpet the colour of moss in a forest, and up some stairs. As an enthusiastic collector of political kitsch I could not take my eyes off a large mural along the way. It depicted a deity of some kind, bearded in a way that made him look like Abimael Guzman, putting his hand encouragingly on the shoulder of a general in nineteenth-century uniform. A very large indian on the right (Continuity? The Spirit of the Land?) brandished a Peruvian flag, while a girl who looked like a 1960s pop star and may have been intended to represent Peru, or Fame, or Honour, looked on. You would have to be a very devoted patriot indeed to find this ersatz depiction of military glory in any way stirring. Below and in front of it, another military policeman with a completely blank face stood at ease. His eyes didn't even follow us as we passed.

The general in charge of public relations settled us down in an interview room. On the table, a chipped, brown-painted statuette of a soldier in the uniform of Peru's deeply unsuccessful war against Chile was carrying out a bayonet charge, under the orders perhaps of Johnny's great-great-grandfather. The room was panelled, and its smell reminded me of the musty tropical atmosphere of the hotel where I used to stay in Salisbury, Rhodesia. A deferential little man came in and whispered something to the general.

'He said it was very important,' he finished up, in a slightly louder voice.

'It doesn't matter,' barked the general.

'*Si, mi general*,' said the deferential figure submissively, and bowed himself out.

People bustled in and out with bulging files; a typewriter clacked behind one of the panelled walls; telephones only rang once before someone answered them. Everything here was done with dash and noise and efficiency. There were nineteenth-century generals (but not a Salaverry amongst them) in seriously bad modern copies on the walls, interspersed with encouraging, energetic slogans: '*JUNTOS SOMOS INVENCIBLES*', '*TOMAR LA INICIATIVA ES TENER LA MENTALIDAD GANADORA*'; Together We Are Invincible, To Take The Initiative Is To Have The Winning Attitude Of Mind. They bore roughly the relationship to Peru's military record in the war against subversion that the paintings on the wall bore to art.

I followed the advice, however, and took the initiative, asking if we could be taken to film the military campaign against Shining Path in the regions around Ayacucho and the Huallaga Valley. That would, it seemed, present no difficulty; the general rubbed his hands at the very thought of it. But, I asked, knowing how such people usually prefer to keep you away from the action wherever possible, would we actually see any fighting?

'All the different forces are going to be there: the Army, the police, the DEA. Be sure you're going to find action. Don't worry about that.' He would fax all the relevant regional commands with the names and details of our team.

'No problem,' he said as he delivered us to the office where we were to fill in the details, give our fingerprints, and sign a form headed '*Constancia*' which said we knew the danger from subversives in the area and the risks involved, and took full responsibility for our own safety. We filled in one for Cecilia, who was waiting outside in the bus. She had thought it best not to come into the Ministry, because she had angered them in the past with her reports about Army involvement in drugs. The general did not ask us who was going with us. He shook hands firmly.

'No problem at all,' he repeated.

'He said there'd be no problem,' I told Cecilia when we climbed into Johnny's minibus, where she had been waiting.

'*Vamos a ver*,' she said thoughtfully: we'll see.

A couple of hours later, back at the hotel, my telephone rang. It was the general in charge of public relations.

'We have a problem with Cecilia,' he said. He sounded embarrassed. I asked him harshly what kind of problem.

'I have to say it in Spanish to Miss Rosalind,' he said at last. 'It is too difficult for me in English.'

Rosalind came in and talked to him, making notes as he spoke. Then she said goodbye to him and read them out to me. She was upset.

'What he said was the following: "In Peru, international journalists don't travel around with national ones. We want you to do a good, Christian job."'

I was infuriated by this, but decided not to reply until I had talked it over with Sally Bowen and with the doyen of the foreign correspondents in Lima, Jonathan Kavanagh. Both of them agreed that they had never heard of any rule that prevented foreign journalists from travelling around with Peruvian ones. I felt, after talking to them, that it was important for Cecilia, who was in a difficult position, that we should back her to the hilt. Rosalind dialled the general's number, and translated my words to him down the telephone, sentence by sentence.

'I have checked with other journalists, and have found that no such ruling exists. Therefore I can only assume that this is an action aimed directly at the BBC. I shall therefore withdraw our request for help from you until I have had time to consult with the British Home Secretary's delegation, which arrived in Lima today.'

It was bluff, and nothing more, but the general made a strangulated noise at the other end of the line. I hoped he did not realise how quick the average British Home Secretary would be to wash his hands of any knowledge of, or the slightest desire to help, a BBC team in difficulties in a foreign country. Then I remembered something else.

'And perhaps you would explain your reference to a good Christian job.'

He spluttered an explanation: it was just a Peruvian expression, it had no political overtones, of course we would be free to do whatever we wanted. He just wanted time to get back to his colleagues before I did anything. His last words were, We can be flexible.

It was all very satisfying; but the satisfaction was brief. When he called back a few minutes later, his voice had a new, less apologetic tone to it. He was sorry, but it would simply not be possible to help us if we wanted to take Cecilia. Quite clearly, his instructions had come from much higher up. My bluff had been called.

There is only one thing to do when you have received a serious defeat: go out and enjoy yourself. We asked Cecilia to bring her boyfriend, whom we had not yet met, to an expensive dinner with us at a restaurant of her choosing. What type of food did she like best?

'Chifa,' she said, absently.

Chifa is a Peruvian version of Chinese food. A few hours later we were installed in a private room at the best Chifa restaurant in Lima. Gilberto, her boyfriend, turned out to be tall and fortyish, with dashing grey wings of hair at either temple. He was a reporter-cameraman who worked for Univision, a Spanish-language service with one of the largest audiences of any cable station in the United States. In many ways he was Cecilia's opposite: large where she was petite, reserved where she was enthusiastic, calm and reflective where she was quick and instinctual. We had all dressed up a little: even Eamonn, who felt uncomfortable in formal clothes. Rosalind had put her hair up in an elegant Edwardian bun, and was wearing a superb black dress. Cecilia wore an obviously expensive orange sweater, with her hair tied back in a kind of chignon. The Chinese waiters looked at the two of them appreciatively, and hung around to give us better service.

When we had ordered and the waiters had left, I told them exactly what had happened with the general. Cecilia reached over without looking and held Gilberto's hand, and his face lost its usual calm, amused expression. They both knew that her revelations about the Army's involvement in the drugs trade had made her some powerful enemies, but they had assumed that her sacking and the closure of her television programme had marked the end of the affair. Now, it seemed, her enemies were trying to get at her again.

'Not through us, they won't,' I said. I looked at Cecilia and Gilberto: they weren't the kind of people you would want to let down. Cecilia gave a little prepared speech about not wanting to be an obstacle to us. She swallowed a little, then said she could give us the name of someone extremely good who would take her place. We would, she said, never notice the difference. She was close to tears. Eamonn chipped in with a prepared speech of his own.

'There's no question about it. We want you to carry on with us.'

He meant it; Cecilia had all the necessary contacts both in Lima and the Huallaga Valley, and the courage to see the thing through. Above all, she needed us as much as we needed her. If we let her go now, she would have no protection.

When Eamonn and I had finished speaking, Gilberto sat back in his chair and nodded approvingly. Cecilia changed colour with relief, and her ears went pink. Rosalind beamed. A Chinese waiter stepped forward with a large flask of sake and began to pour it out. The atmosphere became relaxed and cheerful. Gilberto told us how he had been captured by the Iraqis in Basra at the end of the Gulf War, which he had covered for Univision, and how, when the Iraqis accused him of being an agent for the American-led forces he had shouted out, 'But I'm Peruvian!' and they had let him go in bewilderment, never having heard of anywhere called Peru.

It had been a pleasant, relaxed, amusing evening in spite of everything. As Gilberto drove us home afterwards, the streets were lively and the lights blazed. It was Friday night, and the curfew was not in force until 1 am. People had begun to hope that Shining Path had halted its use of car-bombs for the time being. There seemed to be a little less nervousness around.

Miraflores

These people have become distrustful as a result of their experiences and the losses they have suffered.

Felipe Guaman Poma de Ayala, 1613

The following morning Eamonn and I walked to a tearoom down the road from our hotel, in order to have breakfast and talk through our strategy. Slowly things became clearer. In a way, it helped that we would not be going anywhere with the Peruvian Army. We had only ourselves and our own contacts to rely on now. As we talked over the details of our Huallaga Valley trip, we could see the points where the greatest danger would lie, and do what we could do to lessen it.

We planned the outline of our five reports, which I was particularly anxious should run on consecutive days for a week: I could not remember such a thing happening before in the BBC, and it meant that particular attention would be paid to them. The last of the five would be the interview with Guzman, and we would plan the entire series in terms of the search for Guzman. It would begin in Lima, move out to the Huallaga Valley, take in the policies of the Fujimori government, and end with the Guzman interview.

There was a new tension now, which we both felt: the time for preparation was over, and Steve Morris and Matt Leiper were arriving in Lima that evening. Once we had our camera crew we could start in earnest. Our plane tickets were booked to Ayacucho, the effective birthplace of Shining Path, for the following morning. As we walked back to the hotel, past the well-dressed inhabitants of Miraflores, the persistent dollar-changers, the Andean beggar-woman who held a picture of a beautiful white Madonna and rocked back and forth incessantly, and the guards with their pump-action shotguns and their Los Angeles Police Department shades, I felt once more the full enthusiasm which the days of preparation and worry had eroded.

Rosalind met us. She was in a state of some excitement.

'I've had a message from Macavity,' she said as we went up in the lift. Macavity the Mystery Cat is a character from T.S. Eliot's *Old Possum's Book of Practical Cats*, and Rosalind as a cat owner used it when she talked about Shining Path.

'Six-fifteen this evening. Same place. It seems to be important.'

That's it, I thought, with a mixture of nervousness and elation; they're going to tell us the time of the interview, and how we'll go about getting it. The problem would be if they wanted us to do it soon, and it seemed likely that they would: that way, we would have to leave the country almost immediately afterwards, in order to make sure we did not lose the tape and were not arrested and questioned about Guzman's whereabouts. We could forget the rest of the five pieces which Eamonn and I had painstakingly discussed in the tearoom. Cecilia's position might be difficult as well. But there would be no question about it: if they came up with a time, we would have to fall in with it. It would, I reflected, be an interesting evening: immediately after the meeting with Macavity we were due to go to the British ambassador's residence for a party in honour of Kenneth Clarke, the Home Secretary.

The afternoon was long and difficult. In the course of it we had a curious visit from a man in an anorak and carrying a backpack. He swept into the lobby where we were all sitting, and said he had been sent to us with a message. Something would happen very soon, he said, and hurried out before we could ask him any questions. It could only mean that our interview was about to take place. In the meantime, we had our meeting with our other contact. When the time came to leave, we managed to be late. Worse, we told Johnny we were in a big hurry. He forced his way wildly through the traffic, reaching out of his window and beating loudly on his door whenever we were held up.

It was getting dark as he screeched around the last corner on two wheels and performed a hand-brake stop. Passers-by stopped to watch. We had not told him that he should avoid making us look conspicuous; that way he would realize this was a clandestine meeting, and in his own interests we were always careful to give him no hint about our Macavity dealings. I looked nervously across the road; a curtain was being raised in the house opposite. A man sat in a parked car a few yards away; it seemed suspicious, given the racket we had made, that he was ignoring us completely. It could be, I thought, that the police had been tipped off about our meeting.

Still, we had no alternative but to go on with it all. We were let in, and sat down to wait, looking down at our hands or glancing occasionally at each other's faces.

Six-thirty came.

'We needn't have hurried.'

Rosalind's words broke the silence, and the mood. I grinned back at her.

Six-forty-five.

'We'll leave at seven on the dot,' I said. 'Something must have happened. Maybe the cops have rolled some of them up.'

At seven o'clock an electronic watch somewhere beeped. I stood up.

'Drawn a blank,' I said. I felt certain we wouldn't get the interview now.

We picked up Eamonn at the hotel and drove round to the British ambassador's residence. The drive was full of expensive cars and bodyguards, and well-dressed men and women who had to walk an unaccustomed distance to the door. Keith Haskell, the ambassador, was a bluff, shrewd man, different in background and approach from the starchier type of British diplomat. He was famous for giving good parties. When I had visited him a few nights earlier, his house had been almost empty. Now it was crowded out with people; *le tout* Lima, if such a thing existed now. Waiters pushed their way through the crowds of politicians and businessmen, offering breaded prawns and sandwiches and glasses of good Chilean wine.

I paid my respects to several of the politicians and academics we had been meeting during the previous week. The head of the biggest human rights organisation, a small woman in her late fifties, moved skilfully past a couple of men in generals' uniforms: plainly Keith Haskell enjoyed juxtaposing his guests. The Vice President, a large man built like an Aztec idol, was talking earnestly to a couple of government ministers. He had broken with President Fujimori when the constitution was suspended the previous April, had declared the '*autogolpe*' illegal and announced himself to be the rightful president. The editor of *Caretas*, the magazine which Cecilia now worked for and which had constant problems with the authorities over its outspokenness, was smiling absently at the justice minister, who smiled back at him. I looked closely at the interior minister, who was chatting with the minister in charge of the police. Both seemed completely relaxed, and were laughing at some remark from a tall man in uniform. I was to remember that later.

I was just telling another British diplomat, Russell Baker, that we had been having problems about Cecilia, and asking him to let me know if anything should happen to her after we had left, when the wife of one of the Western ambassadors, a handsome woman in her forties, barged in and began to take him away.

'You don't mind, do you?' she said, looking past me. 'I have to say goodbye to this man.'

Eamonn was deep in conversation with one of the drugs experts from the Home Office in London, who was describing the ludicrous time they had had during their projected trip to the Huallaga Valley that morning: the aircraft would not start and the trip had been aborted.

'Wouldn't have seen much, I don't suppose,' the civil servant said. 'By all accounts they aren't doing anything much to stop the whole thing up there anyway.'

I gravitated to the centre of attraction, where Kenneth Clarke was talking to a group of Peruvian politicians including Carlos Bolona, the Oxford-educated finance minister. Clarke greeted me in the way senior British politicians greet British journalists: enthusiastic yet wary. I rather liked him; anyone who enjoyed jazz and good cooking was likely to be more interesting than most politicians.

'Whatever are you doing here?' he asked jovially.

'I could ask you the same question.'

In fact I knew what he was doing there: I had, by a considerable coincidence, reported on the meeting in Colombia, four months before, where his visit had been arranged. The British prime minister, John Major, was visiting President Gaviria on his way to the Rio Earth Summit; Colombia, which supported the British line during the Falklands War and was now fighting the cocaine trade, seemed a good place to go. As a follow-up, Major offered to send Ken Clarke, currently the man in charge of Britain's anti-drugs effort, to visit Colombia. While he was there, it made sense for him to go on to Peru, where most of the coca processed in Colombia originated.

We said little more to each other. Ken Clarke's attention was soon taken up by some earnest political figure, and Eamonn was signalling to me that we had to go. The plane bringing Steve Morris and Matt Leiper would be landing in an hour or so.

I went back to the hotel while the others headed off to the airport. There was an outside possibility that Shining Path had left a message about the aborted meeting that evening. Anyway, I was tired, and we had an early start in the morning. I was getting ready for bed when the telephone rang. Eamonn's voice came through on our portable phone, distorted by the airwaves and tense with the news he had to tell me.

'They've just announced on Channel 9 that Guzman's been captured.'

Eamonn and the others had been helping Steve and Matt with their luggage in the arrivals hall when one of the security men, recognising Gilberto, came over to him holding a walkie-talkie, and whispered the news to him. I sat on my bed, trying to work out all the angles as Eamonn waited for my reaction. I had already turned the television set on, and was reading the subtitled message: '*Abimael Guzman capturado*'. The studio audience for some chat show burst into applause.

'No wonder our contact didn't turn up this evening,' I said lamely.

'Looks like curtains for us,' Eamonn said. 'It's hard to think there's much point in our staying now.'

'I'd better get on the phone to London and start doing something for the World Service,' I said. 'We can work all that out later.'

'How on earth did you know to be in Peru, of all places?' said an admiring voice on the other end of the line.

I couldn't think of any way to explain, so I said it was just a piece of luck. To me, it seemed the worst luck imaginable.

'But did you get a tip-off?'

That's it, I thought; everyone's going to think we were told to be here for the big moment.

'Not everything has to be done on the basis of tip-offs,' I said irritably.

'No, no, of course not,' replied the woman at the other end of the line hastily. 'I just thought. . . '

'Let's get the piece across,' I cut in. I was angry with her for assuming that I was some kind of stooge for the Peruvian or British governments, and angry with myself for showing my annoyance. Most of all, I found it impossible to think what we should do, now that the plans of seven months or more had collapsed in a single evening.

Surquillo

Then the chiefs should be given the order to have them
tracked down and discovered, wherever they may be.

Felipe Guaman Poma de Ayala, 1613

The house was painted lime green. A high outer wall with
a climbing plant straggling over it faced on to the street; a
door in the wall opened on to a small, hidden courtyard which
led to the house itself. It was originally two storeys high, but a
third storey, smaller and set back, had been added on afterwards.
From the street, this third storey was almost invisible. Beside the
door in the outer wall was a neat metal address plate:

Urb. Los Sauces II
459
CALLE UNO

House number 459, First Street, in the second administrative
area of the urban district of Los Sauces: The Willows. Los
Sauces was a small part of the Lima suburb of Surquillo.
It was an address for the moderately well off. People here
washed their cars themselves, and took their own dogs and
children for walks, unlike the householders of wealthier areas in
Lima. But there were several small parks in Surquillo where they
could go with their dogs and children, and the streets were lined
with ornamental trees. In many ways it was a good place for the
leader of a terrorist movement of workers and peasants to hide;
yet the parks and the general atmosphere of middle-class neatness
were to play a part in the capture. In the building beside number
459 was a little shop which sold beer and soft drinks. That was
to play its part too.

We found out the details about the arrest of Guzman in the

days that followed, much of it from those who were involved. It was a remarkable piece of detective work on the part of the men and women who carried it out. The received wisdom in the Army and most of the confusing proliferation of anti-terrorist agencies was that Guzman was hiding either in one of the shantytowns, or else in some part of the countryside where Shining Path was strong. The detectives at DINCOTE, the National Directorate for Counter-Terrorism, which had dedicated itself to tracking Guzman down, worked on the opposite assumption: that he was somewhere in bourgeois Lima.

DINCOTE had gone through many changes of name and direction (its previous incarnation had been entitled DIRCOTE). Its detectives, few in number, overworked and chronically underpaid, used ordinary, old-fashioned police methods: they followed up every known lead and watched everyone who they thought might be linked to his known associates.

They had come tantalisingly close to capturing Guzman in June 1990, when they raided a house in Monterrico, another middle-class suburb of Lima. Guzman had left the house a short time before, but they found a curious home video of Guzman at a party with some of his closest followers. In the course of it Guzman performed the dance from the film *Zorba the Greek*, smoking a cigarette and waving his arms in the approved fashion. Seven months later, in January 1990, the anti-terrorist police raided another house in the same suburb and arrested Guzman's private secretary. Her name was Nelly Evans de Alvarez Calderon, and she had been clearly visible in the video. Sixteen other people who were arrested in that and other raids were released by the courts for lack of proper evidence.

Nelly Evans came from a wealthy family of English origin. She became a nun in the order of the Sisters of the Immaculate Heart of Mary, but was profoundly influenced by Vatican II and by the ideas of liberation theology. Eventually she turned her back on the disciplines of religion in favour of those of revolutionary politics, and married a former Catholic priest. She moved gradually towards Shining Path; he was less enthusiastic, and their marriage broke up.

With the limited resources at their disposal, the anti-terrorist detectives began a discreet surveillance of all her known friends and relatives, among them her niece, Maritza Garrido Lecca. Maritza Garrido was moderately well known as a ballet dancer but she had, like Nelly Evans, become secretly involved with Shining Path. Later, the more lurid section of the Peruvian press became obsessed with her; 'Beauty and The Beast', said a headline in one magazine, setting a photograph of Lecca beside one of Guzman. She was not, however, conventionally beautiful, with her heavy black eyebrows, low forehead, and hard, lined features.

By May 1992 Maritza Garrido was the covert link between Shining Path's Central Committee and the Party's newspaper, *El Diario*, which was always under threat but was permitted to carry on publishing. In that month she left her previous address and moved into the lime-green house in Calle Uno with her husband, an architect called Carlos Inchaustegui. He, like her, was a leading figure in the Shining Path structure. They rented the house for five hundred American dollars a month from a couple who lived in Venezuela and knew nothing of their political sympathies. One thing distinguished the house from many of the others in this relatively well-off neighbourhood: it had no telephone. Maritza Garrido made her calls from the greater security of a nearby public call box. She converted the ground floor of the house into a dance studio, and began to give ballet lessons.

DINCOTE kept a discreet eye on her, as it did on dozens of possible Shining Path leads. Gradually it came to the conclusion that she was worth more attention; and the more they watched, the more its detectives realised that something strange was going on at the house in Calle Uno. By June 1992, less than a month after she had moved into her new house, its officers set up a full-scale surveillance operation to check out the theory.

The first thing they noticed was that Maritza Garrido was bringing home heavy bags of shopping. When they watched her in the supermarkets they could see she was buying surprising amounts of steak, chicken, fish and bread, and considerably more alcohol (including Chivas Regal whisky at $20 a bottle) than a couple on their own might be expected to consume. In fact she was buying food for six people in the house in Calle Uno: herself and her husband, Guzman and his mistress, and two women who acted as his headquarters staff. Guzman, it seems, liked to have women working for him.

There were other indications. Maritza Garrido occasionally bought men's sweaters and shirts from the 'Extra Large' racks, even though her husband was short and slightly built. The watchers noticed that the curtains of the rooms on the first floor where Guzman lived and worked were always drawn, and at night when the lights were on inside they thought they could see the outline of a large, bearded man. By the third week in August they were certain it was Guzman. Two years earlier, when they had searched the safe house in Monterrico, they had found stubs and empty packets of Winston cigarettes. That it was Guzman and not someone else who smoked them became clear from a minute examination of the Zorba video. They blew up the picture of the cigarette he was smoking as he danced, and could see from the tiny printing on the paper that it was a Winston. They also knew from his past medical records that he was suffering from the painful skin disease psoriasis. Now they sifted through the rubbish from number 459 Calle Uno. Among the chicken bones and the Chivas Regal bottles they found several empty packets of Winstons and jars of ointment. The labels said 'For the treatment of psoriasis'.

Yet the senior men in DINCOTE, each hand-picked by the commanding officer, General Antonio Ketin Vidal Herrera, were under orders from him to keep the discovery of Guzman's hideout secret. Most of the DINCOTE staff knew nothing of it, and no government minister, not even those in overall charge of the police, security, and anti-terrorist operations, was told. General Vidal was determined to carry out the operation against the leadership of Shining Path in his own way. He knew that if the government were involved there would be heavy interference, and the news would leak out. Instead, the operation went forward slowly and carefully, at a pace dictated by General Vidal himself.

DINCOTE was powerfully assisted by Guzman's over-confidence. It was unwise of him to have stayed in the house of a close relative of Nelly Evans after her arrest, and careless not to have seen that Maritza Garrido was scattering so many clues to the fact that she was hiding people in her house. Guzman had developed a powerful contempt for the Peruvian government and its servants. He had out-thought and out-manoeuvred them for twelve years, and as the prospect grew that Shining Path's strategy would succeed, he may have thought he was invulnerable.

The choice of Surquillo for his safe house itself showed a certain hubris. The two Shining Path safe houses in Monterrico which DINCOTE had discovered were less than a mile from Maritza Garrido's house. Guzman seems to have worked on the principle that the safest place for a wanted man to hide is opposite a police station: Nelly Evans was arrested at Number 265, Calle Buenavista, close to the Peruvian Army headquarters off Avenue Angamos, in January 1991; the house where the police had just missed Guzman the previous June and discovered the Zorba video lay close to the Army headquarters on the other side. Its address was Calle Dos 459, in a sub-division of Monterrico called Ramon Castilla. Number 459, Second Street: and now Guzman was living within walking distance of it at number 459, First Street, Los Sauces. He might almost have been playing games with the police.

It all amounted to a failure of the analytical intelligence which had characterised Abimael Guzman's tactics and strategy. His continued freedom was essential to Shining Path's entire future, and his whereabouts were the most important secret the organisation possessed. Yet there was a paradox in all this: the Chairman of the Party could not be guarded by the elaborate system of security and discipline for which Shining Path was famous, 'the thousand eyes and ears of the Party' as it was called, for fear that the secret would become known by too many people. As a result, when DINCOTE began to keep a discreet eye on the house, there were no guards from Shining Path to notice that it was under surveillance and give the alarm. The house contained neither weapons to defend against a police raid, nor any way of escape. Guzman had staked everything he and Shining Path had achieved on the continuing secret of his hide-out. Once that was discovered, it was all lost.

DINCOTE infiltrated its men into the ranks of the street-sweepers in Surquillo, while others discreetly joined the team of gardeners which looked after the little parks at the end of the street and in a cul-de-sac off it. The real gardeners and street-sweepers had no idea that the new recruits were policemen. One of the neighbours told us afterwards that Calle Uno became the best-kept street in Lima during those months, though he hadn't noticed it at the time. It was a delicate operation: by waiting more than two months before moving in, DINCOTE ran the risk that the people in number 459 would eventually realise they were being watched. But General Vidal had to be certain Guzman would be in the house at the moment his men carried out their raid; as a careful observer of events he recognised the danger that the government might collapse in Peru, and that Shining Path could emerge as the force to take over. There could be no mistake now: the blow against Shining Path would have to be devastating, not merely damaging.

The moment came on the afternoon of Saturday 12 September. The watchers had established themselves in a house across the street from number 459, and had taken hundreds of photographs of the people who went in and out. They confirmed that everyone was in the house. The plan which had long been prepared was put into operation. Gardeners began to assemble in the little park opposite. Down at the end of the road there were several street-sweepers on duty. A young couple sat at a table outside the little bar in the building next to number 459 and looked at each other lovingly over a glass of beer. General Vidal drove up in an unmarked car and parked down a side street from which he could watch the lime-green house.

The sun went down. There was power that night, so the streetlights were on and the house was clearly visible. Upstairs the curtains remained shut. Occasionally a shadow crossed them. The street was as quiet as usual. Then came the characteristic sound of a Volkswagen. It drove along Calle Uno and stopped outside number 459. In it were two people: a handsome man in his fifties, Celso Garrido Lecca, who was a well-known composer of shows and serious music; and his current girlfriend, Patricia Awapara Penalillo. He was the uncle of Maritza, and Patricia Awapara was a ballet dancer and Maritza's close friend. They were frequent visitors to the house, which they used as a place where they could be together and carry on their affair; later they both denied having any idea that Guzman might have been upstairs. Neither, certainly, was a member of Shining Path. Celso Garrido was a familiar figure in Lima society and a friend of the unsuccessful presidential candidate and novelist, Mario Vargas Llosa.

Celso Garrido got out of the Volkswagen, locked it, and walked over to the front door. Patricia Awapara joined him. He pressed the bell. Maritza Garrido came across the little courtyard and called out to know who was there. When she heard her uncle's voice, she opened the door. At that instant the policeman who had been sitting drinking with his girlfriend at the little bar next door threw himself across the intervening few yards, hit Celso Garrido hard with his shoulder and stuck his revolver through the partly open door. Half a dozen armed detectives ran forward and forced their way inside. It was done with ferocious suddenness. They ordered Patricia Awapara, Celso Garrido and Maritza Garrido to lie down in the courtyard, near the barbecue where Maritza Garrido had earlier cooked the steaks for the household's evening meal. The barbecue had often been used to burn secret documents.

Inside the house, in the room where Lecca gave her ballet classes, the police found her husband, Carlos Inchaustegui.

'What's going on?' he said in bewilderment.

'Get down on the floor!' he was told.

The police ran through the house. A heavy-set detective threw his weight against a closed door and burst it open: it turned out to be the kitchen. The others raced up the stairs. At the top their way was blocked by what seemed to be a wooden partition and was in reality a folding door. It was flimsy, and they broke it down in an instant, bursting into the sitting room beyond. There they found the keeper of Shining Path's secrets, the psychologist Maria Pantoja Sanchez. They ran on into the office next door. Laura Zambrano Padilla, known as 'Comrade Meche', was sitting there. She had been arrested once before but released for lack of evidence, and had escaped abroad. Now she had returned secretly to work for Guzman. She and Laura Zambrano lived in the two rooms on the second floor.

Meanwhile two other detectives had turned left on the landing at the top of the stairs. They headed through a door and found themselves in a small, plainly furnished bedroom. It was empty.

They threw open the door into a larger room on the other side. It was Guzman's study, lined with books. He was sprawled in an armchair in front of the television, too shocked to move. Beside him was his companion, Elena Iparraguirre, who was also his deputy as leader of Shining Path. The policemen came to a halt, pointing their guns at him. He clearly thought they were going to kill him on the spot.

Iparraguirre was the first to react. She threw herself in front of Guzman, and then attacked the policeman who had led the way into the room, beating at him with her fists. Two other policemen grabbed her, but she continued lashing out at them and hit the gun which one of them was still pointing at her. It went off and the bullet grazed a detective who was standing near the door.

At this point Guzman found his voice at last.

'No more violence,' he said. 'Calm down.' He seemed to be talking to Iparraguirre. Then he looked at the most senior of the detectives.

'Who are you?'

'We're from DINCOTE.'

'You're the ones who killed three of my best men.' He was referring to the deaths of Shining Path prisoners in Campo Grande gaol at the hands of the security police. In fact DINCOTE's part in what amounted to a series of unlawful executions was negligible.

Iparraguirre had got her breath back now. 'Show some respect for Chairman Gonzalo!' she screamed at them. By using his nom de guerre she gave the final confirmation of Guzman's identity; though it was scarcely necessary. The senior police officer pulled out his walkie-talkie and spoke to General Vidal, who was still sitting in his car opposite the house, waiting for news in an agony of suspense. The policeman's voice trembled with emotion as he reported to his commanding officer.

'We've got El Cacheton! Long live the Peruvian Police!'

'El Cacheton' was the nickname the DINCOTE officers had given Guzman among themselves. It means 'fat-face', but there is a hint of respect about it: something like 'the Big Man', perhaps.

Suddenly there was a feeling of anticlimax: apart from the brief struggle with Iparraguirre and the gun which had gone off by accident, there had been no violence. A search of the house later showed there were no guns in it. With the release of tension, two of the policemen found themselves in tears. A third grabbed his chest: he was suffering from palpitations of the heart. One of the more senior policemen put out a tentative hand to touch Chairman Gonzalo. After all this time he could scarcely believe he was seeing him in the flesh.

There were footsteps in the room next door: General Vidal had arrived. Behind him in the doorway was a police video cameraman, who was just in time to record the handshake between the most wanted man in Peru and his captor. Vidal, polite and unassuming, introduced himself. He was careful not to gloat, and Guzman responded courteously.

'How do you do, General? I am Abimael Guzman Reynoso.'

Vidal had prepared his next words with some care.

'There are times in life when you win, and times when you lose. This time you have lost.'

'I have only lost one battle. You yourself know, general, that the Party is everywhere in Peru. We have now advanced sufficiently to be able to win.'

By this time Iparraguirre had regained her self-control. Seeing the video camera, and no doubt realising that the pictures of the arrest would be shown in public, she picked up the miniature red flag with its hammer and sickle which stood on Guzman's desk and held it over his head like a standard. Guzman was still sitting in the armchair where, only a few minutes earlier, he had been watching television. General Vidal walked up and down the small room, looking at the objects on the shelves: a human skull, a model of a rifle made by a prisoner at Campo Grande, a photograph of a dead comrade. Then he settled down briefly and allowed Guzman to speak.

'In the end,' Guzman said, leaning back with the ease of a man who expects to be listened to with attention, 'you can always take objects away from a man. But you can't take what he has here.'

He tapped his head fiercely with a forefinger; he too seemed to be thinking in terms of gestures for television, and no doubt knew his followers would instantly realise he was referring to

'Gonzalo thought'. 'You can't do that, even if you kill him. And if I'm going to die, this will live on through other people. And when we triumph, history will vindicate me.'

He lit a Winston cigarette, the brand which had helped to betray him, and puffed away, his eyes on the camera. It seemed that he expected to be killed soon. At length Vidal told them it was time to go. They stood up, and he asked them to turn out their pockets.

'Don't touch him,' Iparraguirre warned angrily, but it was clear no one was going to mistreat Guzman. He showed that his pockets were empty; hers contained nothing but tissues. One of General Vidal's worries had been that Guzman might try to kill himself, but he had no poison capsules on him, and no concealed weapons. He allowed himself to be escorted downstairs without a struggle. The neighbours who had gathered in the street caught a quick glimpse of an impassive bearded profile as he was driven off in Vidal's unmarked car. They are unlikely to have paid much attention to the small, unremarkable, bespectacled figure of the general sitting beside him.

Lima

[He] was a genuinely learned man whose influence was always exerted on the side of justice ... saying that Your Majesty had sent him to do justice and not to condone robbery and inhumanity. Such a person, mature and considerate, deserves to remain a long time in office.

Felipe Guaman Poma de Ayala, 1613

Vidal had chosen the moment to make the arrest with some care. On 12 September 1992 President Fujimori was out of Lima on one of his regular provincial tours. Across the city, the interior minister, Briones, and Kuba, the minister in charge of the police, were still at the British ambassador's party.

Nothing happened to disturb the party for them: no sudden calls to the telephone, no whispered conversations, no hurried apologies or departures. As we were leaving the party, I walked past Briones and Kuba. They were still talking animatedly to a small group, glass in hand. There was no sign of tension or anxiety, and certainly none of triumph. General Vidal had decided to tell them nothing about the raid he was planning in Surquillo that evening.

A couple of weeks later we went to see General Vidal at his headquarters: a seedy barracks in the centre of Lima, built some time after the First World War. Its grey paint was peeling, and its pipes were rusting. A small, bright-looking detective in clothes that were no longer fashionable checked our names against a list and led the way into the building. A great many men stood around with guns; ever since the capture of Guzman the possibility of a revenge attack by Shining Path seemed strong, and General Vidal's deputy had already been murdered as he walked down the street.

We went into a bright hallway in which muzak of some

indistinguishable type was playing. It followed us up the staircase and into a waiting room, and was there to greet us in General Vidal's office itself: a low-level rhythm with an indeterminate Latin beat, which lay on the air rather like the smell of cooking. Perhaps it was intended to soothe everyone's nerves; perhaps it was an anti-bugging device. A tough-looking character in a leather jacket lounged outside the general's door, cradling a machine-pistol.

Vidal was short and slight and dressed with extreme neatness in a brown checked jacket and brown trousers. His hands were well kept and surprisingly pale. His tie was knotted perfectly, there was no sign of scuffing on his small brown brogues, and he took his glasses off several times to polish the lenses. Everything he said was carefully considered, just like his decision to keep the impending arrest of Guzman from his superiors.

I had the impression that he would regard taking a decision without proper forethought as being the equivalent of dressing carelessly – as the sign, perhaps, of a disintegrating personality. A modest man, he was reluctant to talk about himself. The murder of his deputy seemed to have made him feel that his own life was now likely to be a short one; 'My personal situation is different as a result of 12 September,' he said in his dry, understated way, with a hint of quizzical humour lying somewhere beneath it. But his sense of duty, and no doubt of having done the state some service, seemed to reconcile him to the prospect.

He was as quiet and neat and self-effacing as a hero from a detective story, and like all the best heroes he refused to accept orders if he disapproved of them. He was seeing us privately because he had been refused permission by his superiors to give us an interview on camera. But he was extremely discreet. 'I must ask to be excused from answering Mr Simpson's question,' he said more than once in his old-fashioned Spanish.

A grandfather clock stood in one corner, and there was a rather fine pottery Don Quixote on top of a bookshelf. It was more like the chambers of a trusted family lawyer than the office of a South American secret police chief. Vidal had indeed trained as a lawyer before joining the police. Yet his career was not without blemish: there were allegations that he had been involved in an offshoot of a drugs operation. I found it hard to imagine, looking at the slight, self-controlled man opposite, as he sat with his legs neatly crossed, the hint of a smile on his face still; he had taken great risks over the arrest of Guzman to ensure that the right thing was done, regardless of the consequences to himself.

It was plain that he had given considerable thought to the ethical problem of how a free society should face up to terrorism; plain, too, that he had taken the view that the state must never stoop to the methods of the terrorists, or it will become terrorist in its turn. He would not confirm or deny it when I asked, but I had the strong impression that he had been on an anti-subversion course run by Scotland Yard in Britain, and had returned to Peru fired by these notions. The slow build-up to the arrest of Guzman had given him ample time to work out everything beforehand: whom to inform, whether he should make the news public, how Guzman should be treated once he was arrested. Not all of Vidal's superiors shared his belief that the state had to guard against emulating the terrorism of its enemies.

Vidal himself refused to discuss the subject, but I knew from other sources that the mysterious Vladimiro Montesinos, President Fujimori's lawyer and security adviser, had been involved in drawing up Vidal's instructions for dealing with Guzman if he were arrested. The orders were that the news of the arrest should be kept secret for twenty-four hours, during which Guzman would be interrogated intensively, using whatever means were necessary to get from him the full details of the Shining Path organisation. After that, the announcement of his capture could be made public. Depending on his degree of cooperation with his interrogators, Guzman could either be put on public display and later tried, or – if he were not prepared to talk – he could be quietly killed, as though resisting arrest. The decision would be made by the President and his advisers. These were Vidal's standing orders. He had disapproved of them and, after considerable thought, decided to ignore them.

On the evening of the arrest, with Guzman sitting meekly in his office in front of him and looking perhaps at the clay statuette of Don Quixote and the grandfather clock, Vidal gave orders that the news of the capture should be given to one of the Lima television stations. Briones, the interior minister, heard a report about it in his car on the way back from the British embassy party. Montesinos, the security adviser, heard it first on television. Immediately, the bleeper which Vidal carried with him began to sound. He ignored it, and continued his interrogation of Guzman. Then the telephone rang. Vidal picked it up. It was Montesinos himself. His voice was cold with anger.

'I take it that what I have just seen on television is some kind of joke in bad taste,' he said. It was a curious way to greet the capture of the main enemy of the Peruvian state.

'No, it's true.'

'So why didn't you do what you were told to do?'

'It was a work of expert surgery by the police,' Vidal replied enigmatically.

'Is he [Guzman] there with you?'

'Yes.'

Montesinos slammed the phone down.

Soon afterwards Briones and Kuba arrived. They took little notice of Vidal.

'Why did you use so much violence?' Briones asked Guzman.

'It seems strange to me that you're a military man and yet you don't realise there's violence in war,' he answered, laughing and looking across at Vidal. The two ministers left soon afterwards, and the interrogation began again.

Guzman was prepared to talk about the intellectual and ideological structure of the Party, but he insisted that he had nothing to do with what he called the war, and could give no details about it. Vidal did not believe it, but decided that it was important to retain Guzman's relative cooperation. He was also understandably curious about Guzman's perceptions of the surveillance operation against him.

'What happened to the thousand eyes and ears of the Party?' he asked, meaning Shining Path's army of watchers and informers. Guzman shrugged, with remarkable composure.

'Sometimes we make mistakes.'

'Were you aware that we were closing in on you over the past few days?'

'I've been followed throughout my revolutionary life.'

Shortly afterwards there was shouting in the little hallway outside Vidal's office. The door burst open. It must have been an alarming moment for Vidal; DINCOTE was half-expecting an attempt to rescue Guzman. A dark man in early middle age stood in the doorway, trying to shake off Vidal's embarrassed bodyguard outside. Vidal recognised him: it was Colonel Alberto Pinto, the head of military intelligence and a loyal follower of Montesinos. Some weeks later, a senior intelligence source told us that Pinto had been in charge of a military death squad. Now, like his patron, Pinto was angry. He said that Vidal's office was an unsuitable place to interrogate someone as dangerous as Guzman; he had been able to get in there himself, even though the bodyguards had tried to stop him.

Vidal replied mildly that if he had been someone other than the head of military intelligence he might not have found it so easy. Pinto tried to insist that Guzman should be handed over to him, so that he could be held in Army custody. If anything happened and Guzman was rescued by the Shining Path, he said, Vidal would be responsible; and he gave a strong hint that it would have been better to have killed Guzman instead of bringing him in alive. Vidal stressed that he had carried out the arrests in a lawful way. The argument grew even more heated, with Guzman sitting there and looking from one to the other of them. In the end, Vidal said that since Pinto was only a colonel and he himself was a general, he was ordering him to leave the building. Pinto had no alternative but to obey.

This was no mere inter-service rivalry. By making the arrest public, Vidal may have saved Guzman's life and ensured that he would be treated in a lawful fashion. He had also damaged the interests of men like Montesinos and Pinto in a more specific way. A good deal was at stake: Western governments had made cash and equipment available to the Peruvian government to help with counter-terrorism, and on Montesinos's advice almost all of this had gone to the Army and its various agencies.

DINCOTE was a police department, and so received almost nothing. Some of its more senior detectives had had to use their own cars for the surveillance operations which had ended in Guzman's arrest, and they were not able to claim expenses for doing so. Vidal had succeeded in giving his men the leadership and motivation to continue, but it had been done with no help from the government. It was not altogether surprising that although the governments of Britain and the United States sent him their congratulations that night, and there was a telegram from the Colombian ministry of defence, he received no message of any kind from the Peruvian defence ministry, nor from the Peruvian President.

The next day President Fujimori returned to Lima, and countermanded an attempt by Vidal to present Guzman at a press conference. Together with most of the other journalists in Lima, we waited for ten hours outside the police building where it was supposed to happen, but shortly before 7 pm it was announced that no press conference would take place. Vidal spoke to a friend by telephone from the room where he was continuing with the interrogation of Guzman.

'I am doing things as they ought to be done,' he said. 'There is a lot of pressure on me to do them differently.'

That night the government reached a decision on the way in which Guzman and the others should be presented to the public. A humiliating little ceremony was arranged, in which the people who had been arrested at the house in Surquillo were paraded in front of a police video camera. Guzman, still wearing the clothes in which he had been arrested, was shown behind bars, and was then obliged to strip off his jacket and shirt and show his psoriasis-scarred body. An opinion poll carried out later by the respected news magazine *Caretas* showed that while 22.9 per cent of people said they were repelled by the man who had done such damage to their country, 20.4 per cent actually felt pity for him.

'The peasants here are used to being treated badly,' Sally Bowen said when she heard these results, 'and it makes them instinctively courteous to one another. They don't like seeing someone being treated like an animal.'

The public show achieved one thing: it demonstrated that the composer Celso Garrido and his girlfriend Patricia Awapara had nothing to do with the Shining Path. They too were paraded for the cameras with the others. Iparraguirre, Maritza Garrido,

Inchaustegui and the others gave defiant clenched-fist salutes and answered in the approved way when Maritza shouted out the requisite slogans, while Guzman looked on impassively. The other two looked miserable, and said nothing. They had already convinced Vidal that their presence in the house that Saturday evening had simply been a piece of bad luck, and when they were all paraded together Guzman said of Patricia Awapara, who was standing next to him in the line-out, 'I don't know this young lady; it is the first time I've seen her.' They were released; and Celso Garrido was sent back to face the anger of his wife.

Some days later there was a more formal occasion, when several hundred journalists were brought in to a large room in which was a cage covered with a huge awning. When the awning was pulled back, Guzman was revealed, standing behind the bars. It was a ludicrous business, which Guzman tried to turn to his own political advantage by speaking at length: but because he used the arid ideological phrases of Marxism-Leninism, he failed to sway those who might otherwise have sympathised with him.

The authorities deliberately injected a sense of near-hysteria and a desire for revenge into the proceedings. A number of journalists, encouraged by the Army intelligence officers and security men in the audience, tried to shout Guzman down and yelled insults at him. They ended by singing the Peruvian national anthem. It seemed to be part of a new mood in the country. Having had a serious fright, the middle classes now wanted blood. Many of the newspapers began demanding Guzman's execution, even though the death penalty had been removed from the statute books. After a swift court martial, Guzman and the others were sentenced to life imprisonment; and there was always the possibility that the law would be changed to make a retrospective death penalty possible.

At last we had word from the woman we were supposed to meet on the evening of Guzman's arrest. Perhaps because she thought it would make us feel at home, she suggested the Liverpool Bar, not far from our hotel. Rosalind and I, both experiencing the old nervousness, hailed a vast elderly American car which waited for dollar-paying foreigners at the hotel's taxi rank and drove round there. As the car oozed around the corners we discussed the possibility that we were being set up. Did Army intelligence want to show the links between Shining Path and foreign journalists?

Our contact was waiting for us on the street corner near the Liverpool Bar. She looked rather attractive.

'She's wearing Liverpool red,' whispered Rosalind, who had once been a football photographer.

'It could be Maoist red,' I said.

'Not with those earrings,' she answered. The woman was wearing large imitation pearls.

The café was decorated with framed Liverpool scarves and stained-glass panels of the Beatles. It looked, and was, expensive; but nothing could make that kind of decoration into good taste. As a survivor of the Sixties I had half an ear on the music, which was also by the Beatles. Eventually 'Revolution' came around, as I knew it would:

> And if you go carrying pictures of Chairman Mao,
> You ain't gonna make it with anyone anyhow.

Our contact didn't spot the reference.

She was remarkably serene. She even laughed once or twice. She reminded me of an early Christian who had been through the despair of the Crucifixion and was now convinced that the Resurrection had taken place.

'The Chairman prepared us for these events in his speech of 1981,' she said. 'We know what we must do now, and we shall do it. It's even possible the Chairman wanted things to happen this way. Perhaps he felt that a new leadership was required. He planned everything, you see.'

She smiled at my Doubting Thomas look, her early Christian assurance stronger each time she thought about these things. We were sitting at a table outside, and I had my back to the street. I could see the reflexions going past: there was even a street-sweeper, along Surquillo lines.

'Suppose your phone is tapped? The police could have followed you here.'

She smiled again. 'No one knows of my connections with the Party.'

I nodded, though I wasn't certain if it was true. I finished my *cafe con crema*.

'Will we be able to speak to the person who has taken Guzman's place?'

'We'll see. I'll put your request in. It's possible.' She smiled her Resurrection smile again.

'I don't believe it,' Rosalind said as we left. 'I think they've been knocked for a loop.'

I agreed.

Eamonn was standing at the window swinging his arms when Rosalind and I came back. He had been talking to the news desk in London: interest rates were going up to unheard-of levels, the pound and the lira had dropped out of the EC's exchange rate mechanism, and people at the BBC were starting to say that since Guzman had been arrested there was no point in our staying in Peru any longer. 'I think there's a very good point to our staying,' I said. 'We've just got to deliver on the other things now.'

'Yes,' said Eamonn. He looked out at the darkened city and started rocking backwards and forwards again. 'Drugs.'

PART IV

VALLEY OF THE SHADOW

A Spanish official takes a bribe.

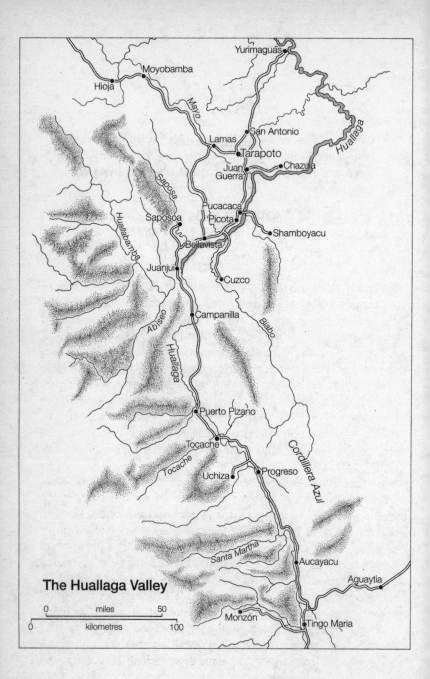

The Huallaga Valley

Drugs

Our rulers were undoubtedly responsible for the widespread custom of chewing coca. This was supposed to be nourishing, but in my view it is a bad habit, and leads to craving and addiction.

Felipe Guaman Poma de Ayala, 1613

Nearly three-quarters of the world's cocaine supplies originate in Peru, which is by far the largest producer of the coca plant. Colombia, the country where the coca is refined and turned into cocaine, grows relatively little itself: in 1992, the year we visited the area, Colombia had only 42,500 hectares under coca. The other main growing country, Bolivia, had a little more: 50,330. By comparison Peru, according to the World Bank, had 230,000 hectares under coca, 154,000 of them in the Upper Huallaga Valley. This meant that in 1992 Peru grew 71 per cent of the world's supply of coca; and the Huallaga Valley, an area around two hundred miles from north to south, grew 47 per cent of the world's supply.

It takes 200 kilograms of coca leaf to make 2 kilos of basic paste. That in turn is changed into a kilo of cocaine base, which after processing becomes a kilo of cocaine hydrochloride. This can then be prepared for sale. The average market price of 200 kilos of coca leaf in 1992 was US$392, which represents a profit of 26 per cent on the cost of production. During 1992 the estimated output from Peru as a whole was 360 metric tonnes of leaf, which represented an estimated revenue of $288.8 million; well down on earlier years. (The figure for 1988, by contrast, was $432 million.)

A family of five living in the Upper Huallaga Valley and growing one or all of the main local alternatives to coca — coffee, cocoa and anatto, a plant from which an orange-red dye is made – would have earned about $305 nett on an average holding of land in 1992. If the same family had grown coca, it would have earned them $4,146, which was close to the average family's income in Peru in 1992. In other words, the only way to make a decent living in the Upper Huallaga was to grow coca.

The food subsidies paid to American or European Community farmers for crops such as corn, rice, milk, wheat, or beef made it very difficult for the farmers of Peru to compete with imported foodstuffs even in their own local shops; and the Fujimori government's decision to eliminate subsidies to its farmers made it impossible. By contrast, the price which the farmers received for their coca reflected accurately the real cost of production. For the farmers of the Upper Huallaga Valley, the logic of the market meant they had no alternative but to grow coca.

Not that growing it earned them much in terms of the international sale of cocaine. In 1990, the latest year for which there are reliable figures at the time of writing, the farmers who grew the coca received 0.15 per cent of that year's proceeds from the overall cocaine industry. 16.5 per cent went to the smugglers, known as *traquateros*, who came to buy the basic coca paste from them. The remaining 82 per cent went to the big cocaine barons who refined it and sent it on to the rich markets of the developed world. As an example of an efficient industry run on free trade lines, it would be hard to fault cocaine; there are few if any distortions here. And so the developed world, through its trade and agriculture policies, is unconsciously encouraging the cocaine industry. The growers, the smugglers and the barons are enabled, by courtesy of the taxpayers of the United States and the European Community, to continue supplying a product which leads to greater crime, corruption and addiction throughout Western society.

The unwitting father of the modern Peruvian coca industry was President Fernando Belaunde Terry, whose two administrations made so many errors in other ways. When he was first in office, from 1963 to 1968, he decided to open up the Amazon River Basin: Peru's New Frontier, as he called it. At the time it was fashionable in the Americas to have new frontiers. The idea caught the public imagination. A trunk road, known as the Marginal, was to be driven along the eastern tropical slopes of the Andes, with spur roads off it cutting into the virgin rainforest.

Making the area productive would, the Belaunde government said, help Peru to feed itself. It would therefore offer new hope to the unemployed drifters who were leaving the villages of the highlands for the big cities. When an earthquake struck the northern Peruvian Andes in 1970, for instance, the refugees moved down to the new settlements en masse. Hundreds of thousands of acres of virgin rainforest were cut down to accommodate the new immigrants. Yet the plan had not been properly thought through, and was unreasonably optimistic. Few of the proposed crops reached the suggested levels, either in terms of productivity or of profit; one of the few exceptions was coca. The big upsurge in the demand for cocaine in the United States during the 1970s ensured that the peasants of the newly reclaimed land would grow the one crop which entirely suited the area.

Then, during the 1980s, Shining Path moved in. Its 'urban columns' were not opposed to the growing of coca in principle. They were, however, deeply opposed to the high-spending culture that the *traquateros* brought with them, as they drove their Honda motorbikes at speed down the dusty streets of the little Huallaga towns. The car dealers in the town of Tingo Maria, in the southern part of the valley, regularly sold more new cars than anywhere else in Peru. It was this conspicuous expenditure that Shining Path wanted to root out. Anyone who was too obviously corrupt, or was involved in prostitution, or took drugs too openly, was liable to be murdered. The *traquateros* were expected to pay contributions to Shining Path. So were the growers, though Shining Path claimed it was acting on their behalf, and in some places it tried (with varying degrees of success and sometimes with none at all) to negotiate better prices for the coca leaf.

In return, the coca growers were expected to join Shining Path's armed groups. As the battle for control between the Peruvian Army and Shining Path grew fiercer, the peasants of the Huallaga Valley found themselves in a terrible position. The Army assumed as a matter of course that the peasants supported Shining Path, and treated them accordingly. The disappearances and deaths began to grow. Shining Path, on the other hand, would accept nothing less than the full loyalty of the peasants. The number of bodies found in the Huallaga River grew.

Both sides swiftly became involved in creaming off the profits from drugs-trafficking. Shining Path demanded payment for allowing the growers to produce the basic coca paste, and for letting the consignments use the roads to the towns; the Army, with its superior logistics, quickly took control of the airfields, both legal and illegal, from which the basic paste was flown to Colombia for processing. The government in Lima tried to make out, with some support from the United States, that Shining Path controlled the drugs trade and earned huge amounts from it. Yet the really big profits were being made by Army officers. And in the meantime the murders of innocent civilians were continuing unabated.

Palace

The Visitors [-General] need to be visited, and the judges judged, if good government is to be installed in your kingdom of Peru.

Felipe Guaman Poma de Ayala, 1613

'I suppose I just knock,' said Sally Bowen.

A large jaguar, carved in stone by someone who had never seen a jaguar, looked down at us from above the enormous door. The street outside the presidential palace was dark, and we were all getting wet from the light rain drizzle. A small hatch, set at eye-level in the door and covered by an elaborate wrought-iron guard, opened after half a minute. A large black shako, of a kind that went out after Peru's war of independence against Spain, appeared in the opening. Dark eyes surveyed us, and the hatch shut again. Then another small hatch lower down on the door opened. Other faces, under other headgear, looked out at us. Sally spoke to them. A hand was thrust out of the hatch.

'Please your pass, John Seemson.'

Inside the hatch they were consulting a list.

'You are six? But you are five.'

We were six; whoever had typed out the list had skipped a line, and put Rosalind's name against Eamonn's passport number. We waited a little longer in the rain while this was explained. Finally the door creaked open, and revealed a large and splendid hall with an imperial coach from the days of the Viceroys standing in its farthest recess. Soldiers were standing round in an extraordinary variety of uniforms, from shakos and bandoliers to camouflage fatigues. Swords that seemed rather too big for them clanked awkwardly against rifles.

'Auditioning for a pageant,' Steve Morris said beside me. It was good to have him and Matt Leiper with us at last.

A deferential man in a suit ushered us into a room decorated with yellow and blue tiles, then a less deferential man took us into a large, gloomily panelled room whose windows were closed, barred, shuttered and covered with heavy brocade curtains. Even the ceiling was of carved mahogany.

We moved everything, as television crews do: the table, the chairs, a model of the Peruvian ship *Huaca*, whose admiral became a national hero after he went down with her when she sank. We were there to interview the President, and we wanted things to look good.

'The rudder's going to be sticking out of his left ear,' Steve said. Eamonn leaped forward to lift the *Huaca* off the mantelpiece altogether, but its lifeboats shook alarmingly and the uniformed aide-de-camp who was helping us to set up looked so agonised that I suggested we might do better to leave the *Huaca* where she was, rudder and all. Finally we were ready. We sat down and drank coffee from small cups.

Someone had told us that President Fujimori timed everything to fit in with the afternoon and evening soap operas on television. Now, when the aide-de-camp knocked respectfully on the door of the next office and went in, he left the door slightly ajar. I could see the President sitting at the far end of the room, behind a desk which was entirely clear of everything except a small portable television set. The light from it played across his impassive features and glinted on his spectacles. The aide-de-camp said something deferential to him. The President held up a small, bony hand, and the light from the soap opera shone on that as well.

'His Excellency will be free shortly,' said the aide-de-camp as he came respectfully out. He closed the heavy mahogany door behind him as though it were made of the finest and most fragile glass.

Alberto Fujimori had won a stunning victory in the 1990 presidential election by mobilizing indian support against the candidate of white, creole, Spanish Peru, the novelist Mario Vargas Llosa. Vargas Llosa had the money, the reputation, the ideas, and the international respect and support. It seemed to outsiders that he could not fail to win. He employed a team of British consultants headed by Mark Malloch Brown, who soon realised that Vargas Llosa had made a terminal mistake by aligning his Libertad movement with the two big conservative opposition groups, Popular Action (which had formerly been headed by the old, discredited Belaunde Terry) and the Christian Popular Party.

So even before the campaign began, Vargas Llosa had become identified as the candidate of the old elite. He did not hide the fact that he had no great enthusiasm for indians, and he surrounded himself with notably European-looking supporters. Mark Malloch Brown wrote afterwards, 'When I looked at the venerable Castilian façade of Peru, I found overtones of white Rhodesia.' Vargas Llosa seemed to be the candidate of the white settlers.

Fujimori by contrast had no serious backing and virtually no ideas beyond a vague call for change; but he was not a European, and the indians, who in many cases had only had the vote since 1979, flocked to him. He looked like an indian himself; he could have been an Ashaninca, and when he put on a *kushma* at a rally everyone applauded the resemblance. His money came partly from fundamentalist and evangelical Protestant groups, of the kind that were experiencing great success in converting indians from Catholicism.

There was a moderately large Japanese community in Peru, which had been founded in the 1920s and 1930s. The Japanese had mostly been poor when they arrived, but the community was now wealthy and well-educated. Fujimori's parents had supposedly come to Japan shortly before he was born; this was questioned by his enemies, who pointed out that if he had been born in Japan he would have been ineligible to stand for the Presidency. His full name was Alberto Fujimori Fujimori, which means that his mother had the same name as her husband before their marriage. In Peru, where illegitimate children are often given their mother's name twice when the father has not acknowledged them, this caused a good deal of often spiteful comment.

Not among the peasants, however. They thought that as an agriculturalist, an Asian and an outsider, he would be their first real representative. They also assumed that he would attract heavy investment from Japan. He went around the rural areas in tractors, waving a notebook to the crowds of indians who gathered to listen to him as though it contained the solution to Peru's problems. His campaign was openly anti-white, and he made a series of racist taunts about people of European origin. He also promised that he would not introduce the kind of savage deflationary measures which Vargas Llosa had warned would be required.

In the end Fujimori won by a landslide, and Vargas Llosa's supporters showed that it had indeed been an election about race by beating up a number of people of Chinese and Japanese origin; though Vargas Llosa himself condemned this behaviour. In August 1990, less than two weeks after his inauguration, Fujimori announced the toughest economic adjustment programme Peru had ever experienced. The so-called 'Fujishock' was much more savage than Vargas Llosa's proposed measures, which Fujimori had condemned as completely unacceptable. When the outcome of the election had become clear, Vargas Llosa told his son Alvaro, who was also his press officer, 'Peru has voted for a president in favour of compromise and trickery, one who won't make any changes but will dedicate himself to organising and administering chaos, and applying sticking-plasters.'

Fujimori told his friends that it was a book by the political economist Hernandez de Soto, *The Peaceful Path*, which convinced him it was his duty to go into politics. He founded a political party, Cambio 90 (*'cambio'* means change) with a number of like-minded people, few of whom knew him personally. After he had been elected he offered de Soto a job in his cabinet, but eventually de Soto resigned, unable to accept the degree of influence which the President's legal and security adviser, Vladimiro Montesinos, appeared to have on the President's policies.

During the election campaign Fujimori was moving ahead in the opinion polls when a legal case pending against him was scheduled to come to court. Fujimori's supporters believed the timing was politically motivated, but the case itself was real enough. He had failed to declare for income tax purposes more than thirty properties which he and his wife owned. If he had been convicted, his campaign would have been finished: the case was being brought against him in the criminal courts, and the Peruvian constitution specified that no one found guilty of a criminal offence was eligible to serve as President. At this critical moment he made the decision which was to affect the whole of his presidency: he turned to Vladimiro Montesinos to help him.

Montesinos, after a brief and turbulent career in the Army, had qualified as a lawyer. He specialised in defending senior military men who were being tried on human rights charges, and people accused of drug-trafficking. In cases where Montesinos appeared for the defence, courts had a habit of returning unexpected verdicts, witnesses changed their evidence, dossiers became lost in the bureaucratic system and never reappeared. By linking himself with some of the worst figures in Peruvian society, he made even senior politicians afraid of him.

Fujimori's defence proved easy enough. Soon after Montesinos became his lawyer, many of the papers were mislaid and the case was diverted to the civil courts. Fujimori had to pay a fine and the tax he owed, but he was still eligible to stand for the Presidency; and when he was elected, his debt to Montesinos was total. Within a matter of months, Montesinos had made himself the most powerful figure in the administration. He was immensely secretive, and only one photograph of him was known to exist. He successfully sued the editor of *Caretas*, the strongly independent political magazine which had offered Cecilia a job when she was sacked by her television company, for describing him as a presidential adviser. Some months later, on Peruvian television, President Fujimori twice referred to Montesinos as being one of his advisers.

Now, waiting in the anteroom to President Fujimori's office, we had completed our preparations for the television interview, and the soap opera had finished. The President came through the big double doors. He could have been a Japanese version of General Vidal: just as neat, just as small, just as self-controlled. He was quiet and dignified; but it was hard to imagine Vidal sitting at an empty desk, watching soap operas. Alberto Fujimori knew something about television: in the 1980s, while he was still a lecturer in agriculture, he was chosen to present a programme about farming. He was at best a wooden performer, but the programme was successful and he became associated in people's minds with serious, positive matters.

It was difficult now, as he sat down opposite me and Matt pinned a small microphone to his lapel, to think that this gentle, self-assured man could possibly be mixed up with anything lurid or discreditable. He looked at me and smiled confidently. Matt asked us both to say something, in order to check the sound-level of our two voices.

'I must congratulate you, Mr President,' I said, 'on the arrest of Abimael Guzman.'

He nodded, which was not good enough for Matt's purposes. I tried again.

'When did you first hear that the police had tracked him down and were going to arrest him?'

The President's eyes flickered.

'Three or four days before; I can't remember exactly.'

We already knew, from a close associate of General Vidal, that the arrest operation had been kept secret from everyone outside DINCOTE. Fujimori cannot have known about it beforehand; if he had, it is unlikely that he would have been so far from Lima when the arrest took place. Perhaps it was nothing more than a diplomatic untruth, to cover over a political embarrassment; but it broke the presidential spell.

Fujimori's English, though reasonably grammatical, was pronounced with such a combination of Peruvian and Japanese accents that a British audience would have had serious problems understanding it. Since it would be something of an insult to him to put subtitles over his English, I decided to encourage him to speak Spanish. Sally Bowen sat beside me to translate, but Fujimori could understand my questions and I understood his slow, concise answers.

I had structured the interview carefully in my mind beforehand. It seemed advisable to start off in a friendly way, by asking him about the success his government had scored with the arrest of Guzman, and the likelihood that he would be able now to keep his promise of eradicating terrorism from Peru by the time he left office in 1995. From there I planned to move on to the problems of human rights, the Army's involvement in drugs running, and the position of Montesinos. How he would answer these questions I could not be sure; he might even walk out. If he stayed, though, I would slowly head back on to easier ground and ask him about his plans for the future. It was important to us that we should end in friendly fashion; my experience of interviews like this is that a visiting foreign television team can usually make one request of a political leader and expect, like Aladdin, that it will be granted. Our wish was, naturally enough, access to Guzman; and only Fujimori could grant us that.

We began, then, gently enough. Soon, though, I directed him towards the subject of Montesinos. I am not a particularly fierce interviewer, and prefer polite persistence to browbeating. Rosalind, who was sitting across the room from the President, noticed his reaction when I mentioned Montesinos. Until that point he had been perfectly relaxed, but now he began to move his foot in an agitated way.

'Do you,' I asked, 'understand the concern that Peru's friends abroad feel, that you should have such an adviser?'

'Well, I have repeated on many occasions that he is not an adviser. He is a lawyer on certain matters. He is a civil servant in the intelligence service.'

'Your ministers haven't seen him and don't know him. Isn't it strange for an unelected official to have so much power?'

'There is no need for them to know. He is not an adviser.'

'It has to be said, it's an unfortunate background that Mr Montesinos has, isn't it? I mean, representing drugs traffickers as a lawyer?'

'Yes, well, he is not my adviser. Some people might question whether he should be operating as an employee of the intelligence service, in which case it might be interesting for the British or US intelligence services to combine with our own intelligence service to investigate the situation. I understand there is very close collaboration between the intelligence services, and such enquiries have not taken place.'

'The history of other countries which have the problem of drug-trafficking shows that there is so much money that it corrupts at high levels as well as low. Is that the case in Peru?'

'At high levels this is not happening, as far as I know, and any other information about this is mere speculation.'

I turned to the question of human rights.

'Organisations like Amnesty International say that the Peruvian Army is responsible for almost as many deaths as Shining Path.'

'Well, probably under previous governments. Not probably, but according to the statistics. There were a lot of reports of "disappearances", not necessarily due to the armed forces. A lot of these disappearances could have been due to Shining Path. But the statistics have been significantly reduced.'

'But what about the way the Army and the police deal with terrorism?'

'Nowadays there is selective intelligence work, collaboration with the people. This is most important. Indiscriminate repression is not being used at the moment.'

Although, as I had planned, I moved the conversation on to less contentious subjects, Fujimori was annoyed. He had expected something much easier, a discussion of the twin evils of terrorism and inflation perhaps, and his extraordinary success in dealing with both of them. He had not been expecting questions about drugs or Montesinos, and he was seriously annoyed to be asked about them at a time when the United States and Britain both seemed to have decided that Peru should be forgiven for suspending its constitution. There was no chance of persuading him to let us see Guzman now.

The President stood up, shook hands and walked silently back into his empty office. He told one of his associates soon afterwards that it had been a serious mistake to have agreed to give us an interview.

To *the* Huallaga

The general rule in our times is one of fraud and violence, and a great deal of infamy would need to be removed or buried deep in the earth in order to avoid occurrences like the one I am about to relate.

Felipe Guaman Poma de Ayala, 1613

I recognised the look on Cecilia's face as she joined us at the Las Americas hotel: a surface sweetness covering an intense excitement. She knew that a good, and dangerous, story was in the offing. We ordered coffee and rolls. The waitresses were middle-class girls who dressed well and spoke good English; they were here for the company of other Miraflores girls, not because they liked the job of waiting. They were inclined to be slow, and some of them got angry if you complained. We waited twenty-five minutes for our coffee.

'My country,' said Cecilia, with a comically sad expression and an accent which sounded like a Californian imitating Mexican. Then we turned to our Huallaga trip again, and the excitement returned to her face.

'This trip dangerous. I, no problem. But Tocache, Aucayacu, Tarapoto, very danger. You must know this. Is OK?'

'Is OK,' I said, though by that stage she was probably asking about my coffee.

Some of the problems were purely logistical: the only place in the Huallaga where there would be a reliable source of electricity was the town of Tingo Maria, so Steve and Matt might not be able to recharge their batteries anywhere else. That meant taking extra batteries, which weighed a great deal; and the plane we were chartering was too small to take much luggage.

'I'd rather take all the camera gear we need, and fewer shirts,' said Eamonn.

Steve and Matt were looking at the front cover of the latest *Caretas*, which showed Guzman behind the bars of his cage and Maritza Garrido Lecca in her ballet outfit.

'Don't think much of her,' said Steve, throwing the magazine across the breakfast table to Matt.

'After a week in the jungle, you'll be desperate for her.'

'After a week in the jungle I'll be desperate for him,' Steve said, looking at the heavy features and grizzled beard of Chairman Gonzalo.

We decided to have one last pleasant social evening before we left. Gilberto and Cecilia drove us to the most attractive restaurant in Lima – one of the most attractive anywhere, I decided later. We headed down through the cliffs to the ocean road, where the Pacific crashes on to a shore littered with derelict cars and rubbish heaps. At the end, a pier exactly like something from the south coast of England pointed out into the water, a Victorian cast-iron creation of struts and curlicues. The lights from a Gothic construction at its far end glittered on the surface of the ocean.

'La Rosa Nautica,' Cecilia announced proudly.

Half a dozen heavily armed thugs were hanging around in the car park: the Rosa Nautica was a favourite place for politicians to eat, and these were their bodyguards. We walked along the pier, with the Pacific breaking against the pillars beneath us. The lights along the coast flickered and grew stronger as the evening drew on. Inside, the restaurant was empty except for the politicians. A waiter showed us to a large wrought-iron table in the middle, and we listened to the politicians arguing and watched the waves breaking outside, until we slowly began to drown the other sounds with our own talk and laughter. A line of pelicans, outlined against the sky, caught the light from the restaurant as they flew past and skidded into the luminescent water. The politicians left. We were alone in the restaurant, as the waves built up and the sky outside became indistinguishable from the ocean, and the waiters came and listened to us and joined in the laughter.

The next morning, just as I was about to walk out of the room, Tira called me from the country house of some friends in Dorset, where she was spending the weekend. She had just come back from a ride across the nearby hills. As I listened to her describing the scenery and praising the qualities of her horse I felt a longing as sharp as pain to be away from Peru and terrorism and drugs and back in the English countryside where things were safe and assured. I could imagine the greenness of the downs, the high clouds, the temperate calm nature of everything.

Yet the sense of excitement and common purpose was too powerful for such thoughts to last long. The Peruvian ritual of a morning handshake for Johnny and kisses for Cecilia, the bustle of getting the equipment into the minibus, the heavy tipping of the hotel staff who had been unfailingly pleasant and helpful, the impatience to get going, all combined to wipe out any sense of reluctance.

'I think we're going to have to be careful about the pilot,' Eamonn said. Cecilia had warned us that the only way to keep out of any trouble from the Army was to have our own plane: that way we could leave a town when we wanted, rather than wait for one of the small scheduled flights that serviced the area. Accordingly, she and Rosalind had chartered a King-Air for us. Eamonn's point was that any pilot we flew with was likely to have trained in the armed forces, and that if he knew the Huallaga well he might easily be involved in drugs-running himself.

We had a large 'American' breakfast at a rickety table in the airport restaurant. It was another entertaining affair; and though the others probably shared my inward nervousness, they seem to have felt, as I did, that the companionship and sense of shared purpose outweighed everything else. I found myself sitting back and surveying them: Eamonn frowning with concentration, thinking out the next stage in the film-making; Steve and Matt tipping their seats back, cool and relaxed, capping each other's jokes and offering each other the openings to make more; Rosalind and Cecilia laughing over something in Spanish, each with the look in their eyes that I had noticed before: a powerful excitement which was working away below the surface. I felt Johnny's glance, and turned to meet it. He, too, had been observing us carefully, almost paternally, with his psychologist's eye. Awkwardly, I switched my attention to the cheese omelette and the abysmally weak coffee in front of me.

Carlos, the pilot, was a short, competent-looking man in his thirties; with him was a thin, pockmarked, wolfish man in co-pilot's uniform and mirror-glasses, who looked as though he were playing the part of the co-pilot in a film about flying to a drugs-growing area in South America.

'Hi, guys,' he said. Although his name was impeccably Latin and he had plainly been born and brought up in Peru, he liked to give the impression that he was an American who happened to have business interests here and was just visiting.

It feels good to have an aircraft at your disposal. We loaded all our gear – a maximum of equipment and a minimum of personal luggage, as arranged – into its small hold, and crowded into its seats with great satisfaction. I balanced a bag on my lap containing some last-minute purchases: five toilet rolls, five Mars bars, and a bottle of whisky.

'I appreciate that you may need all those things on the journey,' Steve said, 'but maybe you could put it on the floor when I film you looking out of the window?'

Obediently I put the bag down between my feet. As we took off Cecilia crossed herself. She caught my eyes and smiled, a little embarrassed. We were heading for an area where no foreigners ever went, unless they were concerned in some way with the drugs trade. Embassies forbade their staff to go near the Huallaga Valley, and the last American journalist to have visited it was garrotted.

The Andes reared up below us out of the clouds, a variegated mix of blues and greys. 'MAX. ELEVATION FIGS. IN PERU BELIEVED NOT TO EXCEED 23,000 FEET', said a note on the map the pilot was studying. The co-pilot was reading an article in one of the more hysterical Lima papers: 'Guzman Caught Because Of Orgy'.

Eamonn said, 'We want the Andes reflected in the co-pilot's dark glasses,' and for a moment none of us was certain whether or not he was joking.

'I'll have to get on to the bonnet to do it,' Steve said.

I dozed. When I woke up we were over jungle.

'The Huallaga,' Cecilia said suddenly, pointing ahead. It was an unimpressive grey-brown, far narrower than the Elvira in Brazil. Rainclouds hung heavily over the forest. Soon the river opened up, with islands and sandbanks lying in it like foam in coffee. The rainforest looked threatening and encroaching.

'Tarapoto, Tarapoto,' said a metallic voice over the radio.

'84 84. Minus 6.'

'Identification.'

'All these bases are controlled by the Army,' Rosalind said. 'They're bound to meet us.'

Rain spattered the windscreen. Tarapoto lay ahead of us, large and dead in the surrounding green. Fires burned around its edges.

'Will it be all right for Steve to carry the camera openly here?' Eamonn asked Cecilia.

She pointed to the gear and shrugged: we had so much, no one could doubt who we were and what we were doing.

Now I could see the red earth of the runway, an elderly control tower with cars and trucks parked alongside it, a horse meekly grazing, men in uniforms looking up at us.

'Here we go,' said Eamonn, and hunched his shoulders in his bull-like fashion. Rosalind and Cecilia gave each other a quick look of support and encouragement. If I'm nervous, I thought, they've got even more reason to be. I raised my clenched fist in a gesture of solidarity. Our wheels hit the bumpy earth and we rolled to a halt outside the control tower.

Tarapoto

At the same time the self-styled Don Diego Suyca and his
Spanish friends were understandably upset by my arrival.
They had formed a settled habit of robbing and maltreating
those who were at their mercy.

Felipe Guaman Poma de Ayala, 1613

For a moment there was silence.

I opened the door and clambered clumsily down the folding steps, my legs cramped after two hours' flying. An Army
officer and a sergeant stood beside the wing of the plane. They
were not smiling.

'*Buen' dia*,' I said in a tone I hoped was cheerful.

'Who are you, and why are you here?' The officer held his
hand out for whatever letter of permission or accreditation
I might have. He rubbed his forefinger and thumb together
impatiently. I ignored him.

'I like the welcoming committee,' Steve said, coming down
the steps with his camera in his arms.

'I'm afraid it's not mutual,' I said.

The air was cooler than I had expected, and there was
a pleasant earthy smell to it, like a newly dug garden. The
co-pilot joined us. Light specks of rain struck the lenses of his
mirror glasses.

'This way,' said the officer. Steve and I went with him.

'That's good,' Steve said; 'the others can do the unloading,
and we'll get beaten up for them.'

The office we were taken to smelled of damp. The chairs
seemed too broken to sit down in. An old yellow curtain hung
from a string across the window. There were files on the shelves,
but they looked empty.

'*¿Periodistas?*'

The man at the desk was fat and had done a good deal of sweating when his uniform was fresher. He had an old, damp-stained ledger in front of him.

'That's right, journalists. *Television ingles.* BBC.'

'We have been expecting you. Everyone in Tarapoto is expecting you.'

'That's nice,' I said to Steve, 'especially since we didn't tell anyone we were coming.'

'Bush telegraph,' he said. 'Works a treat.'

The man behind the desk wrote something in the ledger, then peered at the names on the six press cards I handed him. He took an extra look at Cecilia's and Rosalind's and wrote down everybody's name. Then he handed the cards back to me and scraped his chair back alarmingly on the floor, hoisting up his bulk very slowly as though he only stood up on very rare occasions and was out of practice.

'*Mucho gusto,*' he said, as though we had just walked in. His big hand enveloped mine damply.

Cecilia had found two heavily rusted taxis. Steve and Matt and I travelled in the second one, through the yellowish-green vegetation which had grown up since the forest was cleared, and which gave the impression of wanting to push its way back towards the town. Tarapoto was neat and not unprosperous. There were signs advertising soft drinks: InkaCola and Bimbo. A rooster ran across the street, and was narrowly missed by a motorbike. Our taxis made it up a hill and stopped by the traffic lights which changed from red to green; at least Tarapoto had electricity. Our hotel, El Lily, stood beside the road junction. It was open and pleasant, and a couple of fans kept it cool and relatively free of mosquitoes. There were signs of money and taste in the furnishings: old farm-implements on the walls, and old gadgets – a 1920s typewriter, an even older telephone – standing on tables in the middle of the lobby. On the floor was a cougar-skin. A glass case held large blue and yellow butterflies, though here they scarcely seemed exotic.

When I had unpacked and came down from my room,

which was small and neat and extremely noisy, since it looked out over the traffic lights, two women in their Sunday best sat waiting for us. Both had gentle indian features, and were very nervous. One jiggled her foot continually, the other licked her lips as I went over to speak to them. Rosalind explained in a low voice that they were from the local human rights organisation, which was holding a public meeting in the nearby church hall. They were expecting us there. Everyone in Tarapoto, as the man at the airport had said, seemed to be expecting us.

Rosalind and I walked the fifty yards down the road to the church hall, accompanied by the two nervous women. Old, rusting American cars ploughed by, and young men on motorbikes made their way along the main street with care, trying to avoid the potholes in the road. People stopped working to watch us. Shopkeepers came out and stood on their front steps. A cockerel crowed as we opened the gate and walked into the courtyard of the building. The human rights group met in the church at Tarapoto; but the Church was not strong enough to protect the inhabitants of the town and the murders and disappearances continued.

Inside a large, airy schoolroom about thirty people had gathered. They were sitting patiently in the school desks, and stood up like schoolchildren when we entered. Most of them were women. We moved along the rows, shaking hands, and with a slight movement of the head the first woman showed I was also expected to kiss them.

'They have been waiting here since 9 o'clock,' the elder of our two women guides said. Now it was 12.30.

'How did they know we were coming?'

'We told the local radio station, and for the past three days they have been asking people to come here and meet you if they have any human rights violations to complain about.'

That explained things. It also made me feel I owed something to these people. To come out into the open like this was an act of great personal courage, given that the Army tended to associate human rights with terrorism. I looked round me at the quiet, patient, trusting faces, all of them turned towards us. They were here because they thought we could do something to help them. In that case I would help them. I pulled out my notebook

An Ashanica couple and thier child at Simpatia, in the Brazilian rain forest.
Both are wearing the *kushma*, the robe characteristic of the tribe

Left

(above) Steve Morris (plus camera) and Eamonn Matthews on the road from Shamboyacu, one of the big coca-growing villages in the Huallaga Valley. We have just got away from it unscathed; which partly explains their smiles

(below) The morning after our disaster on the Envira River. My eighty-eight bites are scarcely visible. In the river behind me are the half-submerged trees on which our dug-out canoe came to grief. The necklace was a present from the Kulina Indians whose hallucinogenic *dime* we had drunk

(top) Rosalind Bain

(above) Cecila Valenzuela

(left) Matt Leiper

(right) Abimael Guzman being presented to the world's press

(below) The only known photograph of Vladimiro Montesinos. The photographer who took it in 1983 was beated up, and considerable efforts were made to destroy the negatives

(foot) After our interview, President Fujimori poses for a photograph with me. But my questions had angered him considerably, and he told his officials it had been a mistake to agree to see us

(above) A still from the video of our meeting with Comandante Roberto in the office of the Army's anti-terrorist squad G2 in Tarapoto. He is holding up his hand because he wants Steve to stop filming him

(left) In his office in Tocache, Comandante Alfonso has just realized that Steve's camera is running

(right) Luis Zambrano, the sub-prefect of Tocache, and his wife Daisy. Zambrano, with her support, revealed to us the full extent of the Army's involvement in drugs-running and human rights abuses in Tocache – as bad as anywhere in Latin America

(below) Victor Ushinahua, whose son, daughter-in-law and one-year-old granddaughter were murdered by the Army in Tarapoto

(right) An unwelcome surprise for two members of Tarapota Army intellignce. They had orders to photograph everyone who had come to tell us about the human rights abuses in the town. In this still from the video I am just introducing myself to them: we were taking pictures of them instead

The Empress of the Marginal, the bus we hired to take us to Aucayacu, fords the Pendencia River

Our vehicle is stopped by a group of guerrillas. We knew that if they belonged to Shining Path we would all be killed, probably slowly. It was something of a relief to find they were from the rival MRTA

(*above*) Sally Bowen and her son Rory

(*left*)Gilberto, Cecilia's boyfriend

(*below*) Johnny, the psychologist-turned-driver

and began to write down detailed notes about what I saw in front of me, so that we could report everything in full to Amnesty International when we returned to London. By the time Eamonn, Steve and Matt arrived – Cecilia was off trying to arrange our filming for the next day – the flow of experiences had started in earnest.

A woman in her late fifties stood up, and began to tell her story. She had dressed up for our visit in a frock of blue cotton and a gold necklace, which made her seem more elderly and frail. Yet she was a strong speaker, and showed no sign of nerves.

'The Army came and took my son at four o'clock one morning. He never was an early riser, my poor boy. He was twenty-five years old. They said he was a terrorist, but I know he wasn't. He was *un chico inocente*: he didn't know what these things were all about. He never came back, and they won't tell me what happened to him. All they do is threaten me. That poor little one. . . Why should they have taken him from me like this? I don't know if I'll ever see him again.'

She began to cry. Another woman stood up and gave her story, less coherently and more rambling. I found myself looking at the pictures on the wall: mostly the routine sentimental depictions of Jesus and Mary. But there was a poem, too – '*Si*. . .' It took me a moment or two to realise it was a translation of the ultra-Protestant Kipling's 'If. . .'. Perhaps its list of public-school virtues counted as a moral text and was therefore acceptable.

I had just made out 'Or being lied about, don't deal in lies' in Spanish when there was a movement outside the door. Two men in their thirties were hanging around there. Steve, whose reactions were always swift, swung round and got a shot of them sneaking past the door and peering in. One had a video camera, the other a stills camera. A little murmur of dismay went round the room: they were from Army intelligence, G2 – the group which arrested people and took them off to disappearance and death. The two men were here to check on and intimidate the people who had turned out to meet us. It was a moment of real fear in the audience. Eyes turned in our direction. If we showed that we were afraid, their act of courage would have been wasted.

'Let's go out and turn them over,' Eamonn said vigorously, and Steve took his camera off its tripod and put it on his shoulder.

We trooped out, leaving the people in the hall to watch us go. Rosalind and I were first: I could sense the anger welling up in her. The two men from military intelligence looked poleaxed when they saw us heading towards them, Steve with the camera on his shoulder and filming, Eamonn whispering something to him, Matt pushing the microphone towards them, Rosalind and I calling over to them. I strove for politeness, and shook their hands: they were small hands, which had no grip and sweated slightly. In this town you didn't need to be big to arrest people and torture them or kill them; you just needed to work for the Army. The younger of the two had a pleasant enough face; the other, who was carrying the video camera, was surly and withdrawn.

I asked them who they were. They had not prepared a cover story; why should they need one, to frighten a few people in a church hall? The younger man stammered an unthought-out reply.

'We're journalists. We're from ... Well, we're from a human rights magazine. Yes. We came here to ...' With our camera on him, and Rosalind translating fiercely, he couldn't think of a reason why they had come here.

'Which magazine?'

He wasn't quite sure; he could come back and tell us its name later.

'I'm glad you're journalists,' I said pitilessly; 'that makes you colleagues of ours. But maybe you could answer a question for me: how come if you work for a magazine you're carrying a video camera?'

'I can if I want to,' the older, nastier of the two answered. 'There's no reason why not.' I had the feeling he was angry with his colleague for being so feeble.

'No,' I said, 'but the people inside the hall are very nervous because they think you're from the Army; so would you mind going?'

They turned and went, fast; and as they walked away I told them to come back later with some identification. The younger one said they'd go and get it. The older one scowled and said nothing. We filmed them off the premises.

Back in the schoolroom I felt a little shaken. But I was aware that these people were looking to us to give them strength and hope. If we behaved calmly and confidently, perhaps our calmness and confidence would communicate itself to them. I apologised for having left them, and asked them to continue telling us about their complaints against the Army.

Ana Garcia Java, a heavily pregnant woman in her late thirties, stood up. She had a mouthful of gold teeth, and wore a gold crucifix round her neck. She supported herself by gripping the back of the chair in front of her. Her words were delivered with clarity and confidence: a good witness.

'The soldiers came at 11.30 at night. I knew they were soldiers. They smashed everything up. They said they'd come to take away my son Mauricio. They pulled him out of bed – he was just wearing a T-shirt and some underwear – and then he said something, so they hit him on the back of the head, just here, and he fell down on the ground. I thought he was dead. He's only fourteen, just a boy. Then as they were driving off with Mauricio I ran out and got the number of the car.'

I sat there, making notes and listening like a judge. It seemed to be what they were expecting. I interrupted her to ask questions: how did she know it was the Army, what action had she taken, was her son involved with any terrorist group? It was plain by the end that her son's best friend had been in the Movimiento Revolucionario Tupac Amaru or MRTA, a moderately ineffectual guerrilla group set up along Che Guevarist lines and dedicated to the memory of the last Inca to rule Peru. It was very active in this area. Perhaps Mauricio was a member too, perhaps not. Even if he were, the legal penalty for being a member of a terrorist organisation in Peru was not death. Yet it seemed reasonable to assume that Mauricio had been tortured and killed; it had happened to so many others.

Most of the people in the audience were of indian origin, and were peasants or the children of peasants. One man, however, looked different. He was older than the rest, in his late sixties, and wore a tie. Two ballpoint pens were ranged neatly in the breast pocket of his carefully ironed white shirt. He had sat awaiting his turn, a polite smile on his lips as though he were waiting for an interview at the office of a prospective employer. Finally he got to his feet, a heavy man, sweating a little in the heat, still smiling. I inclined my head, more like a judge than ever; it seemed to be expected of me.

'*Senor periodista, muy buenas tardes.* My name is Victor Ushinahua Torres, aged sixty-eight, a former clerk at the Banco de la Nacion.'

He went on to tell his story, the facts neatly marshalled. His son, daughter-in-law and baby granddaughter had all disappeared, taken away by armed men in civilian clothes. He produced a document and read from it: an officer at the Army base in Tarapoto had replied to his enquiries by saying there was no record of any of them, and the Army knew nothing of the case.

'Here is the official stamp, at the bottom. But why should he tell such a lie? This is not justice. All I want is to know where my son and his wife and their little baby are being held prisoner.'

I thanked him, and he sat down. His gentle, sad wife had been sitting quietly at the back. Now she came and sat in a newly vacated chair just behind him, and put her hand on his shoulder. He reached up and stroked it, fondly but absently, his quick, disciplined attention fixed on the next speaker, or switched to me as I asked my purposeful-sounding, helpless questions. '"And yet,"' I quoted to myself, looking back at Kipling in translation on the wall, '"don't look too good, nor talk too wise. . . "'

One by one the others stood up and told their stories. I made more notes: Dominguez Lopez, with a funny, mobile face like a natural joker, now turning his energies to the effort to get information about his brother. A man in an InkaCola T-shirt and a straggling, unsatisfactory beard talked about the disappearance of his friend. A woman in pink, Mercedes Sanchez de Riga, her eyes red with weeping, wanted news of her husband. No, she couldn't say who had taken him. No, he wasn't interested in politics, just in *futbol*. Outside, rain was falling in drops the size

of a child's fist on the flat green leaves of plants. Anibal Luis Garcia
had lost his brother. It could have been the Army; who knows in
this town?

We went back to the house of Ana Garcia Java, the
self-assured woman whose son Mauricio had disappeared. It
was, relatively speaking, an expensive place, with proper floors
and a yard at the back. Her husband was a well-respected
carpenter. You could see the indian derivation of the building:
the walls were of mud, the roof of split logs under the habitual
corrugated iron. Nowadays Ana went down to the Army base
at Tarapoto at least twice a week to ask for news of her son,
who had disappeared three months before. Would she allow us
to go with her this afternoon? She was happy to, she said; they
might start to take her more seriously. She was certain he had
been taken to the base; she had run out into the street as the
car which took him away was driving off, and she had jotted
down its registration number. Since then she had seen the same
car parked at the base.

She brought out a photograph of Mauricio. He looked
younger than his nineteen years, his arms draped over the
shoulders of his friends, grinning: the kind of boy you see on
every street corner of every town in Peru, not very clever, not
very good, yet pleasant enough. He was always smiling, said
Ana. Her husband, older and more beaten-down, had shuffled
into the room from his workshop at the back. He looked at the
photograph for a moment, and agreed.

'Maybe some of his friends were MRTA, but he wasn't.
He was too young for that kind of thing. Let them take
the terrorists; that's OK. But they should leave the ones who
are innocent.'

He looked at the photograph again, then handed it slowly
back to his wife, as though he didn't expect to see it again.

After the rain, it was a beautiful golden afternoon. We drove
down to the base between a line of palm-trees, the sun in our
eyes and the forest breaking through into the cultivated fields every
now and then. We stopped our ancient taxis near the first guard
post. The two soldiers watched in a paralysis of disbelief as Steve

and Matt plugged up their gear and got ready for the assault on the base.

A good thirty seconds passed before one of the soldiers picked up the field telephone to warn the men further on that we were coming. It was, I thought, like being Pizarro at a battle with the Incas; they had never seen equipment like ours. We had descended from a world no one here could fully understand: we were the only people in the Huallaga Valley who were not afraid of the Army, and neither the aggressors nor their victims could envisage a world where the power to torture and kill meant so little.

I told the corporal at the guard house what we wanted. He told a sergeant, who told a junior officer. In the end an unpleasant-looking captain came out and spoke to us. He wore dark glasses, and his cheeks were cratered with acne. His voice showed the strain of keeping polite to us.

'Of course we know Dona Ana,' he said with a smile that showed a great many teeth, and gaps where teeth had been. 'She is our friend here. We see her often.'

'She's going to be famous all over the world,' I told him with equal pleasantness and equal insincerity. 'Everyone will know about her son and the fact that she comes here to try to get news of him. Is there any news of him?'

'Switch your camera off, please,' said the captain sharply. He was still trying very hard to remain pleasant. He gave us a brief account of the strategic situation in the area. He even drew us a little map in the dust with the key to his car, to show how the base was under constant attack from Shining Path and the MRTA.

'Over there,' he said, pointing to a blank wall, 'we will soon put up a monument to all the men from this Army base who have died at the hands of the terrorists. We're here to finish with a particular problem: subversion. That is our duty.' He was starting to address us as though we were a parade.

It was plain they did not want us to go any farther into the base. The time had come to put on a little more pressure.

'I think now we need to speak to the commander in charge of the base,' Eamonn said firmly.

Like the G2 men at the public meeting earlier, the Army had not prepared any way of dealing with us. The captain simply retreated to the next line of defence.

'Why not? You are our guests,' he said, as though the words gave him a certain amount of pain. He held a whispered conversation with another officer, then led us up a muddy path towards a group of wooden huts on the crest of the hill.

Strictly speaking, I thought, they could do anything with us now, though it did not really seem likely that they would kill us. What was possible was that they might arrange an accident for us somewhere outside the base rather than inside it. Still, there were a lot of us; and although unpleasant things often happened to lone journalists in this area, six of us would be harder to get rid of. If two cars, rather than one, went over a clifftop with defective brakes, people in Lima would start asking questions.

We straggled up three ranks: the captain with Rosalind and me beside him, Eamonn, Cecilia with Ana Garcia, and Steve and Matt at the back. I had asked Steve not to film the base itself, but to be ready to film, in secret, whatever confrontation would now follow.

The captain showed us into a wooden hut with a large map of the area on the wall. Cecilia realised at once where we were: inside the office of G2, the unit which had arrested Mauricio, Ana's young son. Several Army officers, some in uniform, were sitting there already, expecting us. The door burst open and an eager-looking, energetic, handsome man came bounding in and shook our hands.

'Good evening. I am Comandante Roberto. Forgive me, I cannot give you my family names; we have to be careful of terrorists.'

He laughed self-deprecatingly. Everything about him seemed designed to make us trust him: his serious horn-rimmed glasses, his hearty handshake, his enthusiasm, his boyishness. It was about as genuine as the captain's earlier frankness. Comandante Roberto was the officer in charge of G2, and there was nothing boyish about that.

'First, I have a question for you,' he said, adjusting his

spectacles reprovingly. 'Why did you try to shut out the men who came to talk about human rights to you today?'

I told him what had happened at the church hall earlier, and why we had asked the two G2 men to leave.

'But whatever made you think they might be from the Army?'

I explained that too. He shifted his ground quickly.

'But they were only there to help, to explain the position.'

It was starting to be clear that he had decided we were a part of some big communist conspiracy against the Peruvian Army. I had come across officers like him in various Latin American countries in the past: Argentina, Chile, Uruguay, Colombia. They all seemed to feel the same compulsion to act up to the stereotype.

'Why did you make these announcements on the radio, stirring people up?'

I explained that we had made no announcements ourselves: he was unconvinced.

I glanced round as casually as I could to see if Steve was filming. I could tell by the way the camera was pointing, and the way that he was reading a notice on the wall, that he was. I launched into my set piece.

'Can you tell me why this woman has never been given any information about her son, even though the car which drove him away is often seen parked in this base?'

He answered as best he could; there was no certainty about the case, he had made enquiries and no one had heard anything about Mauricio. He produced a book which detailed the arrests made by G2: there was no entry in it for 29 May, the night Mauricio was taken. Another officer, sensing perhaps that Comandante Roberto was not making much of a fist of it, broke in:

'You don't understand. The subversives use the same uniforms and the same type of cars, the same everything that we do. It's part of their tactics.'

'In this case,' I said, 'they seem to have had exactly the same car, with the same numberplate.'

There was silence for a little. Then something awkward happened: one of the security men who had come in at the back of the room wandered over to look at Steve's camera, and saw that the cassette was turning. He realised we were filming after all. There was an angry argument, and Steve tried to placate the security man. Somehow, he kept the camera running, even though he had to tip the camera almost on to its side and the remaining pictures were at a considerable angle.

'We've got a problem,' Eamonn said to me. I did my best to divert the attention of Comandante Roberto by asking more and more elaborate questions. Eventually the security man passed a note to him. As he read it, a look of anger which belied the boyish eagerness passed across his face. He spoke briefly to the captain, then continued talking as though nothing had happened. That seemed significant to me: they might dislike what we were doing, but they were reluctant to stop us. For the first time, I began to believe that we were going to get away with this.

I went back over the question of Mauricio's disappearance: what could have happened to him?

'We, the Army, are under strict orders to respect human rights. If I keep someone in more than two days without charging them, I get into trouble. Maybe it was the police who took him; bad things have happened in human rights here, I can tell you frankly. But most likely it's the terrorists themselves.'

'Why couldn't it be the Army, which simply goes out in civilian clothes, arrests and kills people, and then comes back?'

He had no answer to that. The presence of the car with its numberplate made it hard to suggest anything else.

'You have a duty to tell the truth, you people from the media,' said the captain when the meeting was over and we were heading down the hill again. The lingering red of the sunset was reflected on the dark glasses he still wore. 'You should be very careful.'

I took that as a warning.

'These *militars* are *huachafos*,' said Cecilia as we drove away. 'What is *huachafo* in English?'

'Wanker,' I said.

'Huanca,' Cecilia repeated. It was the name of a Peruvian tribe, and she liked the word.

Later, we went to see the former bank clerk, Victor Ushinahua, in his large, gloomy house on the outskirts of the town. He had agreed to give us a longer interview. Everyone knew him, and seemed to respect him. When we knocked on his door he was as formal and polite as ever.

'Good evening, sir. I should like to thank you for your help in the case of my family.'

He went through his files with us, and I began to realise that the neat arrangement and presentation of these documents, of little value in themselves, represented his hold on sanity and reason in a society where the Army could simply come and kidnap the sons of people as well-established as himself. He read the details from their records:

'Victor Ushinahua Fasanando (that's my son). Born 5 July 1964. (He is twenty-eight now.) Maria Elva Mendoza Coral (his wife – a beautiful girl, sir). Born 25 April 1965. She's twenty-five. Elisabeth Ushinahua Mendoza, born 8 August 1991. She's one. Of course, they had other children.'

He looked round at Danny, a quiet, nervous little boy whom Rosalind had taken to and was slowly winning over. Danny was sitting on her lap, leaning his head against her, but his thoughts seemed somewhere else. Earlier, when she had asked him if he had been playing, he had looked blankly at her and said, 'Why?' Danny didn't, Mr Ushinahua said, do much playing with other children now.

Somewhere at the back a baby was crying. A little girl stood in the doorway, looking on. She was serious and unsmiling, the only one of the group who did not respond to Rosalind's affection.

'It is difficult for my wife and me to look after these children at our age, sir,' he said. 'Difficult for them, too. That's why my son needs to come home.'

I looked at Cecilia, and saw the pity in her face. Quietly, I asked her if she thought they would come back.

'They're all dead,' she said. 'Everyone knows it except him.'

I noticed that when Victor Ushinahua went through the documents, each neatly tied and docketed, he flipped past one file very quickly. I looked at it, and saw it was his son's police record. Victor Ushinahua junior had been sentenced to a term of imprisonment for being part of a group of drugs-traffickers. He had been the link man, driving round on his motorbike. We had heard stories of the Army's habit of breaking into the drugs trade by arresting people from groups like this. They would kill some, and force the others to work for them. That was no doubt what had happened here. The soldiers would have taken his wife because they did not want any witnesses, and since she was breast-feeding the baby she would have refused to leave it behind.

I did not want to ask Mr Ushinahua about any of this. I gave him back his documents, and he put them neatly away in a large file.

'I'll write again to the Procurator Fiscal,' he said. 'Seeing you has encouraged me to do it. I went there with the documents, but he wouldn't see me. He knows where my son is being held. If I write to him again now, he'll have to tell me.'

His wife put her arm through his and held on to him very tightly. She knows, I thought.

'Thank you again for your visit, sir,' he said, holding on to my hand a long time. 'You've helped me very greatly.' He stood in the doorway of his house as we drove off, his arm raised in farewell, outlined against the golden light of the oil lamps inside.

Crossing The River

I moved among the animals who prey upon the poor.

Felipe Guaman Poma de Ayala, 1613

My alarm clock went at 3.35. I dressed by torchlight, and shaved in cold water. Even though I had had less than four hours' sleep, a sense of anticipation and suppressed excitement about the day ahead gave me the energy to get going. By four we were all assembled in the lobby of the Lily hotel, waiting for the minibus which was to take us out of town. I sat down, my feet on the cougar-pelt. A large pale gecko, its organs showing through its transparent skin, adhered to the wall near my head, watching me carefully. The driver still hadn't appeared by 4.30. I turned my head to look at the clock. When I turned back, the gecko had gone.

'I know him. He can't ever wake up,' said the paunchy, unshaven character behind the counter. He eyed the telephone he kept beneath the desk. Cecilia, stung by the notion that her chosen driver should not have been perfect, headed out into the street and stopped a minibus as it passed. The driver agreed to make the dangerous journey, but demanded 300 soles. She came back into the hotel in triumph.

The night air was cool. We crammed into the minibus with all the camera gear. The driver blasted us with salsa music, until we shouted at him to turn it off. We drove out of Tarapoto some way, and came to a building marked 'Casa de Campesino' – the farmer's house. Two men came out and shook hands with us in the darkness. These were Cecilia's contacts, and I looked at them curiously. They were not ordinary farmers: they grew the coca which was sold to the Colombian cartels and smuggled to the United States and Europe in the form of cocaine. As they climbed into the minibus and settled down for a long ride, there seemed nothing noteworthy about them: they were neither rich, nor sinister, nor violent-looking. They were precisely like any other Latin American *campesinos*; and yet the crop they grew was undermining governments throughout a continent. It was hard to reconcile so much crime and greed with the two small figures sitting beside the driver, chatting about the state of the road and the contested result of some local football match.

Gradually, though, I began to realise why they were prepared to take the risk of being seen with us. There was something extraordinary about these two men, after all: as leaders of the local farmers' organisation they had decided to take the risk of showing us the coca-growing area because they wanted to demonstrate to the outside world that they grew it against their will. The growers were some of the cocaine trade's main victims. It was a dangerous crop, which brought inexperienced, backward, peaceable peasants into direct contact with the sharp-minded criminals who collected the coca leaves and sold them to the big organisations. It was dangerous too because there was always the possibility of some intervention by the American Drug Enforcement Agency, whose duty was to eradicate the cocaine trade irrespective of the effect on the *campesinos*. These men wanted to go back to growing the safe crops they had grown in the past; and they wanted us to show that the pricing policies of Europe and the United States made that impossible.

Our minibus jolted horribly over the stony dirt track that led out of town to the Huallaga River. In the darkness this was the worst part of the journey, and it was made bearable only by the approach of dawn. The growing light, which had just been a luminescence in the eastern sky, was now scarlet. It glistened on the surfaces of the puddles that filled the potholes in our road, it lit up the elaborate spiders' webs on the tall grasses by the roadside, it showed us the density of the jungle alongside us. As we rounded a bend on the hillside and found ourselves on the bluffs above the Huallaga, the valley opened below us. But it was filled with a river of cloud, which moved gently downstream in the same direction as the river itself.

For Steve, the opalescent morning light and the valley filled with cloud were irresistible, and we stopped by the roadside so he could film the sun coming up. The clouds were disappearing fast in the growing heat, and soon we could see the river below them. It ran almost straight for two miles or more, not the grey-brown colour we had seen from the air but a dark, steely, glittering band of water, sinister and forbidding. I looked across at the other side of the river. It was bandit country, where the terrorists operated and the coca was grown. Nothing we had seen had quite prepared us for the beauty of it all; but there would be no protection for us over there.

We rattled on down the descending road, through a village where the people were beginning to stir. The women were out building fires and preparing to cook the morning meal; the men were mostly still in bed. Cocks crew; underfed dogs barked at us, then shrank back nervously under cover. At the bottom of the hill the road opened out, and the river lay in front of us, wider than the Rhine at Bonn. The ferry we were to take came beating across the fast-flowing current, thrashing across it in a wide arc, then allowing the stream to carry it in to the quieter waters close inshore. It proved to be four boats lashed together and powered by two outboard motors, each of which had a man to steer it. The problems of ensuring that they were steering at precisely the same angle must have been considerable, yet they managed well, looking across at each other every now and then to check the angle.

The captain of this strange ferry was a man in his fifties with an eccentric taste in clothes and an exaggerated strabismus that made you wonder how he could direct a vehicle like ours so precisely alongside the earth-covered planks that acted as a landing stage. We were no sooner on board than Eamonn thought we should reverse off and get the ferry to come back in so we could film from it.

'I see, it's Cecil B. DeMille time,' Steve said, but he knew the idea was a good one. If you have only one camera there are times when a well-made film demands shots like this. There is usually little problem persuading the people you are filming: they tend to enjoy the experience and rarely mind going through the motions for the sake of the camera. Rosalind threw herself into the business of persuasion and organisation with great enthusiasm, and the boatmen put out into the river again with Steve and Matt on board, while we stayed on the shore in the minibus.

But it didn't work. The current was so strong that nothing short of the half-mile arc described by the ferry in midstream could get it back to the landing stage at the correct angle. After three or four attempts, even Eamonn agreed it couldn't be done.

'We'll do it on the other side, though,' he said, and the set look about his jaw and forehead showed that the current would not stop him again.

We described a reverse arc now, spinning out into the dark, fast-running river until the engines seemed to be making no headway whatever, and then slowly, inch by inch, easing ourselves through the current and into the calmer water along the river's edge. With a double roar of engines the boat forced its way up to the muddy shore where a group of passengers was waiting. Rosalind, with the same good humour, announced to them that they would have to wait while the camera-crew disembarked, the ferry went out into the river again, and came back in. She explained the reasons carefully, though these were people who may well never have seen a television set. The passengers looked blankly at her and at Steve, and sat down patiently to wait for the mystery to run its course.

Steve filmed me leaning on the rail of the ferry, looking grimly at the forest ahead of us. The yellow-green of the trees, the mountains in the distance, the cool water rushing by beneath the boat, made it a place of considerable beauty. But only a couple of weeks before a group of Shining Path guerrillas had come here and murdered a group of passengers exactly like the ones sitting waiting now. They wanted to show that they, and not the MRTA, were the dominant force in the area. I could see the slogans they had daubed on the walls of the huts on stilts beside the landing stage: 'LONG LIVE MARXISM-LENINISM-MAOISM!' 'LONG LIVE THE THOUGHT OF CHAIRMAN GONZALO!' Now Chairman Gonzalo was behind bars, but the slogans remained.

The boat's engines were switched off, and in the sudden silence a vast black sow grunted loudly. A clutch of piglets ran squealing along the shore, and large yellow and black butterflies like our swallowtails played over the puddles of water. A big indian woman came out and welcomed us: would we like to stay for breakfast? We had been on the road for three hours, and it seemed an attractive prospect to eat fried eggs and look out at the river. But Lorenzo, the senior of the two coca growers, was nervous, and wanted to get going.

He was small, and had the neatness and good looks of a Mexican band leader. By allowing Cecilia to talk him into escorting us to the coca fields, he had taken a big risk. He thought the other coca growers would be worried about us, and he wanted to reach them before the dealers arrived. They, he knew, would be bitterly hostile to us. Only the support of the growers would protect us from them, and the growers would need a little persuasion; hence, no breakfast. We climbed into the minibus and ate a handful of Matt's nuts and raisins each as we headed along a road of orange mud towards the first of the coca-growing villages, throwing up big drops of orange-coloured water each time we hit a puddle.

Castilla was a neat kind of place, like the picture of an Anglo-Saxon village in a child's history book. Its huts were of clay and were roofed with thatch. Animals rooted around on the grass in front of them, and because they kept the grass cropped the village looked tidy. A man rode across the road ahead of us on a small frisky horse. He balanced a machete in his lap and pulled at the reins with one hand to keep the horse under control, and waved cheerily to us with the other.

'There's a man who doesn't realise we've come to film him,' said Matt.

He was right. When a group of villagers gathered round the minibus and began talking to Lorenzo, their friendliness noticeably faded. Life is difficult enough for coca growers without bringing in the television cameras.

'But this is what we've been saying we wanted,' Lorenzo argued despairingly, leaning out of the minibus window as though he were trying to meet them halfway.

The next village was forty minutes' drive away. We stopped and talked, and got nowhere. We drove on to Huanipo. The villages were no longer neat, and no longer quite so prosperous now. This was guerrilla country, as the slogans on the wall showed:

'VIVA EL MRTA!' 'COMANDANTE ROBERTO VIVES EN EL CORAZON DEL PUEBLO!': 'Comandante Roberto Lives In The Heart Of The People.'

We assumed this was not the Comandante Roberto we had met at the Army base in Tarapoto; if he lived in the heart of the people, it would be for a different reason. This one appeared to be a local leader of the MRTA, who had been captured or killed in the area round Huanipo. Other slogans were in red, and were the work of Shining Path. Huanipo had the misfortune to lie on the battlefield between three mutually antagonistic armies. It was ugly and straggling, and there were few animals around. No doubt they were in danger of being handed over to whichever group demanded them. Two children looked out at us from the doorways. A woman ran round a hut to see who we were, then ducked back out of sight again. There were vultures in a nearby tree, and the smell of sewage was everywhere. It did not seem like the kind of place to announce that we wanted to film the drugs trade.

We were only ten minutes out of Huanipo along the dirt road, with a steep drop to a little, dark, silent tributary of the Huallaga on our right /and a wooded hill on our left, when we saw them: eight figures in rough approximations of military uniform, carrying rifles. The driver stopped almost immediately. They kept on coming towards us.

'Oh-oh,' Eamonn said.

No one else said anything at all. We were either about to get some good pictures, or else a bullet in the back of the neck. Our lives rested on the group's political orientation. If they were MRTA, we had no serious problems. If they were Shining Path, they might kill us outright, or they might torture us before they killed us. They might of course let us film them and then allow us to go on our way with a friendly wave; except that I had never heard of a case where a foreign journalist had survived being captured by Shining Path.

In the interminable time it took the guerrillas to reach us, we sat there, silent and serious; the others knew as well as I what the consequences could be. The driver was terrified, moving around in his seat in an agony of nervousness. But Lorenzo, the coca grower, seemed unworried. That, I thought, was a good sign. He knew this area, and if they were from Shining Path he would die as unpleasant a death as the rest of us.

'We are from the MRTA,' said the eldest of the group. He can only have been about twenty. There was a general release of breath in the bus, and the driver sat quiet at last.

'Do you mind if we film you?' Eamonn asked, and we all took the opportunity to get out of the bus and shake their hands; it was simply a way of expressing our relief.

They had no objection whatever to being filmed; indeed, it gave them a great deal of pleasure. At least three of them were under fifteen. They looked tired and hungry, and they said they were the advanced guard of a contingent which was planning to attack an Army patrol in the area. We had seen the Army in one of the villages we had passed through, but it was no part of our job to tell them that. Now they wanted to prepare themselves for the camera. They pulled their scarves over their faces so they could not be identified. While we were waiting, Steve and I went over to the side of the road to relieve ourselves.

'The trouble you get me into,' I said, referring to Rumania and all the other awkward places where the two of us had worked together.

'Oh, I don't know. They look like nice boys to me.'

'You won't say that if you get a bullet in the back of the neck.'

'They wouldn't do a thing like that,' Steve said; 'they'd make me splash my trousers.'

The patrol was ready now, although the youngest member was having difficulty keeping his scarf over his face. The leader reached over and put the safety catch of his rifle into the 'on' position. When they had marched down the road, and we had asked them to look as natural as they could look with their faces covered and the embarrassment of being on television, Steve and I went over and interviewed the leader. His opinions were copy-book ones:

'We are trying to make things better for our own people, so they don't die of hunger. We don't want exploitation. We want the levels to be equal, so there are no more exploiters and no more exploited. The only way to do this is to take up arms to change the situation.'

What about Shining Path?

'They are in error. They look for us and fight us. We don't seek them out.'

He wouldn't say any more. I thought he seemed more worried about Shining Path than he was about the Army. Now, though, he wanted to get going. He jigged from one foot to the other, the desire to play-act on television giving way to his wider concern, which was the operation he and the young boys with him had been ordered to carry out. The Army had been in the area for three days, he said; and he added naively that there were eighty MRTA guerrillas in the area preparing for a battle. So much innocence and ignorance combined with so much firepower, I thought, looking at this youth with his red scarf and air of responsibility, and the children who followed him.

No wonder the local people sympathised secretly with the MRTA: these were just local boys working on a vague, instinctual, enthusiastic mixture of ideas from Che Guevara back to the mediaeval outlaws of Europe, robbing the rich for the sole reason that they were rich and giving to the poor because they were poor. The leader looked round. The others were cavorting round because they thought the camera was still on them, aiming at nonexistent threats in the bush and putting on expressions of assumed ferocity. By comparison with them, the Army and Shining Path were serious, and dangerous. A sixteen-year-old reached through the open window of the bus and shook my hand with playful ardour.

'*Mucho gusto*,' he said, and laughed, showing his gappy yellowish teeth. Meeting us had made what was left of their day: of their lives, perhaps.

We were late, and Lorenzo was getting worried again.

'These boys will fight the Army today,' he said. 'Maybe that could make big problems for us later.'

Coming across an MRTA unit had been an extraordinary piece of luck for us, but our efforts to film the coca growers and their relations with the *traquateros* had so far come to nothing. We rattled along the red earth road, between high clumps of thick, weedy, insect-gnawed bushes, with the dark little river below us and the hillside on our left. The road turned sharply right where a stream came down the hill to join the river. It had turned into a slough of red-brown mud, and the driver gunned up his engine at the sight of it. We were halfway through before the wheels sank.

Blue and black butterflies five inches across settled on the pool of mud, and the raucous noise of parakeets in the trees rose to a new height as we climbed out. Lorenzo turned away as though our last chance had gone. Everybody else went round searching for rocks to put under the wheels, as the stream flowed into the slough of mud and spread, dammed now by the arrival of the minibus. We put our backs against the minibus and heaved. The engine roared, black smoke filled the air, mud splattered our clothes, the minibus sank back into its slough. Of all the things that could happen, I thought, this is the most stupid. We fetched some more rocks and set our weight against the rear of the minibus a second time, while the butterflies flew up and the parakeets screeched all over again. This time the bus moved a little. We tried harder. It moved more. At last its front wheels got a purchase on drier earth, and we found ourselves left behind in the slough as it roared its way out.

'Another triumph for Rohan Man,' said Matt sardonically; it was a reference to the shop that made the clothes he and Steve were wearing.

'Tell the driver we can't have another delay like this,' Eamonn said to Rosalind. The driver nodded seriously, but seemed to feel as I did: if the road was bad, it was bad.

A pony laden down with green plantains had to move out of the way for us, and a dog burst out of the undergrowth, its lips curled back over its teeth, barking hysterically at our wheels. We were getting near another village.

'Shamboyacu,' said Lorenzo, pointing through the windscreen. It was past midday, and it had taken us more than four hours to get here from the river crossing. The sun went down shortly before six. It was not advisable to drive in the dark. We each did the calculations, quietly.

Shamboyacu was holding the annual celebration of its foundation, a quarter-century before. Feeble yellow and red bunting straggled across the main street, and there were flags in front of every house. We drove through the village to the main square, a big open unpaved area where people sold things from piles of goods on the ground, children played football, the local radio station was being relayed over loudspeakers, horribly distorted, and there was a general sense of insistent enjoyment. People swarmed round our minibus, peering in and sometimes reaching through the window to shake our hands, as the MRTA had done earlier. A white dog sniffed round a pile of T-shirts in the football colours of Peru and Brazil, and cocked its leg on them. A child of three chased it off with a stick.

Lorenzo was deep in conversation with a man dressed in a green T-shirt and shorts, who had no teeth whatever. Rosalind translated for our benefit:

'. . . only here to help us. They're very discreet. I've seen them on the road already, when . . . [he dropped his voice]. Nothing to worry about. . .'

'. . . to get everyone's agreement.'

'Sure. Of course. No problem.'

But as he turned away his face seemed to show that there were plenty of problems.

By now Rosalind, the one-time football photographer, was listening to the excitable, heavily overmodulated commentary from the loudspeakers.

'It's Italy and Argentina,' she said, with a kind of reverence.

'Gooooooooooooooooooooooooooooooooooooooool,' raved the commentator, in the Argentine fashion which has now been picked up throughout Latin America and beyond. People stopped to listen, more interested in the commentator than in the fact that a goal had been scored. Anyway, it seemed to be a recording of an old match.

Rosalind went with Cecilia to buy chocolate. When they came back she explained to us what was going on.

'This is where they do the deals,' she said, pointing out at the market square. 'The growers are out with their families. The ones with bags over their shoulders are the *traquateros*. Some of them are Colombians. They keep their money in the bags – quite a lot of it.'

There were dozens of *traquateros*, moving through the crowd with the ease of men who knew their power. Most of them were young. Their only competition came from other *traquateros*; the coca growers were far too weak to stop them or rob them of their money. The coca-growers were the natural prey of the *traquateros*: this was a Darwinian industry, in which one species battened on another and fed off it.

A crowd of children had gathered round our minibus like midges round a cow. The *traquateros* stayed away from us, and the coca growers, who might otherwise have regarded us as friends and allies, still thought we were Americans. Not everyone was hostile: a boy about as old as the MRTA leader, wearing a red hat with a legend on it that said in English 'Surfing is life-instinct' handed a plastic bowl full of cut sugar cane through the minibus door. Matt pulled out his Swiss Army knife and opened up the saw attachment on it. Then he began cutting up the sugar cane.

'Always knew I'd find a use for that,' he said, wiping the sticky liquid off the saw.

Outside, it seemed to me that the atmosphere was becoming more hostile. It was not good to be mistaken here for Americans. To the growers and *traquateros* alike, the Americans were their enemies: the growers because they were believed to destroy the crop, the *traquateros* because they interfered with the trade and encouraged the governments of Peru and Colombia to take action against the dealers. In a place like this there was such a vague notion of the outside world that they were scarcely aware who an American, a German or a Briton really was. Foreigners, Yanquis, Europeans all seemed to merge into one general category for them, and were all potentially hostile.

The other problem we had was that the head of the Shamboyacu coca growers, a good friend of Lorenzo's, was away. All the negotiating had to be done through the mayor of the town, a thin, unimpressive little man who was dressed in a carefully ironed white shirt with long sleeves to show his significance in the community. He and Lorenzo stood apart from everyone else, while the *traquateros* gathered and watched them intimidatingly. Lorenzo was summoning up his last powers of persuasion; the mayor was making the despairing gestures of a man who wants to present himself as even weaker than he really is. At last Lorenzo walked back to the bus, and before he could tell us what had happened the loudspeakers sprang into overmodulated life again. It was the mayor.

'Friends and colleagues, our guests here are from television and they would like to talk to you.'

'Damn,' Eamonn said. 'We're in serious trouble.'

'Just go along with it,' Cecilia said.

But there was nothing to go along with. By making it a matter of public debate the mayor was washing his hands of the affair, and had opened up the possibility of even greater opposition than had existed before. By now Steve was asleep. If he had tried to get the camera out to film it would have caused a riot.

A tall, thin man in his twenties, wearing a green eyeshade, was arguing strongly that we should be allowed to do what we wanted. We were not Yanquis, he said; anyone could see that. The growers needed all the interest and help they could get, in order to give people in the rich countries abroad an idea of what they were suffering here. His clothes were spattered with mud, and I assumed he had come from the hills outside Shamboyacu where the coca was grown. The *traquateros* said nothing, but it was noticeable that they were beginning to bunch together.

Then Cecilia did what she could. 'We understand that you don't like American policy here. We've come to show that there's a serious economic problem for you. We don't have anything to do with the Americans, and you shouldn't think we necessarily agree with them.'

It was neatly put, I thought, especially that 'necessarily'. If she had been on her own here, working for Peruvian television, she would probably have said she had nothing but contempt for the Americans and wanted to show them up. But she knew about our need to stay impartial. Her words had an impact on the crowd in general, who were immediately attracted by her youth and looks. But the divide between the growers and the *traquateros* was as wide as ever.

The mayor took back the microphone. People pressed in around him, particularly the *traquateros*.

'Tell me, friends and colleagues – are you in favour of letting them stay here or not?' It was, I noticed, no longer a matter of letting us film.

The *traquateros* gathered around him roared out 'No.'

'Impossible,' Lorenzo said quietly, as the shouting and cheering died down. No one had shouted yes; directly they had seen the reaction of the *traquateros*, the growers had gone quiet.

'This is why they suffer,' said Lorenzo. 'A few powerful people say no. That is enough.'

Now the decision had been taken, the *traquateros* seemed prepared to make themselves unpleasant.

'I think it's time to go,' said Eamonn.

'What's the matter?' Steve asked, waking up. 'Were we trying to buy on the wholesale market rather than retail?'

The driver hadn't waited for instructions: we were already on our way. I looked back at the market square. The *traquateros* were gathered round, congratulating each other. The growers were drifting off. The mayor, clearly visible in his white shirt, was still standing there with the microphone in his hand. He was on his own.

We headed back towards the Huallaga. It is depressing and humiliating to be run out of town, especially if you have no pictures to show for it. Eamonn and I decided that I should at least record a piece to camera about it, when we had got sufficiently far away from Shamboyacu. Cecilia was very low: she felt it was her arrangements which had let us down. I explained to her that if you could tell your audience what had happened it was as good as being able to show them with pictures. I didn't exactly believe it myself, but she cheered up a little after that.

We turned a corner and drove into the village of Alfonso Ugarte – and right into the middle of the Army.

'No problem,' Cecilia said, 'film, film.'

It was clear the soldiers didn't welcome us, but they did nothing until an officer came over and asked us politely to stop. The patrol was a small one, and they were doing their best to be nice to the villagers. A giggling girl brought out a large bowl of milk, and the soldiers scooped it out with a coconut shell. Behind her, on the wall, someone had painted the slogan 'STRUGGLE OR DIE FOR THE REVOLUTIONARY CAUSE. LONG LIVE

THE MRTA.' The village, like the others we had stopped in, was always between two fires. The peasantry of Peru had never been anywhere else since the Spanish Conquest.

The soldiers were merely there to show their presence; they were not even checking documents. They were dressed as carelessly as the MRTA patrol we had met. The villagers took little notice of them, and were not friendly; though when their truck failed to start a few people lent a hand to push-start it. Everyone wanted to maintain a strict neutrality towards them. We watched the soldiers leave. Then someone said, 'There's been fighting down the road.' The MRTA patrol had found the Peruvian Army at last. A dozen or so people had been killed or wounded, and this patrol was moving between the villages trying to restore calm. I thought about the twenty-year-old leader, and the thirteen-year-old who hadn't remembered to put his safety catch on, and the sixteen-year-old who had reached through the window – this window – and said, '*Mucho gusto*.' By the time we reached the area where the battle had taken place, it was all over.

We crossed the Huallaga by the ferry at sunset.

'We filmed the sun come up, and we'll be filming it come down,' Steve said, setting up his tripod.

'And we haven't had breakfast yet,' Matt put in. He didn't seem worried about it.

When we walked in the Lily Hotel in Tarapoto the paunchy man in the stained T-shirt was still at the reception desk. He had not shaved in the intervening time, and he looked extremely shifty. Quietly, he reached for the telephone below the desk. The action reminded me powerfully of the time Steve and I had gone back to our hotel in the Rumanian city of Cluj, when we were filming undercover at the height of Ceausescu's police state; the same casual movement of the hand to the phone, the same unwillingness to meet our eyes. The next morning the security police in Cluj had arrested us. Now, as we walked upstairs carrying the television gear, the receptionist watched us go. I looked back: he was holding the mouthpiece of the phone so close it was impossible to hear what he was saying.

Upstairs in my room I found that the little marks I had made on my suitcase no longer seemed to be quite aligned. Did that mean my case had been searched? I was too tired to care. There was electricity, so I turned the fan above my head full on to cool down the unbearable temperature and keep off the mosquitoes. For a few minutes I leafed through an old copy of the *Spectator*. In this disturbing, lawless place it seemed very comforting. Then the magazine slipped from my hand, and I fell asleep.

Campanilla

The coca-growing Indians who live along the entire length of the Andes have a reputation for ill-treating those who are unfortunate enough to work for them. What they save by underpaying their labour, [they] spend on bribes and presents to the Spanish authorities.

Felipe Guaman Poma de Ayala, 1613

'*Senor*, your luggage?'

It was the fat receptionist from the night before. There was, I decided, something guilty about his manner, as though he hoped some small act of service might atone for having betrayed us the night before.

'Bugger off,' I said in English, with a gesture which showed what I meant. He shrank away, and I lumbered downstairs with the luggage myself, sweating in the early morning heat. I might be cutting off my nose to spite my face, but it was the only way I could express my dislike of his presumed treachery. Perhaps, I reflected, he had only been telephoning his mother, or his girlfriend, and not section G2 at the Army base after all. In that case all he had suffered was two words of abuse, neither of which he would have understood, and he had been saved the trouble of carrying my cases downstairs. I said good morning to Cecilia and asked her if she had slept well.

'Yes – except for one mosquito huanca.'

She had found us two taxis to take us to the airport: a shiny Toyota Crown that could have belonged to a Lima politician, with blacked-out windows and no numberplate, and a smashed-up Datsun with a sagging ceiling, a rusted interior, no window at the back, and a rear door which had to be held to prevent its coming open at corners. Eamonn and I travelled in this. We knew our place.

It was a considerable relief to see our King-Air waiting at the airport: a little sign that our plans were working, and that we had a certain independence. Tarapoto had been tricky, but our next stop, Tocache, was likely to be even more dangerous.

The airport was named after Heroe Nacional Capitan Jose Abelardo Quinones Gonzales, who had achieved his prominence for some act of bravery in the war against Ecuador in 1941. Until then I had not known that there had been a war between Peru and Ecuador in 1941. It was a good year for wars. When I asked around, no one could tell me who won, from which I assumed Ecuador did. An Army officer, the man who had met us when we arrived at Tarapoto two mornings before, came bustling up. Where were we going? What were we doing?

'Oh,' I said, trying to be irritating, 'here and there, a little bit of this and a little bit of that. You know how it is.'

He stood around irresolutely. Our pilot must have filed a flight plan, so they knew we were going to Tocache, but it would have been hard for them to see exactly what our purpose was in all this. Were we sympathisers with the subversives, who wanted to make as much trouble as possible for the Army? We had made an arrangement with Comandante Roberto to ring him that morning, in case the colonel in charge of the Tarapoto base was prepared to give us a formal interview on camera. It seemed unlikely, and Comandante Roberto must have guessed he would not too, but it was part of the phoney openness of the G2 people that they should have offered it. Rosalind rang the base.

'Is Comandante Roberto there?'

'I am Comandante Roberto,' said a voice which was plainly not his.

'This is Rosalind.'

'Who?'

'Rosalind. From the BBC.'

'*No se*,' was the answer; 'don't know.' The phone went dead.

Carlos, the pilot, was alone this morning. Eamonn and I had already decided that he was not, after all, an Army spy. He had managed to obtain permission for us to fly low over the Huallaga and film it, but he said he thought that if we tried to fly too close to the illegal airstrips (from which the coca supplies were flown), the Peruvian air force would shoot us down.

'Because they would think we were drugs runners?' I asked.

'But of course,' replied Carlos, looking carefully away.

'It's what I told you when we first started talking about all this,' I said to Eamonn quietly. 'In these Latin societies there is no centralised power structure, so people aren't all working for the state, or the Army, or the intelligence outfits, or anything very much except themselves. There isn't any single great efficient organisation, and if we can just dodge our way between the various small power-centres we'll be OK.'

He nodded. It was true, but it wasn't any kind of insurance. If we stumbled on anything too embarrassing, the Army in one place would shoot us, whether there was a big overall organisation or not.

The plane rumbled down the uneven airstrip and headed up into the air. Sitting sideways down the side of the plane, we lurched to the right in a line, like toy soldiers falling over. Then we levelled out at our cruising altitude. Tarapoto was now a series of little interconnecting squares of green with oblong roofs of grey and rust-red separated by orange, dusty roads. Steve, leaning over Matt, was filming through the window, his face streaming with sweat, dark patches growing visibly on his back and under his arms. It was normally a short flight to Tocache – not more than twenty-five minutes – but we would take twice that long because we wanted to film from the air. It was a pleasant business, and I relished the security of it. Up here, there was no one to stop us filming, no one to be nervous of. After a decent night's sleep, everything seemed relaxed and enjoyable. If only, I thought to myself, real life were provided with the kind of warning music you get in films when the dangerous part is beginning. Here there was nothing but sunshine and the roar of the engines.

We hit the lowest bank of clouds, a little above the level of the hilltops.

'We need to be well over to the left. Tell him to dip it,' said Steve to Rosalind. She explained to Carlos.

He looked back over his shoulder and pointed.

'All the light green stuff you can see down there on the hillsides is likely to be coca,' he said.

It was the first time the word had been mentioned between us;

he obviously knew what we had come for, even if the Army had found it difficult to work out.

I looked down; the coca was a cabbage-colour from this height, yellow and green. The plantations were hidden from the roads but generally placed on the side of the hill that received the most sunlight. The Huallaga Valley beneath us looked extraordinarily peaceful, with smoke from a fire drifting gently across and obscuring some of the yellow-green patches on the hillsides. In this area the drugs barons were starting to diversify. Cecilia had found evidence that they were planting poppies for heroin alongside the coca.

'I'll do a piece to camera now,' I said to Eamonn. I wiped the sweat from my forehead and plastered my hair down as best I could. Steve sweltered and grunted under the effort of keeping the camera still for the twenty seconds or so that I was speaking. What I said was scarcely very analytical: I merely described the coca plantations I could see out of the window, and tried to inject some sense of the nervousness we felt; more, I think, through my tone of voice than through the words I used.

'Campanilla,' said Carlos a few minutes later. We peered down to our right. A neat little town lay below us, with straight streets which looked well maintained from this height, and houses which were not just shacks. The plaza in the middle was laid out in the form of a Union Jack, with a couple of pathways like a St Andrew's cross on top of another couple in the shape of a cross of St George. There seemed to be a statue, or perhaps a fountain, in the middle. Probably from the ground it would be an ordinary, scrubby little Peruvian town; from this height it looked charming. One particular house, on the edge of the town, was very grand: a big white-pillared mansion set in beautifully kept lawns. Four white horses were grazing in a paddock.

'Who lives there?' I asked Cecilia.

'His name El Vaticano.' We laughed, but she was serious. 'Real name Limiliel Chavez.' She said it again for extra emphasis. 'The biggest drug man in Peru. He is our Pablo Escobar.'

El Vaticano was the only Peruvian with the standing in the drugs trade to match the big Colombian dealers, though even he was said to have had his occasional difficulties with the Medellin and

Cali cartels. If this part of Peru was indeed an effective province of the Colombian drugs empire, then El Vaticano was its prince: not entirely independent, yet not entirely part of someone else's power-structure either. Looking down at his delightful house, I felt a sudden longing to pay him a visit. Close to the house, the main road out of Campanilla became wider and straighter.

'The airstrip,' Cecilia said excitedly.

This was the place from which the coca under El Vaticano's control was flown up to Colombia. It looked very tempting.

'What would happen,' I asked Cecilia, 'if we just landed there?'

Knowing her courage and enthusiasm, I was a little shocked by her answer.

'We would all be killed.'

It was presumably true, or she would have tried it herself. I looked down at the gentle countryside below, the estate of a man whose taste was clearly good, at the charming little town. Perhaps not now, I thought, but I'm determined to see that place from ground-level at some stage. And interview El Vaticano as well.

We had done as much filming as we needed to do, and Carlos flew on to Tocache. We had already talked it over with him: he was nervous about the place.

'Is Tocache nice?' I had asked, pretending I knew nothing about it.

'No, difficult,' he said. He wouldn't elaborate.

Now he insisted that we had to take off by 4.30. The air force, supposedly trying to curb drugs flights from the area, wouldn't let us fly any later than that. He was not in favour, clearly, of spending the night there, and neither were we. Cecilia had told us that our only chance to get away in safety was to spend as few hours in Tocache as we possibly could. To stay the night somewhere where we could be tracked down might be fatal.

We talked over the last details. We would bring as little equipment with us as possible, so that we could make a run for it if necessary.

'It's like standing on the plank and watching the sharks circling,' I said, on the assumption that if someone starts to talk about feeling anxious, it helps the atmosphere.

'We might as well get in the habit,' Eamonn replied. The others grinned. Rosalind was smiling mildly. I couldn't tell if she was hiding her anxieties, or was not anxious at all.

We landed almost exactly at 10.30. The runway was rather better maintained than the one at Tarapoto. Half a dozen planes were parked on the grass at the runway's end. A line of little tented booths had been set up in the absence of an airport building.

'Looks like one of those laid-back Club Med holiday places, only they've got Bacardi labels on their Kalashnikovs,' Steve said.

I could see as I looked out of the aircraft window that the men sitting at trestle-tables in the booths were very rough-looking characters indeed, who made the soldiers we had met at Tarapoto airport seem like Grenadier Guardsmen by comparison. Some of them wore elements of Army uniform; others were in the blue fatigues of the Peruvian Air Force. They all looked very interested in our aircraft. It was something of a test of character for us to get out of the plane at all. I cast round for something positive and encouraging to say.

'At least we don't have so far to carry all the gear.' It sounded pretty feeble.

We said goodbye to Carlos, the pilot, and he reminded us to be back by 4.30.

'Look out for yourselves out there,' he said, and grinned sympathetically.

We walked the twenty yards across the grass to the nearest of the booths. A fat, heavy-featured man in Army uniform sat at a trestle-table. He was very dark, with the curved nose and high cheekbones of the archetypal indian. He was reading a newspaper, and his rifle lay on the table in front of him.

'See what it says on the stock?' Eamonn said in an aside to me, while smiling encouragingly at the soldier.

I looked down. 'NAZI' was inscribed on the wooden part of it with a ballpoint pen, the letters cut in deeply as though the owner really cared about it.

Eamonn continued his charm offensive by pointing at the picture on the front of the man's newspaper. It was Maritza Garrido Lecca, Guzman's landlady, dressed as a ballerina. Eamonn grinned encouragingly. The soldier's face did not lose an iota of its hostility, but he put out his arms like an aeroplane and moved around in his seat a little. It seemed to be a joke. Perhaps he thought that was what ballet dancers did.

'You are staying for a few days?' he asked.

'We're not yet sure,' I said eagerly, pretending that I really wanted to give him as accurate an answer as possible.

He looked at me in a speculative kind of way, as though trying to work out the best place to hit me. You would not want to see a look like that if you were tied to a chair.

All he said was, 'There are two taxis here.'

He held up two massive fingers as thick as the branches of a young tree. Then he hoisted himself up, gripped his rifle, and wandered off in search of the two taxis. After a pause we followed him. When we caught up he was leaning on the roof of one of the worst wrecks I had ever seen. Its boot was held on with a piece of rubber tubing, and one of the rear tyres had a jagged hole the size of a fifty-pence piece in its side and no discernible tread whatever. The soldier lumbered off, having presumably given the driver instructions about us. I felt sorry for him, as he sat behind the wheel. He looked a seriously frightened man.

The aircraft had been hot, and we had done a lot of sweating. Now all of us were dehydrated, Cecilia more than anyone. I went over to the little open-air bar and bought soft drinks for everyone. Under the hostile eyes of a group of Army men at a nearby table we sat and drank them, and waited.

We were in Tocache for three reasons. The first was that it had one of the worst records of murder and disappearances in the entire Huallaga Valley. The second was that the commander at its Army base was reported to be deeply involved in the smuggling of coca to Colombia. The third was that the former mayor of Tocache, Luis Zambrano, had investigated all these things. Cecilia had made contact with him and found that he was prepared to tell us, on camera, of his findings.

A blue Landcruiser drove up. It contained two men who Cecilia had hoped might help us. It was clear from her face as she walked back to us after speaking to them, however, that they had let her down. They were simply too scared of the Army commander, Comandante Alfonso, to do anything. Alfonso had the power of life and death here. The Landcruiser drove off. In the silence, the heat settled like a heavy weight. Flies swarmed around us. A chair scraped on concrete. We could feel everyone's eyes on us.

There was a buzzing sound in the distance, louder than any fly. A motorcycle was heading down the road towards us. 'Zambrano,' Cecilia said, in the voice of someone who is witnessing a miracle after despair. We prepared to follow him into the town.

Tocache

He was able to face death with tranquillity because he
knew himself to be a loyal subject and his conscience was
clear.

Felipe Guaman Poma de Ayala, 1613

The forest had once covered Tocache, and you could feel its
amputated presence everywhere: in the heat which wrapped
round us like towels at a Turkish bath and turned our clothes
into damp, shapeless rags, in the rank grasses which grew in the
gaps between the paving-stones, in the rich, over-ripe vegetation
which smelled as unwholesome as flowers on a mass grave, in
the dark clouds banked up to enormous heights overhead, in the
yellow puddles from the last downpour. This was an unnatural
place, and it had an unnatural atmosphere. Perhaps twenty per
cent of the world's coca paste originated in the area around
Tocache. Enormous quantities of money passed through here,
yet the town itself was very poor: the only paved street ran
around the Plaza de Armas in the centre, with its obligatory
fountain (out of operation) and its bust of San Martin, noseless
and tarred black. Near the fountain a pomarosa tree fought to
survive the competition of tougher, ranker plants.

Most of the buildings in the town were one storey high,
and the shops did little business. There were few customers
in the Salon de Belleza Rosita, the Bar Capricorn, the Libreria
Cesar Vallezo, the Bodega Vista Alegre. The Soda Fountain had
been burned out. A few shops sold vegetables and fruit, mostly
imported from abroad – and this in an area where a pencil would
grow if you planted it. '*Se Alquila*', '*Se Vende*' said the signs on
half the shop windows: For Rent, For Sale. In the midst of so much
natural richness, Tocache was a little clearing of impoverishment

and dearth.

The inhabitants stared at us with hostility as we rattled through the streets in our two disastrous taxis, which might have come from a wreck heap. It was too hot to be indoors. A woman leaned against a doorpost making lace. Under a sign that read 'Doris Mariza Ortiz and Brothers', the brothers in question sat on the kerb beside Doris Mariza herself, who tucked her skirt modestly between her thighs as we drove past. She said something about us which made the brothers scowl. As usual, they will have thought we were gringos, perhaps from the DEA, come to make trouble. A roughly chalked menu on the blackboard outside the San Miguel café showed the degree of poverty here: vegetable soup, chicken with rice and a soft drink for one sol: a fraction of a penny.

Zambrano turned right off the main street and we rattled down a side alley. The window beside me, which had been jammed closed, fell into its slot as we hit a rock in the middle of the street. The stench from something dead filled the car briefly. It was not yet noon, but the clouds covered the sun, making it gloomier and hotter than ever. Ahead of us Zambrano made another turn, and our two taxis followed. He stopped outside a small grey-painted house with bars over its windows. We took the equipment out of the rusted cars: the others looked as nervous as I felt. Zambrano looked nervous too as he led the way into the house. There was no sign of life inside: it could have been uninhabited.

Inside, a large room opened up. A couple of wide, shallow steps went down to a sitting area. Its size and emptiness made the room cool, but it was not uninhabited after all, merely short of furniture. Two armchairs and a sofa were in the lower part of the room, and a table and chair stood in front of a small bookcase filled with school texts. There was nothing much else. Apart from a calendar on the wall and a few empty boxes marked 'EC Aid', the place was unfurnished. There weren't even any curtains. Everything that Luis Zambrano and his wife had owned was destroyed in a fire at his old house. The fire happened soon after he had made his first public criticisms, to a local radio station, of the way the town was governed.

Sitting in his armchair and facing me, he seemed smaller than ever. Yet he had a very real presence. This was not a man you could easily ignore. He was thirty-nine now, and unemployed. He had been the sub-prefect of Tocache, the equivalent of its mayor, until President Fujimori's suspension of the constitution in the *Autogolpe* of 1992 deprived local officials of their jobs. Earlier, he had been a schoolteacher, specialising in history and geography. In 1989, he became interested in politics because of Fujimori's call for people to come forward and join a new force to contest the 1990 presidential election and transform Peruvian society: the cause which Fujimori called Cambio 90. Zambrano, who had never had anything to do with politics in the past, was fired by enthusiasm, and organised a campaign for Cambio 90 in Tocache. For him it represented the best way of bringing the town under the rule of law, instead of the rule of the Army and the murder gangs.

Fujimori duly became President, and Zambrano, his supporter, became sub-prefect of Tocache. He felt the victory of Cambio 90 empowered him to introduce radical change in the town. When he walked into his office for the first time that October he found hard evidence of what he had previously assumed: his predecessor and the whole staff of the prefecture were totally bound up with the drugs trade. Each time a plane took off from one of the illegal airstrips around Tocache, carrying basic coca paste to the factories of Colombia, a payment of $7,000 was made to the local authorities.

There had once been a suggestion that they would invest at least part of the money in public works: sewerage, water, lighting. Zambrano found that no such investment had ever been made. Each month there was a meeting of the senior government officials in the town: the Army commander, the police commander, the chief prosecutor, the sub-prefect. Zambrano attended his first such meeting:

> It was decided which drug running 'firm' would be used, how many flights they would have, and how much they should pay for each flight. The drug trade is coordinated from the military base here, headed by Comandante Alfonso. Wherever his men are stationed there is an airstrip which the drugs traffickers can use, under Army protection.

For each drugs flight that took off from the local airstrips,

Comandante Alfonso received $5,000. The police commander received the same. So did the public prosecutor. The sub-prefect, who unlike them had no power to interfere with the trade, received only $200 per flight: still a considerable amount of money in Peru, sufficient to keep a family comfortably for a month. There was probably at least one flight every day of the week. The profitability of each plane-load of coca paste may be judged by the fact that the traffickers paid bribes of more than twenty thousand dollars per shipment in Tocache alone. Another payout was made, with rather greater care: $1,000 per flight to Shining Path, to permit free passage of the coca paste to the airstrip.

At this first council meeting, with the police and Army commanders sitting round the table with him, Zambrano made it clear he was not interested in receiving the sub-prefect's share for the drugs flights. The degree of moral courage required to make a stand like that would be very great indeed. I looked at the figure opposite me and tried to imagine the sleepless night that would have preceded it, the slight unsteadiness of the legs, the dryness of the throat, the nervous movements of the hands.

Most of the people round the table probably thought he was simply holding out for more money than the $200 on offer. His predecessor, a man called Santa Maria, had protested that it was insufficient, and the drugs traffickers agreed to raise it to $500. Forty-eight hours before the election in April 1990 Santa Maria was murdered. Perhaps it was part of Shining Path's campaign of assassination against local politicians; perhaps it was the drugs traffickers or their friends in the Army, who were annoyed that someone was demanding more than his share.

The others around the council table were puzzled when Zambrano spoke. They looked at him. He repeated that he did not want any money, no matter how many planes might take off from the Tocache area. There was a brief silence, then the Army commander laughed.

'In that case there's more for everyone else,' he said, and the figures round the table joined in the laughter: a little relieved, perhaps, that the oddity had been dealt with. No one seems to have regarded it as an implied criticism of the general attitude. That was so deeply ingrained that it was regarded as utterly natural. If Zambrano chose not to take advantage of his position, he was no threat to them: he was merely a fool.

Behind the apparent unity of corruption, though, a serious battle was being fought out. The Army was trying to ease the police out of the drugs trade, in order to increase its own profits. For more than a year before Luis Zambrano was elected sub-prefect, the Army and the police had been competing with each other. Often they arrested people under the other side's protection. The Army was the more effective force, and many people assumed that Zambrano was planning to side with the Army and get rid of the police altogether. The thought that he might not want any part in the dispute does not seem to have occurred to anyone.

Within a matter of months the police had withdrawn from the drugs business of their own volition. The new head of the police in the area, a man named Santos, had been strongly influenced by his training with the American Drug Enforcement Agency. He moved his headquarters to a large new base which was built at Santa Lucia, not far from Tocache, where a small number of technical advisers from the DEA, probably only eight in all, were based. Comandante Alfonso, the Army commander in Tocache, took the police commander's share of the bribes after that, giving him $10,000 per flight. He now controlled, single-handedly, 20 per cent of the world's supply of coca paste.

A normal tour of duty for an Army commander in the Huallaga Valley was a year. The posts changed hands often, either to restrain corruption (the official version) or (the more realistic one) in order to spread the profits around more. Comandante Alfonso had been in Tocache two years, which argued that he had powerful protection: it was in someone else's interest, presumably, to keep him there. Alfonso must have been paying a sizeable amount in kickbacks to his superiors. Now that there was a possibility that the police and the DEA might raid their operations, Alfonso and his men had had to move their own airstrips northwards, so that they would be further from Santa Lucia. Two of them, little more than enlarged dirt roads, were built by Army engineers, using government money earmarked for the fight against terrorism.

Fewer Shining Path guerrillas were now operating in the area than previously. The Shining Path military command had ordered many of the more experienced fighters to Lima and the surrounding area, in the expectation that the final battle for the capital would shortly begin. Thanks partly to the arrest of Guzman it did not happen, but the leaders did not return. There was now surprisingly little terrorist activity by Shining Path in the area of the Huallaga Valley. President Fujimori, whom Luis Zambrano had played a small part in bringing to power, had insisted to us in our interview with him that the cocaine trade was in the hands not of the Army but of Shining Path. He and his ministers had succeeded even in persuading some Western diplomats of this.

In Tocache, however, Zambrano insisted that Shining Path's involvement was relatively slight. It received money from the big cocaine syndicates, both because it had the power if it chose to interfere with the drugs flights, and because it claimed to represent many of the coca growers, who performed the primary and by far the least profitable function of the cocaine industry. At times in the past, Shining Path had succeeded in forcing up the price of the coca leaves and the basic paste. Its representatives did not, however, sit at the same table as the other leaders in Tocache; they played their part in the discussions through intermediaries.

From time to time, Zambrano said, the intermediaries had another function to perform: negotiating the release of Shining Path guerrillas who had been captured by the Army:

> The main aim of the Army commander in this area is to maintain the state of emergency. Whenever the Army has caught a Shining Path leader, it has always set him free. That is after a payment of six thousand, or eight thousand, or ten thousand dollars, depending on his degree of responsibility. So Shining Path operate with impunity, because they know they will always be set free.

The Army's position in Tocache and the rest of the Huallaga Valley was extraordinarily profitable for the officers, and no doubt through them to their commanders at regional and perhaps national level. To ensure that the Army maintained a powerful presence in the area, it had to be able to demonstrate that the threat of terrorism was a serious one; therefore it was not in the Army's interest to defeat terrorism there. The regional commanders must have realised this. Maybe they did at national level as well.

The Army represented the only law that existed in Tocache. It was judge, jury and if necessary executioner in every case. Zambrano told us that a great many of the disappearances here, and there had been more than a hundred, were entirely separate from the war on terrorism:

> In general, those who die are innocent of subversion. They are detained because they owe money to a drugs trafficker. Or perhaps someone will go to the Army base and say 'So-and-so has sold my drugs, my coca leaves, and hasn't paid me. So will you, Comandante or Capitano, get the money from them and take a percentage?' The person is then arrested and tortured, and later he is found with a placard over his corpse, trying to make out that the killers were Shining Path.

The Army would, on request, kill people who did not settle their bills, in exchange for a proportion of the debt. It would kill anyone who was denounced to them, if the necessary price were paid. It would kill anyone who hindered the transport of drugs, or set up a rival and less generous 'firm'. And, Zambrano said, if a man's wife went off with her lover, the Army would provide its services free. Civilised standards had to be maintained in Tocache.

By no means all the killings were laid at Shining Path's door. Increasingly, indeed, the Army preferred to demonstrate openly that a good proportion of them were its own work. There were no repercussions; no one came from Lima to investigate. The only person who had spoken about them in public was Luis Zambrano, and someone had set fire to his house as a result. His political mentor, President Fujimori, took no notice whatever of Zambrano's denunciation, nor of the danger it placed him in. Zambrano had done his best to investigate reports that people had been taken to the Army base and tortured and killed there. He had interviewed several people who had survived their ill-treatment, and they had told him that they had been held in some kind of underground tank, near the helicopter pad. He had not seen it himself. As for the bodies of those who were murdered, they would be washed up along the edges of the Huallaga River, on the little beaches where women washed their clothes and the children played. The bodies were usually weighted down with stones which had been whitewashed.

'You can find those stones at the Army base,' Zambrano said.

I asked him what was likely to happen now that he had given us this interview: surely it would be extremely dangerous?

Perhaps it will be; I don't know. All I know is that it is my duty to say these things. No one else will have the courage to do it if I don't. This is a town where everyone is scared. I am scared too, I don't deny it. But you cannot always live on your knees, afraid of what may happen. That is no way for a free man to live. I am a free man, and I am doing what a free man should do. I do not want to live on my knees.

His glance was as calm and firm as ever. When Eamonn, who did not understand Spanish and had not grasped the strength of what Zambrano had been saying, walked over and suggested a whole range of new questions, I was irritable with him; yet it was really my own emotion which had upset me, together with a sense of the intrusiveness of television. Steve changed the camera position slightly and focused on Zambrano again; but while I was getting ready to ask another question Zambrano interrupted in his even, almost flat, clipped voice.

'It is very important for me that you should be here. I have thought it all through, believe me. I know the difficulties involved, but they are worth it.'

While he had been talking his wife Daisy had come in and was sitting quietly, listening to what he had to say. At the end of the interview we filmed them together, talking about ordinary household matters. She was also in her late thirties, a drawn, strained, quiet, gentle woman, even more slightly built than he was. Yet seeing them side by side, I did not feel, as I had with Ana Java who came with us to the Army base at Tarapoto, or with Victor Ushinahua, the retired bank clerk whose son, daughter-in-law and granddaughter had disappeared, that the Zambranos were either weak or the victims of men more powerful and evil than they were. On the contrary, their firm, self-controlled air gave them the appearance of real inner strength. Daisy smiled a little more than her husband, though she was plainly worried by his decision to speak to us. On the other hand, it was equally clear that he had talked it over with her, and she had agreed with him. She was not the kind of woman who would just listen to what her husband told her, and meekly accept it.

Their three children, two girls of ten and eight and a boy of six, came in from another room, where they had been having their midday meal. They wore neat, crisply ironed school uniforms, and Zambrano held the little boy's hand tightly and began explaining to them why we were there and what was going on. They were serious children, as quiet as their parents, and they listened carefully to him.

'You mustn't on any account tell anyone at school that these men have been here. Do you understand?'

The children nodded, their eyes on his face.

'It's very important to keep quiet about it. Otherwise Daddy could be in trouble. All right?'

The three children nodded solemnly. They had seen trouble already in their lives. They knew they were different from other children because their parents were different. They kissed him goodbye, one by one.

'Now hold each other's hands,' he said, and they went out through the back door. It creaked shut behind them.

'Will you go to the Army base?' Zambrano asked me.

'Yes. We'll go there right away.' I was almost looking forward to it now.

'Because you must be careful. Comandante Alfonso is a very angry person. He could get in a rage, and then I could be in trouble. He might send people round to kill me. Don't tell him you came round to see me. He'll find out later, but it's best he shouldn't know yet.'

We packed up the gear and lined up to shake hands with the Zambranos. I was last in the queue. I kissed Daisy on both cheeks and gripped Luis's hand. His handshake was as firm as ever. I could do nothing except tell him that if he got into trouble he should contact Cecilia, or even the British embassy in Lima, and I would move heaven and earth to help him. He smiled. Perhaps he was reflecting that heaven and earth would take a great deal of moving, and Tocache was a long way from London. We climbed into the two dreadful taxis. The other wouldn't start, and in ours Eamonn's door flew open as we finally moved off, and the glass fell out of the rear-view mirror. We waved. Luis and Daisy stood in the doorway of their temporary house and waved back. Then, as I watched, they turned to go indoors. Luis put his hand comfortingly round his wife's waist, and stood aside to allow her to go in ahead of him. The door closed.

Tocache Army Base

I was appalled at his conduct towards these feeble
and defenceless people. I felt I had no option but to join them
in their misery.

Felipe Guaman Poma de Ayala, 1613

I was worried about time. It was now sixteen minutes past one:
we had a good deal of filming to do in the town, we had to go
to the Army base and tackle Comandante Alfonso, and we had
to get back to the airport and take off before 4.30. If we failed
to do that, we might have to stay the night in Tocache, which
could prove very awkward indeed. Cecilia was looking anxiously
at her watch. I trusted her judgement: she had been to this area
before, and knew the problems.

Before we left Lima she had shown us her television report
on the Huallaga Valley. It was as good as anything of its kind
I had seen, and I determined to copy several of her techniques.
As it turned out, we were also to use some of her best footage
in our reports. She had used a small Video-8 camera to film from
the cockpit of her plane as it landed at a small dirt airstrip like
the one at Tocache. At the end of the runway was a Colombian
plane loading up with basic coca paste. She had been threatened
at the airstrip and was followed by half a dozen *traquateros* on
motorbikes: she had filmed them through the back window of her
taxi. Then she had found the commanding officer at the local Army
base and demanded to know why he allowed shipments of cocaine
from his territory. Finally she had recorded a radio conversation
between the ground control at an illegal airstrip and a Colombian
pilot who was coming in to land. The word 'Uncle' is a codeword
for the drugs shipment:

Ground control: The Army is here. They've coordinated things and given us the green light. They have said there are no problems with my Uncle.

Colombian pilot: Only the Army?

Ground control: Only the Army. No other forces can enter. Anyway, if they do, the Army will let us know.

Enormous thunderclouds had built up in the sky, towering above us, and the atmosphere was oppressively hot. If there was a storm now it would be serious for us. The greens of the jungle foliage took on an extra intensity because of the light. Steve filmed the river banks, where the bodies weighted down by white-painted stones had been found, then decided he needed a better shot of Tocache from the other side of the river. We drove down to the small rusting suspension bridge. A soldier was on guard, and the taxi driver stopped. The soldier stood up very slowly and ambled over towards us. He seemed very interested in us.

'Ees beeg screw-up,' I said as the driver told him who we were.

The soldier peered in at us, one by one, then went back to the other taxi and peered at them. There was a pause. Then, as though it was too hot to take any action, he waved us indolently on.

'No ees beeg screw-up,' I said, and the others laughed with relief.

The thunder grumbled around us as Steve got the shots we needed to weld the interviews and the street scenes together. We might be short of time, but if we failed to make a good rounded film out of this, then everything would be worthless; including Zambrano's interview. Up on the hillside overlooking the town the coca plantations stood out startlingly yellow-green in the leaden light. A wall of rain was beginning to fall on the empty fields, a little higher up, where the white fungus had wiped out the newer coca plantations. Steve grunted as a drop of rain the size of a small beer mat fell on his hand while he was adjusting the focus. A red light began to flash on his camera to show the tape was coming to an end.

'It's telling me it's time to go,' he said.

We asked the drivers to take us to the Army base. It was close to the centre of the town, down a short turning. I was surprised by the ordinariness, the mundanity of it; yet to most people in Tocache the base was as fearful a place as Auschwitz. We stopped at the guard-post, and the soldier on duty checked with his superiors by field telephone. There was another pause. In the suffocating heat I looked at my watch: two fifty-seven. We had to be back at the airstrip in an hour and a half.

'*Por favor.*'

The soldier waved us in.

We had an alarming walk, past a platoon of soldiers, tough and ugly, who were cutting the grass with machetes. They raised themselves to look at us: they had big, flat indian faces and pockmarked skins. Outside the gate, a powerful-looking figure with thick, patent-leather black hair was waiting to greet us. He waved at the camera and asked if it were running. I made the kind of noises you make if you are denying something, though I knew Steve well and could be certain without checking with him that it was. I looked round at him and Matt, with Eamonn beside them: they looked tense, but they were clearly doing the business.

'Come in, come in,' said the powerful-looking character.

'Who is this?' Eamonn asked in a whisper.

'I can't imagine he's in charge,' I said; it seemed unlikely that the commanding officer would come out to greet us.

'Then why has he got "Alfonso" on his T-shirt?'

It was on his shoulder, clearly printed, and I had not noticed. At the door to his office he shook hands with us, a rougher handshake than Zambrano's but just as firm. He was heavy-set, but in excellent physical condition. His biceps strained the short sleeves of the T-shirt, his stomach was trim and he was barrel-chested. He looked very powerful, and very menacing. He invited us into his office, and found chairs for us. Someone brought us cold drinks.

Rosalind sat beside me. Matt was in the doorway, and Steve perched on a chair, resting his camera on his knee, the lens pointing straight at Alfonso as he lowered himself into his chair.

Christ, I thought, he must notice the camera's on. He seemed not to do so.

I started questioning him. I didn't want to be too specific, because Zambrano had asked me not to say we had interviewed him beforehand. I was afraid that if I showed too precise an awareness of what had been going on it would be plain to him where the information had come from. I began with questions about subversion and the security position. He answered in vague terms, then said he thought he should call his commanding officer, who was at Tarapoto. He picked up the phone on his desk.

It was an awkward moment, given that the people at Tarapoto knew all about us and had discovered that Steve was filming them surreptitiously. He looked down at his desk, then up at me. It was obvious he was being told all about us. Then he looked at the camera. His face became darker and nastier.

'Watch out,' I said quietly to Steve and Matt; 'he's on to us.'

Steve looked away from the camera, in that careless way that cameramen only have when they want you to think they are not filming. Alfonso put the phone down. He looked extremely angry. Somehow I had the impression he had been told to get rid of us as fast as he could. But Alfonso had too much belief in himself for that: he wanted to have a little fun with us first.

'The general instructed me not to answer your questions, but I will anyway.' He tried to smile, and merely succeeded in looking menacing. 'But I will only do it if it is, in your phrase, "off the record", "on background". Agreed?'

I agreed, and felt badly about it. A promise is a promise, even to a psychopath, and I like to keep my promises. I could tell that Steve had left his camera running, even though he had put it on the floor. Matt continued to point the microphone in his general direction. This meant we would have sound but no pictures. Rosalind translated my questions firmly and clearly. Outside the door, Eamonn was keeping an American-educated captain, Alfonso's second-in-command, in conversation; he was anxious that the captain should not come in and realise what we were doing.

I knew that if I were as blunt with my questions to him as I had been at the Army base in Tocache, he would throw us out. Instead, I was elaborately polite.

'I am sorry to touch you on a difficult subject, but it has been alleged in Lima and elsewhere that you are in charge of the drugs trade here, and receive payments for the drugs that are flown out from Tocache.'

'As a member of the Army, I don't see drugs. I have orders that I'm not to fight drugs. For me, "drugs" is a word that's not in the dictionary. I have nothing to do with them. Nothing.'

Outside the door, his second-in-command was assuring Eamonn pleasantly that they didn't even know where the illegal airstrips were. It was the standard line of the Peruvian officer when asked about drug-running: the Army's job was to fight terrorism, and it was for the police to combat the drugs trade. It had nothing to do with them.

Alfonso was lying politely to me, and I was pressing him with equal politeness. Rosalind noticed that each time he said something which was obviously not true he would look down to the right. It happened many times.

'And what,' I asked him, 'about the allegations that serious human rights abuses are carried out here? In the United States and elsewhere, organisations like Amnesty International say that Tocache is the place where it happens.'

'There has been no proof that I have tortured anyone,' he answered. 'There have been clashes. My people, my officers and troops, have died, and some civilians have died too. The terrorists call it violating human rights, but that's war, isn't it?'

'And you can give me an assurance that no murders take place here at the base, and there's no torturing done here either?'

He looked down to the right and said he could give me that assurance. 'There is no murder, no torturing, and there are no rapes either.'

I had not mentioned rapes. The next day, when we talked it over with someone who knew the town well, he told us that a number of women had been raped at the Army base, and that Comandante Alfonso was responsible for many of them.

At the end of the interview I thought I should make one thing absolutely clear to him: that he should no longer think he could run the base, and the town, with the same impunity as in the past. We might not represent the law, we might have no physical power, but we had the curious status of a *deus ex machina*: we had descended from a world he could scarcely imagine, to tell him that everything he did would be known about in countries he had scarcely heard of. I also wanted him to know, when he came to hear of our interview with Luis Zambrano, that Zambrano must be left alone. So I said to him three times, using almost exactly the same words each time, which Rosalind duly translated, that the eyes of the entire world would now be on Tocache, and that everything which was done there would be known about. It would be the most famous town in Peru. I smiled at him with deliberate insincerity.

Even so, it became clear as we finished our interview and he showed us out, that he still thought he was playing a game with us. He allowed us to film the entrance to the base, then offered to show us the new installation of which he was particularly proud: the helicopter pad. Zambrano had told us that Alfonso kept his prisoners there, so he must have taken us to see it in order to mock us. Overlooking the open circle with the large white 'H' on it was a wooden hut with shuttered windows and a padlocked door. I noticed one other thing too: the long pathway down to the heli-pad was lined with rocks which had been painted white, like those that had been used to weight the bodies of people who had been murdered.

As we walked back from the heli-pad, Steve was continuing to film covertly, and Matt was taking photographs. I could hear the shutter clicking. It seemed inevitable to me that Alfonso knew what they were doing, and I asked them both to stop because I thought our position was still a tricky one.

'Where are you going to spend the night?' Alfonso asked.

'Oh, we're not too sure: we won't decide until later.'

'You should stay with us. We're going on a night patrol tonight.'

It was tempting, but I said no. It would, I thought, be altogether too dangerous. Things can happen in the dark.

'Anyway, if your plane can't take off, you can be our guests.'

I felt like Jonathan Harker being invited home by Dracula.

'And don't forget, everything I have said to you is off the record.'

He shook my hand powerfully, and I waved goodbye. In the car I told Eamonn that, unpleasant though Alfonso undoubtedly was, I had given him my word that what he had said to me would not be used. Eamonn was anyway annoyed with me: he had been standing outside the office and had heard only the polite tone of my questions and not the actual words. He assumed that I had failed to tackle Alfonso about the key questions of drugs and murder.

'We can just fade out the off-the-record part,' he said. 'It doesn't sound as though he said anything to you anyway.'

Rosalind argued that I was being overscrupulous. She was probably as annoyed with my attitude as Eamonn had been, though she did not show it.

'For one thing, you've got to allow him to defend himself if you're going to let Zambrano accuse him of doing all these things. And for another, he's a psychopath and a murderer, and someone like that shouldn't be protected.'

A promise is a promise, I was going to say, but I decided not to. In the end, I allowed my scruples to be overcome. When the reports were edited we used the sound of Alfonso's replies which Matt had recorded after the camera had been switched off. I still don't feel altogether proud about it.

We reached the airstrip at 4.20. The thunderclouds had moved away a little. Our plane was fuelled up and ready to go, the same unpleasant-looking soldiers were on guard duty, the same slack-featured woman stood behind the bar.

'Very, very look in,' Cecilia said earnestly. She meant we should be extremely careful.

'Well, we've got to get some pictures here,' said Eamonn, setting his jaw.

Steve set up the tripod and began filming. A man in uniform came running over, a Hollywood cliché of a Latino drugs runner, to tell him to stop. Steve, in his usual way, looked up from the eye-piece and stood back as though the camera had been switched off. The Hollywood drugs smuggler started haranguing him, but Cecilia, as swift as ever, distracted him by asking sweetly whether she had paid the taxi driver the right amount. He began discussing it with her while Steve started packing up some of his gear. The camera continued turning.

It felt very good indeed to sit in our plane and watch Tocache slip away below us. We relaxed and laughed and imitated the people we had seen and talked about the awkward moments. I looked round at the others, and tried to think when, if ever, I had worked with better or more steadfast people. Three-quarters of an hour later Carlos, the pilot, pointed ahead at a rich valley between two mountains shaped like sugar loaves:

'Tingo Maria.'

It was the one place in the Huallaga, Cecilia said, where we could feel safe; it was too big for anyone to come and get us in the night. Two taxis delivered us down a long drive, and our hotel lay before us: a delightful sprawling bungalow built fifty years before out of mahogany logs from the rainforest which lay all around us. The floors creaked, and elderly porters, who doubled as waiters, greeted us politely and carried our luggage to our rooms. There would, the ancient receptionist promised, be hot water, and electricity until midnight. Even if the hot water was a figment of his imagination, my room was clean and delightfully cool.

Eamonn and I, anxious to forget the earlier irritability between us, helped each other with enthusiasm but not much efficiency to put up our respective mosquito nets. They were not needed: the pleasant breeze off the Huallaga River just below the hotel kept the insects away. I sat on the verandah and read, while the sky turned from cornelian to amethyst. Bats the size of my two hands swooped past, skilfully avoiding the swaying basketwork lampshades decorated with patriotic red and white streamers, which gave an oriental tone to everything. The mountains, which were covered by the thick rainforest, disappeared in the gloom.

Later we sat at a table on the verandah in a little pool of golden light and dined off a splendid dorado fish from the Huallaga, recalling to each other the looks on people's faces as we turned up somewhere unexpectedly, the cunning actions of Matt and Steve, the subtleties of Cecilia and Rosalind. Around us frogs and crickets gulped and chirruped, and the little streamers of crêpe paper rustled in the night breeze. Fireflies flashed overhead, small golden arcs of light in the surrounding darkness. The waiters cleared the plates, smiling, and left us alone as we sampled the Laphroaig I had brought and drank the hotel's watery coffee. Slowly, under the influence of the mildness of the night, the conversation, and a little alcohol, the fears and tensions and emotions of the day began to fade.

Tingo Maria

Even to set these facts down on paper is enough to make
me weep tears.

Felipe Guaman Poma de Ayala, 1613

I woke late. I had stuffed my ears with earplugs in order to
keep out the racket of the crowing cockerels before dawn,
and had failed to hear the lesser noise of my alarm clock. The
morning was bright and wonderfully cool, and the breeze stirred
the wickerwork lanterns as the others sat at breakfast.

Three parrots squawked loudly from their cage by the reception
desk; a dozen other birds I could not identify cawed and clattered
and hooted and whistled and trilled from the bushes around us. A
kite soared in the up-currents, scarcely moving its wings. A small,
undistinguished bird landed on the rail of the verandah. I asked
Steve if he knew what it was.

'An l.b.j. – little brown job.'

By daylight, the hotel had the look of somewhere in the
African bush: the well-kept lawn, the ornamental trees, the
way the wooden buildings stood on brick columns to protect
them from ants, the corrugated iron roof, all gave it a British
Empire appearance.

We were due to spend the whole day in Tingo Maria, interviewing people who had evidence to give about human rights abuses in
our next stopping place, Aucayacu. A Canadian priest who lived
in Aucayacu, Father Bob, had arranged for them to come to the
parish hall of the main church in Tingo Maria so they could speak
to us in relative safety. It would have been much too dangerous for
them if we had spoken to them in Aucayacu itself. Even here we
had to be careful not to attract attention. The military were less
active in Tingo Maria and it was not a centre for coca production,

but the Army in Aucayacu came under the control of the base here. The plan was for us to go in two groups, three in one car which would leave at 9.30 and three in another car at 9.45.

Tingo Maria turned out to be as charming as a little town in the Alps. Trishaws powered by motorbikes buzzed up and down the roads. They were called *moto-cholos*, '*moto*' being the short form of 'motorcycle' and '*cholo*' meaning a half-breed or, more particularly in South America, a Peruvian. An ancient woman, dressed in black and bent almost double over her stick, stood in the middle of the road while the *moto-cholos* politely moved around her, not sounding their horns. The work of a local commercial artist was in evidence everywhere: few blank walls lacked his distinctive touch, as he advertised a make of motorcycle, InkaCola, a restaurant, a bank. The bank's wall carried an eight-foot parrot in green and red, which advised people that there was no better place to put their money.

I was in the second car with Steve and Matt. We moved the camera gear into the parish hall as quickly and unobtrusively as we could. There was an atmosphere of great nervousness, and a woman came out and made urgent gestures to us, her voice cracking a little as she directed us to the hall where the people from Aucayacu were waiting. Eamonn introduced me to a little, smiling, wiry man who shook my hand with a nervous enthusiasm.

'I guess people call me Father Bob.' He laughed, and the strain showed.

I found it difficult to get much information from him. His voice would trail off as he told me one anecdote about life in Aucayacu, and I would find he had switched to another before the point of the first one had been reached.

There was another person in the room, a man who smiled at me and stood up politely, holding a briefcase under one arm. We shook hands. He was nervous too, I could see, but as he started talking not even the distraction of the camera could deflect him from his story. We settled him down so that the light shone behind him and silhouetted him. He had come to tell us about his friend, a man called Pedro Davila. He dug into his briefcase and pulled out some photographs: Pedro Davila with a group of people, laughing and drinking beer; Pedro Davila receiving some kind of diploma; Pedro Davila meeting an important local politician; Pedro Davila lying dead, covered with blood and unrecognisable, his hands and ankles tied.

He had been the director of the government's centre for agricultural development in Aucayacu. People began complaining that money which the government was investing in local projects in the Upper Huallaga Valley was not getting through to them. He arranged a public meeting, and agreed to report the complaints to the Ministry of the Interior in Lima. When he did so, one of the leading newspapers devoted an entire page to the scandal. Davila started getting death threats. The man reached into his briefcase again and brought out a piece of paper crudely inscribed in red ballpoint.

'*TRAIDORES. ADVERTENCIA DE MUERTE*': 'Traitors. Death Warning.' Whoever had written it had wanted to give the impression that it came from Shining Path; in which case it might have been better if the name of Shining Path's leader had been spelled correctly. '*Presidente Gonzolo*', it said, instead of *Presidente Gonzalo*. It is hard to think that members of an organisation as fixated on the cult of its leader's personality as Shining Path might get his name wrong. Three days after Davila returned to Aucayacu he was murdered.

'Who did it?' I asked.

The man shrugged. 'The Army, of course.'

'And why did you decide to speak to us?'

He arranged the briefcase on his lap and shrugged again. 'Pedro Davila was my friend. He had two children. I liked him.'

Our next interviewee was a woman. She looked middle-aged, but was probably only in her thirties. Like the others, she was putting her life in our hands by coming to speak to us, and she did so unquestioningly, not really wanting to know how we planned to hide her identity but trusting to it that we would. We set up the camera behind her, in the reverse of the usual interviewing position, so that only the back of her head showed. The disadvantage was that I was in the picture, face on, the whole time.

She told us how, some months before, her husband and one of their sons had gone in a boat across the Huallaga River to work on his farm, which lay on the far bank of the river. He took several of his labourers with him. There were fourteen of them in the boat in all. Shining Path had been very active on the other bank of the Huallaga in the past, and the Army must have thought that anyone crossing the river was likely to be a Shining Path sympathiser.

> The Army came out of hiding and seized my husband. They tortured him there. My twelve-year-old son saw they were tor-turing my husband, his father. My son started to shout, so they smashed his teeth. He cried out because they were torturing his father, and so they smashed his teeth. My husband said, 'Let my son go home.' They said, 'When he grows up he'll be a terrorist.' So then my husband said, 'Well, kill me, but spare my workmen.' They did not listen. They killed them all. None of them escaped.

There were, she said, several witnesses, people who hid in the thick jungle vegetation for fear of being killed themselves. They saw which unit carried out the murders, but nothing was done about it. Indeed, no one from the Peruvian military had ever been found guilty of an abuse of human rights. When they went to search for the bodies of the fourteen who had been murdered, they came across thirty more bodies from other massacres. Almost certainly the murderers were not from the Army base in Aucayacu, but from the Peruvian Marines, who are known to have carried out an operation along the river in April 1992.

There was a gentle knock at the door, and a younger woman dressed in her best clothes came in: a smart blouse, long brightly coloured earrings, neatly pressed jeans. Steve, as before, sat her opposite me. It had been very difficult for me, on camera, not to show my feelings when I was interviewing the previous woman. This time it was to prove impossible.

The Army had arrested her husband at home in May 1992, almost five months earlier. She saw the men who did it, and would have gone to the base in Aucayacu that night to plead for his release, except that any woman who went there at night-time was liable to be raped and perhaps murdered. So she went the next morning and was told the Army had not arrested him. The following day she went back, accompanied by her doctor, and saw the commanding officer, Comandante Esparza. He had the reputation of being a killer on the scale of Comandante Alfonso in Tocache. He told her not to come back: the terrorists, he said, had captured her husband.

By now she was weeping in a way that was heart-rending, her mouth open, tears pouring down her cheeks, fighting for breath, locked in the misery of remembering what it felt like to go through what happened next.

'Do not hope to see your husband,' they told me. Then on the 11th I found him, at 9 am. I found him in pieces. We never found his torso. His head had been cut off. His arms were all cut up. His legs were burnt.

She found the legs and arms by the side of the road. The head was a little further along, on a rubbish-tip. There were pieces from several other bodies nearby.

As she wept, she said again and again, 'My husband, my husband.' They had been married only a few months earlier. According to someone I spoke to later, he had never been suspected of any terrorist activity; he was a young man, and that was enough in Aucayacu.

The woman had stopped crying now, though her body was still shaken by spasms, like a child's. She pulled out a picture of him, as his remains lay in a coffin: an unremarkable man with indian features, badly bruised and cut. I looked at the picture, and recalled the slogan of the eighteenth-century campaign in Britain for the abolition of slavery: Am I not a man, and a brother?

There was the sound of low voices, as other people from Aucayacu came and told their stories to Rosalind and Father Bob, as well as to me. Outside there was the sound of car-horns, and the cheerful noise of *moto-cholos*, and children laughing and playing. It was like a mediaeval painting, in which a saint is being martyred in one part of the canvas, while in another the ordinary street life of the city continues, people trade and fight and laugh and play as though nothing of any significance is going on. In the Huallaga Valley, the actions of the Army and its martyrdom of ordinary, unremarkable people seemed to be part of the pattern of everyday life, nothing more.

*

That evening we swam in the hotel pool, and went to the bar for our nightly pisco sour with inflamed eyes. Cecilia, who had been working while we relaxed, came back to the hotel having discovered, after a great deal of difficulty, a driver who was prepared to take us to Aucayacu. Everyone else had refused, regardless of the amount we were prepared to pay. The road to Aucayacu, and the town itself, were regarded as too dangerous. She also had a suggestion to make to me.

'I think El Vaticano want speak with BBC. You want speak with him? I think never journalist ask to interview him. His agenda empty. Maybe he say OK. Maybe he like.'

El Vaticano owned the splendid estate at Campanilla which we had seen from the air. He knew everything about the drugs trade in Peru, and a great deal about what happened in Colombia, the United States and Europe. He was at the centre of a web of great evil and cruelty.

'We can *escribir la carta* tomorrow,' Cecilia said, in the mixture of Spanish and English with which we communicated.

'How will we get it to him?' I asked. 'I don't suppose the postman calls in Campanilla too often.'

Cecilia said nothing; but I could see she had a plan.

The man who had agreed to take us to Aucayacu arrived. He was a former policeman who had been involved in operations against drugs smuggling and had been forced into retirement because of injury. He carried the scars of his wounds on him. Now he wanted to discuss the journey to Aucayacu.

'People will think you are Americans from the intelligence service of the DEA,' he said. He put his finger to his head, like the barrel of a pistol. 'In that case you may be all right because you are foreign journalists, but I'll be killed.'

'I think he's trying it on for more cash,' Rosalind said quietly, after translating his words.

Cecilia disagreed, and it soon became clear where the trouble lay.

'It's my wife. She says she'll be a widow if I go. The money's fine – I just have to convince her.'

He left to try to do it.

'We could hire the vehicle from him,' I said.

Steve added, 'And we could put a sign on it that said "Gringo-vision".'

An hour later, as we were starting dinner, the driver came back. His wife was still unhappy, but he thought he'd convinced her. We liked him better for that, and invited him to join us.

Over dinner he became expansive, and started to talk about his time in the police. With the air of one who was taking a serious risk, he waved his glass of beer around and closed his eyes as he took a deep pull from it. He had, he said, trained with the DEA, and had plenty of praise for the Americans and for their bravery. He had left the police because of the bad pay and corruption, and because the Peruvian officers hid when there was danger and left the men to face it. But more than anything else he hated the Army, which had betrayed them time and again to the '*narcos*'. In the operation where he was wounded the DEA had had to get the Army's permission to enter Uchiza, the town they were searching, and the Army had warned the '*narcos*'. We slowly began to realise that instead of being a nuisance, this man was a useful source of information.

'Would he do an interview, do you think?' Eamonn asked me.

'I doubt it, but we ought to try.'

'We rarely found any drugs,' he was saying. 'The Army and the drugs traffickers work hand in hand. At every secret airstrip you'll find the military. When we launched operations with the Americans, the Army would warn the traffickers, and the drugs would be moved to a different place. They'd be hidden somewhere else.'

At dinner, two men sat near us at another table. They were large and unpleasant-looking; Cecilia took one look at them and said '*Milicos*,' in a quiet voice. I remembered the word from my time in Argentina: it was an insulting term for soldiers. One had a flat, open face, the other wore dark glasses, had abysmal table manners and laughed in a braying way with his mouth open, showing what he was eating. Eamonn suggested what the big joke was: 'You should have seen his face when I cut his leg off. . .'

I assumed they were there to spy on us, or perhaps pick a fight; soon they began to get seriously drunk.

Then the singing started:

'... *de mi patria ... la fortuna .... alegria del corazon* ...'

'Why don't we go over to them,' Steve suggested, 'and say we're doing a feature on folk music?'

'You could say we were talent spotters,' said Matt.

Eamonn capped it: 'Opportunity Knocks! And all the way from Tingo Maria, Peru, we have. ...'

The two men were getting seriously drunk and potentially quarrelsome now.

'Maybe you should go and sing them some of your national songs,' I said to Matt, the Scot.

'I could always sing them "The Northern Lights Of Old Aberdeen Are Home, Sweet Home To Me",' he said.

'Go on,' I prompted him.

'Will I?'

'Just softly.'

'You don't sing "The Northern Lights of Old Aberdeen" softly.'

'All right, slur it.'

He started to slur it, but it was wasted on the *milicos*. They were at the stage of dropping bottles.

'Hey little girl, why are you looking at me?' the one with dark glasses began singing to Rosalind. She stared at him and then looked away to show her contempt, but he was too far gone to know or care. Soon afterwards they lumbered off, and I thought I heard one of them being sick in the driveway. If they had indeed come to check us out, they had not made a good job of it.

The Empress of the Marginal

The roads and bridges were not well built or formed into a connected system, so that each king was more or less isolated in his own territory.

Felipe Guaman Poma de Ayala, 1613

Our would-be driver, the man from the drugs police, woke Steve a little before seven o'clock by beating on his door. He was desperate to speak to someone. Steve went to fetch Rosalind from the shower so she could translate. The man was deeply embarrassed and humiliated: his wife, he said, had hidden the keys to his vehicle, so he couldn't drive us to Aucayacu. He had come over in a *moto-cholo*.

'You know what women are like,' he said humbly.

Rosalind gave him another of her looks; that was not the kind of thing you said to her.

'I don't see why he couldn't do what all the other cops do round here,' Matt observed when I told him: 'torture her to find out where she'd put his keys.'

The driver went off to try to find another vehicle. It did not seem particularly hopeful, given the problems Cecilia had had the day before.

'Ten to eight, and we're already into Plan B,' said Steve.

But there was no Plan B. Cecilia drummed her fingers on the table, Eamonn made out his latest outline for our programmes. The rest of us talked quietly and waited for something to happen. A mist drifted between the folds of the hills, like a Chinese watercolour from the T'ang Dynasty. Somewhere a pack of dogs was barking hysterically. It started to rain, then stopped, then started again. In the kitchens of the hotel a radio played salsa music. The waiter brought Cecilia the cordless phone. She spoke into it for a moment, then told Eamonn the driver had found something. She sounded dubious. The two of them went off to inspect it.

The rest of us packed our things and stood around waiting. If we could not get to Aucayacu because no one would take us, it would be a serious setback. Without good, strong pictures of the town, all our interviews of the previous day would be pointless: the key element would be missing. There was no airstrip there, so we could not fly. The time was getting on. Unless Eamonn and Cecilia came back with a decent vehicle large enough to take us all, and a driver who did not mind the risk, we were in real trouble.

There was an insistent, triumphant, deep-toned hooting down the long drive that led to the hotel. We went out to see what it was. An ancient green and cream Dodge bus, with a big roof rack, a flat windscreen and the names of destinations painted on it in red was lumbering towards us. Cecilia and Eamonn were hanging out of the door, waving in triumph. We stood on the steps of the hotel, clapping our hands above our heads and cheering at the sheer style of this solution to our problem. The bus turned in front of us and stopped.

I examined it with delight: I loved the local buses of Latin America, which always seemed like fairground vehicles and demonstrated such loving detail in their painting and lettering. This one was a beauty. 'MARGINAL', it said in giant red curlicued capitals over the front; the Marginal was the road which had been built in President Belaunde Terry's time to open up the rainforest, and it linked all the little towns in the area. Over the driver's side of the windscreen was the name 'AUCAYACU'; over the other half it said 'HUANUCO'. Along one side of the bus, executed with elaborate serifs and underlinings, they were repeated: 'Aucayacu', 'Tingo Maria' and 'Huanuco'.

'And you know what it's called?' Eamonn said proudly. 'The Empress of the Marginal!'

In fact the words '*Empresa del Marginal*', which appeared on the other side of the bus, meant 'Enterprise of the Marginal', which was rather less glamorous and was the name of the company which ran the buses. Even so, I preferred to think of her as the Empress; some myths are more important than literal truth.

Eamonn and Cecilia had hired the Empress from the *Empresa*. She was one of the buses that did the Aucayacu trip regularly, and the driver knew the road and was not particularly scared; though he had apparently had serious trouble from both the Army and Shining Path in the past. But Shining Path had been a little less active in the area in the previous few days, and he was prepared to take his chances with the Army. His name was William. He was an easy-going, phlegmatic man, a little fatalistic perhaps. It occurred to me even then, before I discovered exactly how good he was, that he made an ideal driver for a television crew.

We posed for several team photographs with the Empress as she stood in front of the hotel, while the green and yellow parrots screeched at us from their cage and Matt sweated in the early morning heat, trying to get us all into the shot. Then he set up his camera on a makeshift stand, put it on the timer, and ran round to join us. For a group of people who were about to go to the nastiest town in Peru along a road infested by the world's most unpleasant guerrilla group, we were very jolly and carefree. We had, I suppose, learned to live for the moment; and that moment, in the safety of Tingo Maria and with the pleasure of encountering the Empress still strong upon us, was a delightful one. 'Day is sunny,' I jotted down in my notebook, 'company good, situation amusing and charming. Whatever may lie ahead, this is pure enjoyment.'

We set off, with the Empress rumbling and shaking her way down the unpaved drive, hooting and waving to the hotel staff. Inside, the Cambridge-blue paint on the metalwork had been rubbed and chipped by the pressure of countless elbows and knees and hands. Most of the seats were split, and dirty yellow-brown foam rubber boiled out through the rents as though it was desperate to be free. We took a seat each, and spread out; the Empress had probably never been so underutilised in her entire existence. Eamonn and I discussed the structure of the report we would do in Aucayacu, but a good half of my attention was on the town and the road. There was a great deal more to be seen from the Empress than from a car, and the feeling of being on a jaunt still gripped me. William, the driver, aware that Steve's camera was likely to be on him, combed his hair carefully in the mirror, taking both hands off the wheel to do it.

The road was good outside Tingo Maria, but there were distinct signs of recent Shining Path activity here. Slogans in red paint covered the walls: '¡Socialismo o Muerte!' '¡Viva el Presidente Gonzalo!' '¡Viva la guerra popular!' and, arguably the clumsiest slogan in political history,'LONG LIVE THE STRATEGIC BALANCE!'.

Trenches had been cut in the surface of the road to slow down Army vehicles and buses at key ambush points, and had now been inadequately filled in. We felt moderately safe in the Empress, however: she gave us a protective colouring which a minibus or a couple of taxis would have lacked. A bus was so familiar a sight that no one looked at us closely, or noticed that it contained so few people. There were only the six of us, plus William the driver and his assistant, or conductor, whose name was Palacin. At a roadblock, a soldier waved us on carelessly without even noticing that we were gringos. William had pasted stickers that read 'Jesus es Amor' and 'Capricorn' above his steering wheel. He had two music tapes, which Matt had to ask him to switch off from time to time when it was interfering with the soundtrack of Steve's filming: they were 'Super Balades 92' and 'Explosion Latina'. Absit omen, I thought.

We drove northwards for fifteen kilometres along the Marginal, and made good time. Ahead of us was a Toyota truck overflowing with people. They waved and sang as Steve leaned out of the open door of the Empress to film them. But they continued along the Marginal, and we turned off to the left.

'From now on is rocky road,' said Palacin. Figuratively as well as literally: this was Shining Path country.

We stopped on a bridge and got out: Eamonn wanted a driving shot of the Empress. Rosalind coached William, and I added some familiar words: '. . .y no mirar al camera', don't look at the camera. Steve climbed up a small hill on the other side of the bridge to get the shot. Insects sang loudly; the river, a small tributary of the River Santa Martha called the Pendencia, ran brown and green through the trailing weed below. A brilliant blue bird, some kind of kingfisher, darted upstream. An enormous hornet, its yellow legs dangling like an undercarriage, buzzed around. Heavy vegetation filled in every available space, like hatching in a Renaissance engraving. The small Bailey bridge on which we had stopped was unremarkable in every way except that, according to Father Bob, eighty people had been massacred here some months before. The Army blamed Shining Path, the local people blamed the Army, and no one had bothered to investigate. The bodies had been thrown down the steep banks of the river and lay in the rank vegetation, festering, for some time. A small battered sign on the rock gave the bridge's name: 'Puente Sobrevilla'.

It was ten o'clock, and getting hot. Eamonn walked up and down in his bullish way, head down, swinging his arms together and clapping his fist into his open palm, thinking of sequences.

'Could you ask him to drive as fast as possible, in the same direction?'

The driver did it to perfection.

'*Fenomenal*,' said Rosalind; 'terrific.'

We applauded him, aware how difficult it was to get people to do this kind of thing correctly.

A mile later we reached another Bailey bridge, larger and comprehensively destroyed by Shining Path a few months before. Now a group of engineers was rebuilding the bridge, but William had to take the Empress down a muddy slip-road into the waters of the Pendencia itself.

'Hey Meester Heetchcock,' Cecilia called out to Eamonn, as he walked backwards and forwards alongside Steve, directing him as he filmed the Empress ploughing through the coppery Pendencia, the water reaching up to her numberplate. Cecilia was an advocate of ciné vérité, and disliked the delays that these production shots entailed. I explained to her, knowing that she found it obliquely flattering, that we were working for the best television company in the world; its standards were very exacting. She nodded, but still looked at her watch.

A man laden with a heavy tray jumped aboard as we struggled out of the river.

'*Helado,*' he shouted: he was an ice-cream seller, who supplied the buses that forded the Pendencia.

'*Si, por favor,*' I replied, and rooted around for money to buy enough for everybody.

'No, no, no,' said Cecilia. 'Here water is from river. No ees flavour vanilla; ees flavour cholera.'

'Ah,' I said.

She pointed out some buildings which had been shot up by Shining Path. The pockmarks in the walls looked recent. Where, I asked William, did he think Shining Path were now? He waved a vague hand towards the mountains. All he knew was that driving to Aucayacu had become a little easier since the arrest of Abimael Guzman, the 'Presidente Gonzalo' whose name appeared all the time in lurid red paint on the buildings along our way.

In the shimmering haze, a line of figures walked towards us. I shifted nervously, my knees jammed against the yielding back of the seat in front of me. We stopped. The men wore T-shirts and dark glasses.

'*Policia,*' Cecilia said. William nodded. We were near a big police base, and this was a roadblock. Steve was filming away. The policemen saw him and started getting angry. There was shouting.

Cecilia got off to speak to them.

'I am the only one who speaks Spanish,' she told them. Rosalind, whose Spanish was perfect, fumed at this and at the thought that Cecilia was doing something so dangerous on her own. Cecilia argued with the policemen for a little, then announced that she was going to speak to the commander in the base close to the road. The rest of us stayed behind.

A couple of policemen climbed on board to keep an eye on us. They looked extremely tough. One sat with his backside on the dashboard and his feet on the rail by the door. We were prisoners. William gazed straight ahead through the windscreen: he knew that the police were capable of doing unpleasant things to him and Palacin. Steve tried to get a brief shot of our captors and was spotted. It was another awkward moment and there was more shouting, but Steve kept the cassette from being confiscated.

I could see Cecilia's white T-shirt in the distance: she had almost reached the police base, accompanied by the leader of the patrol. She had insisted on going alone, though it seemed likely to be dangerous for her. William put 'Explosion Latina' on his cassette player, and one of the policemen rattled the sling-swivel of his Kalashnikov rifle to the beat.

It started to get very hot in the bus. None of us spoke.

After ten minutes I saw Cecilia's white T-shirt again. She was walking towards us, laughing and joking with the head of the patrol, who seemed to be positively fawning on her. Our guards got off, smiling awkwardly and saying they were sorry. Cecilia climbed aboard. We headed off waving.

'What on earth was all that about?' Eamonn asked.

Cecilia was airy in her reply, and waved her hand a lot: 'They wanted to wipe Steve's cassette. That was why I said I was the only one who spoke Spanish.'

She put her arm round Rosalind, guessing that she had been annoyed by this denial of her role. Rosalind gave her arm a friendly squeeze in reply.

'And. . . ?'

'And so I said to them that you were English, and this kind of thing would never happen in England, so you wouldn't be able to understand the concept. I said I wouldn't know how to find the words to explain to you that they wanted to censor your pictures. So they said OK, we'd better go on.'

We laughed aloud, and she sat there, enjoying our praise for her cleverness. Rosalind gave her a kiss. Yet I thought of the hostile policemen my colleagues sometimes had to deal with in England, and of all the politicians who supported them and longed for greater censorship over television; and I mourned the fact that Cecilia's view of English freedom was not necessarily always a reality.

We drove on, the Empress shuddering and rattling over the uneven road. Now, though, there was another noise, louder even than the bus engine and the rhythm of 'Explosion Latina'. It was only when I looked into the sky to my left that I saw what it was: two helicopters hovering over an open field beside us. They carried the word 'POLICIA' on them. I started to ask Cecilia what it was all about, and saw that the enjoyment of her triumph earlier had completely vanished. I was shocked: for the first time since I had met her, she looked genuinely scared.

'Is very danger,' she said quietly.

Men in camouflage fatigues with black caps were jumping out of the helicopter. I spotted one of them, who looked like an American, tall and fair with a bristling moustache.

'Let's stop,' I shouted, 'it's the DEA.'

It was extraordinary that we should have run into them like this. The second helicopter was wheeling round overhead, keeping an eye on us and on anyone else who might attack the patrol. The bus crew were as worried as Cecilia.

We got out, and Rosalind and I went forward, while Steve and Matt kept a few paces behind us, filming us. Eamonn walked beside them. I began to feel really scared myself: the DEA was carrying out an operation, and they might easily shoot us before they found out who we were and what we were doing.

'You all right?' I asked Rosalind, turning my head to look at her. She was, of course; I think she was less frightened than I was.

The first man in the patrol came through the bushes by the side of the road. He looked in both directions and covered the advance of the others. Curiously, neither he nor any of the rest seemed to be particularly interested in us; I had no need to say 'Y no mirar al camera' to them. I spotted a short, pleasant-looking character who had earphones attached to a Walkman round his waist. He was chewing gum, and he had round granny-glasses on. He could have come from an episode of 'M.A.S.H.'

'Hello,' I said, and held out my hand.

'Hey, great, you're English!' he said, pulling out the earphones. He introduced us to another American, and then to the tall, fair-haired man I had seen first; he proved to be the Peruvian officer in command. He agreed that we should film them briefly.

'Man, you were taking some risk comin' up to us like that,' said the second American.

There was another risk now. A large group of villagers had gathered in the roadway, attracted by the noise and presence of the helicopters. Everyone had seen us shaking hands with the DEA men. I now understood why Cecilia was so worried: especially when she explained that William had told her there was a Shining Path ambush on this stretch of road the previous Wednesday. Word of our meeting with the DEA would be with Shining Path very quickly. It would be no good explaining that it had happened by chance. This was an organisation which didn't believe in coincidences.

We sat in the bus as Steve filmed the DEA men moving on down the road, and talked over what we should do next. Cecilia felt that this had done us a great deal of damage. She thought we should carry on now, but that we should head back to Tingo Maria in the afternoon before it got dark rather than spend the night in Aucayacu. Eamonn disagreed.

'I don't think there is any damage,' he said.

I was strongly influenced by Cecilia's reaction, until Eamonn reminded me that there was supposed to be a carnival in Aucayacu that night. That would make good pictures, I thought, and like any chairman at a divided meeting I suggested that we should make up our minds in Aucayacu itself in a few hours' time.

'I no worried me, worried you,' Cecilia said, and I believed her. 'If we are stopped by Shining Path,' she went on in Spanish, 'you must tell them about the Shining Path people you've met in Europe. They'll know the names, and they might be impressed. It's your only chance.'

I jotted down the names in my notebook so that I wouldn't forget them at the critical moment. I just hoped they wouldn't be needed.

The Empress headed on in the direction of Aucayacu. It no longer seemed like a jaunt now; it was a serious undertaking, in which we had put our foot badly wrong. Behind us, one of the helicopters put down in the road outside a school. Steve filmed from inside the bus this time. The children poured out, cheering and shouting. No doubt they cheered everyone who passed by here, whichever side they were. They cheered us too, and we waved back at them.

The village, the anti-drugs patrol, the helicopters faded away behind. The greenness of the tropical foliage settled around us. It was the last stretch of open countryside.

'Aucayacu very close now,' said William. He and Palacin seemed more nervous than any of us now. And, I thought, they're the only ones who've been here before.

Aucayacu

I had the impression that all the demons had been let out of Hell to torment our wretched people.

Felipe Guaman Poma de Ayala, 1613

'Who Are The Terrorists?' asked a large notice in the red and white of the Peruvian national flag. It was fixed on to the wall beside the Army base in Aucayacu: the centre, according to our witnesses the day before, of so much violence and repression. The answer to the question was set out underneath, in language which became increasingly deranged.

1. DELINQUENTS who kill innocent people.
2. DELINQUENTS who kill old people, women and children.
3. DELINQUENTS who assassinate soldiers and policemen.
4. DELINQUENTS who destroy our own country.
5. DELINQUENTS who destroy families, bridges and roads.
6. DELINQUENTS who do not believe in God or the Fatherland.
7. DELINQUENTS with an ideology which has failed everywhere in the world.
8. DELINQUENTS who do not respect our red and white flag, and want to replace it with a dirty red flag.
9. DELINQUENTS, cowards and terrorists who, for fear of vengeance for their acts, do not show their faces.
10. DELINQUENTS who are not worth looking at, and

219

whom we should reject and fight against implacably.

Who, I wondered, was responsible for this? It might have been Captain Esparza, the Jehovah's Witness whom so many people from Aucayacu had described to us in terms that made him sound like a psychopath. Esparza had recently been withdrawn to Tingo Maria, but the noticeboard sounded like his work. He had trained abroad for three years, perhaps in the United States, and was a curious extrovert who would drive around the town in a jeep with the hi-fi blaring out rock music. According to some people we met, Esparza had a sense of honour. He even interrupted the local drugs trade for a couple of weeks, until his superiors ordered him to let it resume. This was probably the reason for his withdrawal.

Yet he was in charge of men who raped and murdered with impunity. For this, he had nothing more than the standard Army excuse. One of Father Bob's colleagues met Esparza in the street in Tingo Maria, and told him angrily that he was responsible for the deaths of a lot of people.

'That was because of the war,' Esparza answered. He seemed to feel, according to the man who met him, that because Shining Path killed a lot of innocent peasants, that was the way his men should behave too.

In one month, according to the Catholic priests in Aucayacu, Esparza's men killed fifty people. When their relatives went to see him, to ask for information, he would say blandly that they had been killed by Shining Path; or, depending on his mood, 'They have gone to St Peter.' Every person who was arrested had to give the names of two other people who were involved in terrorism; these would then be arrested, and required to give two names each in their turn. It was a system which brought terrible suffering.

On the day we arrived the Army was conducting a widespread arrest operation throughout the town. We stood outside the base in the hot sunshine, reading the crazy definition of terrorism and waiting to meet the new captain, whose name was Omero. So far we had got nowhere. A succession of surly NCOs had told us to wait: Captain Omero was out. As we waited, a line of soldiers came in, together with a man in civilian clothes whose face was covered with a hood. He carried a gun, and was presumably an informer: a Shining Path man who had gone out with the patrol to identify others, and who had been given the means to defend himself against revenge attacks.

We decided that Captain Omero had no intention of seeing us, and left to get some pictures. The town was in a state of considerable tension, and the Army was everywhere, patrolling in jeeps and trucks, moving from house to house on foot, setting up roadblocks. We had already been stopped at one roadblock on the way in. Soldiers little older than children had demanded money from us, and when we had refused they grinned and let us go on filming. They had set up a control centre in a building overlooking the roadblock. A large sign above it said '*Consultario Dental*'.

'That's where you go to get your teeth kicked in,' Steve said, and he may well have been right.

Three years before, Aucayacu had been thoroughly infiltrated by Shining Path. Then, it was the terrorists who set up the roadblocks, and went through the streets picking up innocent people and torturing or killing them. The Army scarcely showed its face in the town, and the local officials either did what Shining Path wanted or were killed. Then the Army's line changed, and it decided to take the town back. It was a fiercely contested operation which lasted many weeks, but at last the Army was successful. Almost everyone in Aucayacu, except those who were open supporters of Shining Path, was glad. Then the Army began to root out anyone it thought was guilty of sympathising with the terrorists. The reaction was as bad as the anarchy that had preceded it.

The soldiers were keeping a careful watch on us. When we filmed in the place by the river where a number of bodies had been found, they used their radios and observed us from nearby rooftops; but they did not stop us. Cecilia and I left the others and went to visit the local radio station, in the hope of getting more information about the situation in the town. A small, smiling man, Segundo Ramirez, assured us that everything was entirely normal, and that there were no difficulties with the Army or anyone else. He peered at me nervously to see if I seemed to accept all this. When I said nothing, it seemed to make him more uneasy than ever.

'People like the Army here,' he said as we left.

Our taxi driver told us, 'There's no law, no authority of any kind, in this place. It's terrible.'

By this time we had decided that we must stay the night in Aucayacu: it was too powerful a place to leave. William, the bus driver, wanted to go back to Tingo Maria but promised to be there at six the following morning. The consequences for us if he did not turn up were best left undiscussed, I thought. We went to Father Bob's church, an unremarkable place a few hundred yards from the Army base. Military trucks went up and down the street all the time. A large, crude wooden cross had been set up in a feeble patch of garden in front. On the wall of the church were the words '¿Donde estan?', 'Where are they?', but the last four letters had been painted out. Underneath were seventeen oblongs of white paint: it looked as though there had previously been a list of names there. The Army, which passed this way many times a day, had objected to the memorial.

The house behind the church, where Father Bob and a couple of other priests lived, was airy but suffered badly from ants and mosquitoes. At six, as the light went and filming outdoors became impossible, a chorus of frogs set up a terrific racket in the marshes behind. It was the kind of house where you felt surrounded by hostile forces, almost a prison. I soon realised there were some powerful tensions among the priests there. There had been four of them, but only two seemed to live there now. As I listened to Father Bob talking it became clear what the nature of the tensions was.

Father Bob had done some brave things. He had agreed to allow us to film him, and he had arranged for the witnesses to go to Tingo Maria to be interviewed by us. But it was also obvious that the dangers of being in Aucayacu had undermined his spirit and his desire to carry on. You could sense the fear welling up in him, making his voice and hands tremble. He had been under such strain for so long, imagining the soldiers coming to the door and taking him away, that it had worn his reserves of strength to nothing. He had taken the risk of inviting us here, yet he seemed to baulk at allowing us to film much lesser things.

In the end, having got nowhere, Eamonn suggested that we

should start the interview. Father Bob was nervous even about that now, and made a number of suggestions which seemed intended to delay the whole thing: shouldn't we, for instance, have a meal first and record the interview afterwards? He seemed like a soldier of the First World War suffering from battle fatigue.

We set up the camera in his church, and I looked at his tense, intelligent face. That was, perhaps, his problem: he could imagine only too well what it would feel like as the boot smashed into his face, the cosh into his kidneys, the bullet into his stomach. He had lived with these imaginings for too long. Each new case of the Army's brutality, far from raising his determination, provided new details of violence and horror for his imagination to work on. He had seen the bodies, he had buried the dead. He suffered everything they had suffered. I felt sorry for him, but I had a job to do and he was not making it easier.

Time and again as I asked him a question about the Army's involvement, he would turn it round and evade it. No, he couldn't say the Army was particularly bad. Many of its officers had tried to do their duty. And Captain Esparza? Captain Esparza had gone now, and things seemed to have changed. How many people had died here in the last year? He couldn't say for certain, you heard so many stories, it was necessary to be accurate about these things and accuracy was impossible. It was hot in the church, and the television lights made it hotter. I felt myself getting angry. Why, I wanted to ask him, did you tell me yesterday that the Army was the source of real evil in the town, that Esparza was a psychopath, that more than fifty people had died in a period of a month?

Instead I plugged away, certain that I would be able at last to break him down, just as the anguish of being in Aucayacu had come close to breaking him down. The temperature must have been in the upper nineties. A black moth as large as a bat fluttered around the camera lights. Thunder rolled around the red clouds over the hills outside. At last I seemed to be getting somewhere. Why, I asked, does the Army fight the war this way? You'd think that if they carried out a genuine hearts and minds campaign, people would support them.

I think it's because the Army – this is the only way they know how to deal with the situation. There's not much of an intelligence service that exists. So the only thing that's left to them is what they know: which is to fight a war like a conventional war, only it isn't a conventional war. So they use tactics which have been used in other countries, which is pick people up, torture them, use informers, and in that way try to win the war, you know, and in that way try to eliminate the enemy. The same mentality I guess that soldiers would have in a conventional war, only in a situation that is not conventional.

At last he had admitted that the Army tortured people and were fighting a war here. I thought I would press him on more personal things. Do you, I asked, sleep easily at night? I knew from what he had told me that he did not.

'Most nights,' he answered, with a rueful grin. 'Some nights not so much.'

Which were the nights when he didn't sleep so well?

When people come to us and you know that they're torturing and you know that they're eliminating people. That becomes very difficult because you feel powerless, like, what do you do? We scratch our heads, and we search for all the different ways we can do something, you know, like getting information out, collecting information. But that doesn't, like, stop. And that's been our big frustration: how do you stop this method of dealing with people, with human beings? The Church believes in life, you know, and it doesn't matter if the person is guilty or not, that's not the question. You should have a justice system that judges that; because we can't build a country without justice, and right now there's not a lot of justice in Peru.

We were almost there. Unlike the evasions he had given me earlier, it even sounded moderately strong; yet given the terrible reality of Aucayacu as he had outlined it to us the previous day, it was disappointing. We packed up the gear and left Father Bob. At a little poverty-stricken shop opposite the church we stood and had a coffee.

Rosalind was not willing to judge Father Bob as harshly as Eamonn or I, and she put up a good defence of him. He had, she rightly said, been through a terrible time in Aucayacu, and done what he could to protect people from the Army. And although he had been reluctant to say on camera what he had said to us in private the day before, we would not have known what the real situation here was without his help. And, she added, more tellingly still, no one who had not been through the experience themselves, daily and nightly for years, had any real right to criticise someone who had.

But Eamonn had been brought up as a Catholic, and his toughness and straight-dealing rebelled against everything we had heard.

'A man in Bob's position,' he said, 'could actually bring all this to an end if he wielded enough moral authority. He could stage a march to the Army base, and they'd never dare to do anything about him because it would be headline news everywhere if they did.'

I could imagine Eamonn in a priest's vestments going down to the base at the head of a group of angry townspeople, demanding to see the officer in charge. He certainly would have the moral authority to do it. I agreed with him, though along more typically Protestant lines: if Father Bob did not feel he could face up to the realities of life here, he should have left long before.

'It's all that Sixties sub-liberation theology,' I ended up, trying to lighten the atmosphere a little. 'I expect they sing "Where Have All The Flowers Gone?" and "Blowing In The Wind" at hymn-time.'

At this point one of the other priests came up to us. Father Edmundo was good-looking, moustachioed, plumpish, and possibly gay, and Rosalind had guessed already that he was a useful source of information. Now he told her everything: how he and the nuns attached to the church had to go behind Father Bob's back when someone was arrested, and appear at the Army base to ask for their release; how nothing was done unless they took action; how it was always going to be the next case that the church would take its stand on, but never, somehow, this one. Rosalind, fair-minded as ever, told us at once what he had said, and apologised to us; as though defending someone you think is being unfairly attacked requires an apology.

We wanted to get the atmosphere of moral equivocation out of our lungs, so we headed down to the main square. People were promenading round the Plaza de Armas, walking arm in arm, laughing, buying ice cream and nuts coated with caramel at the little stalls by the side of the road. This was the fiesta we had been told about. The only light came from the hissing bottled-gas lamps on the stalls: there was an electricity blackout in Aucayacu that night, and most nights of the year.

Music, grossly overmodulated and distorted, pumped out of the loudspeakers: dreary disco music, of a kind you could hear in a thousand small towns across the globe. The Army had set them up, and soldiers manned the battery of electronic gear from which the music originated. The Army was very keen to remind people of its organising and controlling presence here. In the otherwise pleasant square, with its obelisk and its neatly kept flowerbeds, obtrusive, irritating signs had been set up everywhere: 'Do Not Walk On The Grass. (Military Base).' 'Do Not Leave Litter. (Military Base).' 'Do Not Set Foot Here. (Military Base).'

As we wandered anti-clockwise around the small square, I saw a face I remembered coming towards us in the crowd: it was the man who, the day before, had come to Tingo Maria to tell us how his friend Pedro Davila had been murdered after making a public complaint about corruption in Aucayacu. His eyes caught mine and held them as we came closer and closer through the crowd. There was a brief unspoken dialogue in our looks: a fleeting panic, reassurance, relaxation, sympathy, relief. He said nothing to his wife, who glanced at Steve's camera and then looked shrewdly into her husband's face. There was, I thought, relief in her manner too as we walked past each other without saying a word.

We were not staying at the hotel in Aucayacu: everyone, including Father Bob and Father Edmundo, had warned us that if we did we would run the risk that anyone could come there during the night and take us away. Instead, reluctantly, we went back to the church. Father Bob seemed to notice our change of attitude towards him, and perhaps he understood the reason for it. He went out of his way to be friendly, and I felt bad about being so critical of him. Who was I, as Rosalind had said, to question the behaviour of someone who had gone through so much?

Steve and I, as the eldest, were awarded the two single rooms. Rosalind and Cecilia shared another, and Matt and Eamonn slept on the floor of the main sitting room. Before I went to sleep Father Bob showed me the hole beside my bed that a bullet had made during the last Shining Path attack on the Army base a little way across the fields. It was just about at kidney-level.

'The rumour is there'll be an attack tonight,' he said. 'Sleep well!'

At three in the morning I started up: there was a series of violent crashes and explosions, and wild blue and white light stabbed across the sky. All the cockerels in the area began crowing in unison. Then I heard the rain rattling down on the roof like small chunks of shrapnel, and I knew it was a thunderstorm. I put in my earplugs and slept.

Juanjui

Arms ought to be withheld from [those] who have a reputation for being mad or violent.

Felipe Guaman Poma de Ayala, 1613

The sound of hooting in the road outside told us that William, the driver of the Empress of the Marginal, had turned up, as he had promised, on English time; which is the expression used in South America to mean exactitude. It was two minutes before six o'clock in the morning, and just getting light.

Father Bob and two of the others began celebrating mass in a small room off the sitting room. Steve and Matt crammed in with them; the rest of us stayed outside. The celebrants began to sing a hymn which sounded familiar. After a few bars it became clear what the tune was: 'Blowing In The Wind'. Eamonn and Rosalind and I doubled up with laughter. And yet even as I laughed, I felt annoyed to have been proven so right.

'I didn't think much of Acu-yacu,' said Eamonn. He made it sound as though we had been watching a poorly produced documentary of which he disapproved. I nodded. I hadn't thought much of Aucayacu because it had frightened me. That was the difference between us, I reflected: Eamonn judged things by the way they affected the work we were doing, and I judged them on the basis of how they affected me.

We were kings of the road again, and it felt good to be out of the place. Even so, there were dangers here. We came to a bridge over the Pendencia river which had been blown up not long before by Shining Path. Two tree-trunks had been placed over the five-foot gap in the middle, at the width of the Empress's wheels. William edged his way up on to them, and slowly negotiated the critical distance. I looked down: the Pendencia was flowing angrily after last night's thunderstorms, fifteen feet below us. We all applauded when we reached the other side. William, used by now to our curious ways, made us a little bow from the driving seat.

Steve's camera had been accidentally damaged in Aucayacu, and a replacement was being sent out from Miami. He and I were recalling the time, four years earlier, when we had worked together in Chile and he had to replace his camera because it, and he, had been drenched with liquid sewage from a police water-cannon.

'It just perpetuates the myth that South America is a dangerous place to work in,' Steve said.

'Great,' I said, 'we'll go back as heroes.'

'I'd settle for going back.'

I looked out of the window: some Shining Path group had painted 'VIVA EL MAOISMO' on the wall of an abandoned house. But Shining Path was having a much leaner time of it now in the area around Aucayacu: the drugs runners had given up paying Shining Path their dues, and were just paying the Army now.

We came to the police base where we had been stopped the previous day. A large, ugly character dressed in black climbed on board and waved his finger at us. Assuming this meant 'Everyone out,' I gave him an angry look and ignored him. Then I realised he was waving us on, so I changed the look to a weak and ingratiating smile. A little later the driver of an oncoming vehicle waved urgently to us: there was a police roadblock round the next bend. The Empress was going at around twenty miles an hour, but William shifted out of his seat and Palacin slipped into it, jerking sharply on the steering wheel to prevent the Empress from driving off the road into the thick greenery. William had left his documents behind, and did not want to face the police without them. When we reached the roadblock there was a line of seven unhappy-looking figures standing beside a truck. Without documents, they had an unpleasant choice: pay a bribe, go to gaol, or perhaps face being press-ganged into the Army.

At the charming hotel in Tingo Maria we said goodbye to William, Palacin and the Empress with genuine regret. Both men were doing well out of the trip financially, and now it was

over they claimed to have enjoyed themselves; which is what we
habitually did ourselves. There were more team photographs, and
then the Empress headed off down the road. I watched her turn the
corner, her tyres flicking up little pebbles, as unwieldy as ever. If I
had the money, I thought, I'd buy that bus off them now. I'd park
it in the quiet London square where I live, and drive to work in
it every day.

We sat round a table on the verandah and ordered breakfast: eggs
with pale yolks, bacon for the carnivores, toast and a good deal of
red substance that might have been jam. It was all very enjoyable.
Cecilia, though, was working. I could hear her clacking away on
an ancient typewriter in the manager's office. Finally she emerged
with a smile that combined triumph and a certain shyness, and
handed me a piece of paper. It was the letter she had composed
in my name for El Vaticano, and it was a splendid work of the
imagination.

This is a translation:

Senor Limiliel Chavez,
Campanilla.

Dear Senor Chavez,

My name is John Simpson, and I am the principal journalist of
the English network BBC Television of London. The medium for
which I work is one of the most important in Europe, Australia and
Canada. Our news reaches an audience of more than 100 million,
and in addition it has 99 per cent credibility among the people of
Europe.

I am writing you this letter to request a cordial interview
exclusive to the BBC. We understand that you are the most
representative figure in the Huallaga and the Department of San
Martin, and we consider it very important for the entire world to
hear from you the reality for the inhabitants of this troubled area
of Peru.

As a journalist I have interviewed many different world figures,
many of them clandestinely, and I have always respected the conditions which have been laid down for these interviews. You can
rely on this guarantee.

From the 18th to the 23rd September we have been working in

the Huallaga, and have come to understand some at least of the realities of life in this area. I can assure you that I do not share the opinion of the North American press about the problems here; which is why I would like to speak to you.

John Simpson

Tingo Maria, 23rd September 1992

'Just one thing,' I said, ignoring all the other things that were far more questionable. 'Why is the BBC believed by only 99 per cent of people in Europe? Don't you think we should have a little more pride in ourselves than that?'

Cecilia never found it easy to understand the English sense of humour. Now she took me entirely seriously. 'If you is saying one hundred, is too much. El Vaticano no think real. If say 99, he think: OK, is real.'

'Oh well,' I said, 'we want El Vaticano think real.'

Somehow, though, in spite of my habitual optimism, I doubted whether El Vaticano would agree. He was too deeply involved in things that did not bear examination; why should he reveal anything about them to us? I was happy to try Cecilia's letter, but I was certain it would come to nothing. The important thing was to get a better insight into the nature of the drugs trade. How, I asked, did she plan to get the letter there?

She smiled sweetly at me: always a dangerous sign. El Vaticano, it seemed, had a deputy, or adviser, who was also his lawyer. This man lived in the drugs town of Juanjui. His name was 'Loco' Alvan; 'loco' meaning crazy. The two of them sounded a great team.

'I think is possible see Loco Alvan. Only problem is go Juanjui. That is beeeeg problem.'

She laughed, and her eyes glistened. I knew then that she was as determined to try as I was.

Our pilot was not on English time. Indeed, he was two and a quarter hours late. Because he was not there to sweet-talk the soldiers and chivvy them along, we had trouble when we reached Tingo Maria airport. They wanted to search us for drugs.

'Search yourselves, search the Army,' Cecilia raged at them, and the soldiers gave up sheepishly. She grinned triumphantly, and I put my arm round her in congratulation and affection.

Eventually the pilot turned up with a credible explanation. The co-pilot who always insisted he was Canadian but had a strong Peruvian accent was with him again.

'I can't stand the way these guys do things down here,' he confided to me. 'Back home, we do it all so differently. I just cain't understand 'em.'

We had to break the news to the pilots that we wanted to stop off at Juanjui on our way back to Lima, in order to hand over a letter. Cecilia held up the letter and waved it. Juanjui was not the kind of place a sensible pilot would want to land, so they took their time discussing it between themselves, and with their office in Lima. Eventually they agreed. Cecilia and I argued about whether I should go with her to hand over the letter to Loco Alvan. She wanted to go alone, on the grounds that it would be safer. I knew it would, but I did not want a repetition of the incident at the police post on the road to Aucayacu, when we had allowed her to walk into danger on our behalf.

I would have to come too, I said: no question about it. Then with a flash of inspiration I copied her tactic, and invented the clinching argument. The BBC, I said, making it up as I went along, had a rule that no one was allowed to go to dangerous places alone; I might be sacked if it became known that I had broken the rule.

'Have you made *testamento*?' Cecilia asked; she had obviously decided to give way, in spite of her better judgement.

'Yes, and I've left everything I own to Eamonn.'

'In that case,' Eamonn said, 'hard luck.'

It took us only about twenty minutes to fly to Juanjui. The airport was reminiscent of all the other drugs towns where we had stopped in the Huallaga Valley: a heavy Army presence, hostile and questioning, a run-down little terminal building, the feeling of being watched. Cecilia and I left the others in the snackbar.

'*Adios, los muchachos y la muchacha*,' I said, regretting that I was leaving them. They waved to us with a certain finality.

We walked out of the terminal and found ourselves at the end of a short street close to the centre of the town. It was fearfully hot, but it was a dry heat rather than the usual humidity of the Huallaga Valley. Little whirlwinds of dust flickered in the roadway: Juanjui did not seem to have experienced the previous night's thunderstorms. There were no taxis, just a solitary *moto-cholo*. The driver, fat and sleekly dressed, caught our eye. We climbed aboard.

The *moto-cholo* was new and uncharacteristically comfortable, with shiny red plastic seats stuffed with thick foam-rubber. The driver kept it clean, and his motorcycle engine was well maintained. As he started up and we headed down the short side street which led to the town centre, I could see that Juanjui, unlike the other towns we had visited, was a place where the drugs money had genuinely trickled down to the ordinary inhabitants. The shops were full of electrical and electronic gadgets, the bars were full, there were plenty of new cars, and people were well dressed.

This did not make them feel better about us; or more particularly about me. In fact it gave them a more personal reason to dislike me, since they assumed I was an American working for the DEA, which was trying to take their livelihood away from them. Our *moto-cholo* moved slowly, and we were painfully conspicuous as we sat in the open back of it. Cecilia, pretty and fair-skinned, attracted everyone's attention first, and then they would look to see what kind of man she was going out with. I tried to hunch down in my seat, but it was no use.

The Army was everywhere, driving in jeeps and trucks, marching around. For once, their vehicles looked new and well maintained. The drugs money had reached down to the ranks too, it seemed. Perhaps Juanjui was a drugs democracy, where everyone got their share. In the Plaza de Armas, which looked like every other Plaza de Armas, children were playing a game of football. Even they were dressed in decent clothes instead of the usual rags. The streets were decorated with bunting, which fluttered overhead and announced the forthcoming fiesta in the town.

'We should stay and film it,' I said to Cecilia, but I was just trying to convince her I wasn't scared. She drew her finger across her throat and laughed.

We were looking for someone she knew who might take the letter to Loco Alvan. She did not want us to deliver it: finding Loco would take too long, she explained matter-of-factly, and he might kill us. I was still thinking about that when we reached the place where her friend lived: a flat over a shoe-shop. Since she had never been able to visit Juanjui herself, she didn't know the place. We spent a good deal of time trying to work out which was the right door. People began to notice us and gather round.

'Dirty gringo,' someone shouted from a car, reaching out and trying to grab me as he drove past.

We dodged across the road and into the open hallway. The door shut behind us, and for a moment I felt a little better. Then I could hear shouting outside. A crowd seemed to be gathering. We went upstairs. It was stiflingly hot, and the place smelled of people and decay. Cecilia had no idea which was her friend's room, and we knocked on several without reply. There was a muffled shout from one of them. Cecilia opened the door and a fat man in his twenties, wearing only a pair of grubby underpants, jumped out of bed. Cecilia, ignoring the underpants and the rolls of fawn flesh, asked him if he knew where her friend was. He scratched his head and yawned, and looked bewildered.

A middle-aged woman in a skimpy, torn dress had been listening. Now, shiftily, she came up, rested her broom against the wall and put in her contribution. Yes, she knew Cecilia's friend. She had watched him go out about ten minutes ago. He always went to the same place at this time of day, the Restaurant Sindi. She looked from Cecilia to me, then back to Cecilia, trying to judge our reaction. Somehow, I felt she was lying. There was more noise from the street outside: the crowd hadn't yet gone away, and I thought I could hear someone shouting about gringos. I glanced at Cecilia; she seemed unaware of it. Since I had complete faith in her ability to get out of the tightest situation, I let her take the decisions and make the running.

It was hot and stuffy in the building, but at least we were safe from the crowd here. Cecilia went up and down the corridors calmly, banging on doors and asking for her friend. A few minutes passed. Then she decided it was time to go. I put my shoulders back, and prepared for the worst.

Yet for some reason the crowd, having called for the gringo to come out, had drifted off when the gringo insisted on staying inside. Only half a dozen men of the street-corner variety were hanging around outside when we emerged, and they said nothing. I may have looked a little grim: I was certainly prepared to sell my life dearly. As it was, we merely whistled up our *moto-cholo* and climbed in. The onlookers moved away as we spluttered off down the street. We bumped comfortably up and down on the new foam-rubber seats every time the wheels hit a rock in the unmade-up road.

'Restaurant Sindi?' said the moto-cholist when we had got a little way away. '*No se.*'

I very much doubted myself whether the place existed, but it seemed safer to find Cecilia's friend than to go and see Loco Alvan ourselves. We spent ten minutes driving up and down the streets in the area.

'No Restaurant Sindi,' said the moto-cholist at last.

'I know other place,' Cecilia said.

We bumped along, and found an undistinguished, sun-blistered doorway. This time Cecilia felt it would be better if the driver asked the questions. He got out, extracted the key from the lock and put it in his pocket, as though we might drive it off while he was gone. Then he banged on the door.

A crafty-looking youth opened it and peered out at the driver, then at us. He disappeared. His place in the doorway was taken by a much older man with a remarkable squint. He managed, by cocking his head to one side like a bird of the rainforest, to keep his left eye on the driver and his right on us. He opened his mouth: his teeth seemed to have been inserted in the wrong places: there were long incisors on the bottom row, while the ones at the top were short and regular.

He came over to us as we sat and sweltered in the *moto-cholo*, turning his head so one of his eyes rested on me and the other on Cecilia. No, he had never heard of Cecilia's friend. No, he was certain he would have heard of him if he had lived there. But no such person lived there. Sorry. Very sorry. The eyes flicked round, taking in the driver and Cecilia and leaving me out, then switching back to me and leaving out the driver. He wore plastic sandals but no socks, and his toenails were curled and deep brown.

'You lying bastard,' I said, smiling at him and shaking his scaly old hand. It was like handling something in the reptile house.

'*Si*,' said Cecilia, doing the same. Then, when the driver started up and we headed off she said, 'He scared. All scared. No want killed.' She made a little gun out of her childlike hand and waggled her thumb. Then she laughed.

'Maybe we leave Loco letter with him.'

'No,' I said, 'he'll never pass it on.'

She nodded.

'I think we should go and give it to Loco in person,' I said. I listened to my voice saying the words, and thought, Why do I get myself into these things?

'No. Too *peligroso*, see Loco.'

The moto-cholist, listening, seemed to agree.

We headed through the main square of Juanjui for the fifth time. Cecilia was absorbed in her own thoughts. Then she nudged me.

'Maybe we go see Loco,' she said.

I gave her a little salute, to show how splendid I thought the idea was.

'Dear John,' she said, and squeezed my arm a little. I was touched; she reminded me very much of my elder daughter. Then I realised I was going to be practised upon.

'Better I go see Loco, you stay *moto-cholo*. *¿Si?*' She nodded her head, as though it were sympathetic magic and I would start nodding mine too. The moto-cholist looked round: he knew what was going on, and wanted to see my reaction.

'I can't,' I said feebly. I thought of what my grandmother, a charming but fierce lady with the general approach to life of a Sir Henry Newbolt poem, would have said if she had known that her grandson would let a woman go alone into a den of gangsters.

The moto-cholist turned away, disappointed. Cecilia tapped her finger irritably on the side of the vehicle. She told the moto-cholist where Loco Alvan lived. I had the impression he knew anyway. It is not often that you can spot unwillingness from the set of someone's back, but the moto-cholist, without turning round, showed he was not a happy man.

Loco Alvan lived behind a high wall which hid an extensive garden. Cecilia got out and went over to the grey-painted metal gate, seven feet tall, which was shut. She had told me to stay with the *moto-cholo*, but I went anyway. I think she was glad of my company; this was a place where, for all her resourcefulness, she could simply disappear. She was nervous, and I could feel the signs in myself. She banged on the rusty grey metal of the gate. It yielded a little, and we could see inside.

Three men were standing there, drinking beer and laughing. They all had big bellies which hung over their waistbands. They wore T-shirts, and had guns in their belts. None of them had yet had his weekly shave. They looked across at Cecilia and laughed some more, ignoring her deliberately for a while. Finally one of them came over.

'*¿Si?*'

'*Senor Alvan, por favor.*'

She had put on her kittenish voice and expression. The men it was directed at usually went weak at the knees. Not this time. He called out something, and another man, also unshaven and big-bellied, came over. It was Loco Alvan in person. He looked extremely tough. His T-shirt said 'Co-op Bank'. He was probably in his late thirties, but looked considerably older, with sharp, active eyes. They moved to my face. 'Gringo,' he was thinking.

I understood why he was nicknamed Loco: he looked capable of flying into a wild rage on very little pretext; and I might just have provided the pretext.

El Vaticano and Loco Alvan: between them, presumably, they were responsible for most of the raw material that became cocaine and crack on the streets of the world's cities. On its way there, the cocaine – or rather the money it generated – bought off police chiefs, attorneys-general, sometimes prime ministers. The fabric of social and political life in various pleasant little ex-colonies up and down the Caribbean had become thoroughly rotted by the combination of cash and savage violence which the cocaine smugglers were prepared to hand out, impartially.

I heard of a man who had spent his life-savings on buying

a deserted island in the Bahamas: one night he was beginning dinner with his family when they heard a high-powered boat approaching. A polite man knocked on the door and came in, holding a small valise. He opened it up on the table: it contained a large number of $100 bills in packets.

'This is for you, if you leave here for good by midnight and never come back,' he said.

The owner protested that he had lived there for years, that he had young children, that it simply wasn't possible.

'You're all dead if you don't,' the polite man said.

The family cleared out by eleven o'clock, and the cocaine runners had bought themselves a useful staging-point on the way to Florida.

Cocaine is not like heroin: it does not necessarily wreck individual lives quite as fast, or quite as completely. But the money it generates enslaves entire communities. Policemen are paid off, judges give the right verdicts, politicians pass the right laws. And underneath the money is the threat of real violence.

Loco Alvan, as second-in-command to the man who provided well over half of the raw material for the entire world trade in cocaine, knew that he could certainly deal with the consequences if it were necessary to kill Cecilia and me. Peru was one of the countries whose fabric the cocaine money had rotted, and here in Juanjui the only law was the Army, which had been corrupted totally.

'*No es gringo*,' Cecilia said of me quickly. '*Es ingles.*'

There was, I thought, a faint relaxation of his jaw muscles.

'*Si*,' I said. I reached out my hand. It slithered with his in the drenching heat. For once, I managed to stop myself gripping too strongly.

Cecilia started to explain why we were there.

'Senor Simpson is a very important man, and he wants to interview Senor Chavez. Speaking as a Peruvian,' she went on with enormous sincerity, 'I think it would be very good if Senor Chavez agreed.'

To my surprise, Loco Alvan seemed interested.

'*Momento*,' he said, and disappeared inside the gate. While we were still trying to work out what was going on, he opened a door a few yards along the wall.

'*Oficina*,' he explained: and indeed it was a very small office. On the walls were the certificates which testified to his legal training, and a calendar with a naked girl on it; under glass on his desk were photographs of Loco drinking, Loco standing with his hands on his hips, Loco smiling. Cecilia scarcely noticed these things: she was in persuasion overdrive.

'Senor Simpson has interviewed many famous people,' she said. I nodded modestly. 'Including Pablo Escobar,' she added, making up anything that she thought would help.

I stifled my instinctive denial. Pablo Escobar was the biggest cocaine dealer in the world.

'Ah,' said Loco Alvan, looking at me with a new respect; 'Uncle Pablo, huh?'

I shrugged, in a way that I hoped would be ambiguous.

'Senor Chavez may very well be interested. I shall ask him.'

I produced my last visiting card, bent and sweat-stained. It went into a drawer with God knows what others. Cecilia motioned to me to bring out the carefully typed letter: Loco Alvan held the envelope by the corners, as though anxious not to dirty it, then put it into the drawer as well. The interview was over: I put my hand out to shake his, but he reached up and laid his heavy arm round my shoulder. Awkwardly, unwillingly, I matched the movement, and we stood entwined for a moment or two, the English journalist and the Peruvian who knew the secrets of one of the biggest drugs operations in the world. I stayed like that until I thought it was safe to disentangle myself.

Outside, we climbed into the *moto-cholo*. The driver started up with obvious relief, and lurched off down the road. Loco Alvan stood outside his office and waved us goodbye. The gun showed through the material of the T-shirt as he raised his arm.

'To the airport,' I said. When we were out of sight of Loco Alvan I took Cecilia's arm and raised it in the air like a boxer. She leant over and kissed my cheek. The sense of having come so close to the centre of the web and then escaped from it was intoxicating.

'*Senor Simpson es muy famoso*,' I said, imitating her voice and fluttering my eyelids.

'He have made interview Pablo Escobar,' Cecilia answered. We spent the rest of the journey to the airport laughing. Half an hour later our plane lifted off from Juanjui.

El Vaticano never did give us an interview. He seemed interested enough, but heavy rains washed out the telephone lines between the Huallaga Valley and Lima and we were unable to arrange anything before we left for England. One day, I promised myself, I would come back and try again.

Our plane stopped at Tarapoto to refuel. As we sat in the airport café, drinking InkaCola and waiting, a familiar figure entered. It was Victor Ushinahua, the bank clerk whose son, daughter-in-law and granddaughter had disappeared. He was seeing his mother off on the small scheduled flight to Lima, and had come into the café to buy something for his grandson, the solemn, reserved little boy called Danny.

Danny stood there looking at us for a moment; then Rosalind took him off to make a fuss of him. Victor Ushinahua held out his arms and embraced me, tears welling up in his eyes. The day after we had interviewed him, he said, someone from the Army base in Tarapoto had taken pity on him and told him what everyone else had guessed long before: that his son and daughter-in-law and their baby had all been murdered by the Army several months earlier.

He looked across at Danny, who was listening gravely to Rosalind as she held him in her arms and talked to him.

'So there is just us now, sir,' said Victor Ushinahua. 'And I am not young any more.'

PART V

WITH THE REAL PEOPLE

The spirits of the river sing a song, accompanied on the flute by two indians sitting on the cliff-top.

San Antonio de Sonomoro

They wandered like lost souls in a world they did not
understand.

Felipe Guaman Poma de Ayala, 1613

'*Negabehage; adoge; pomena.*'
'*Negabehage; adoge; pomena,*' I repeated obediently: hello,
thank you, please. They were my first and only words of the
Ashaninca language, and I repeated them with relish. The biggish,
broad-faced, aquiline-nosed indian woman sitting opposite me
smiled encouragingly and nodded. Bertha was an Ashaninca
herself, and worked for an indian rights organisation in Lima.
She had agreed to go with us to her home village and translate
for us when we filmed there.

'One different word you is wanting,' said Cecilia. 'Important;
useful for you.'

I looked at her.

'Huanca,' she explained to me. '*Huachafo,*' she said to Bertha.

'*Kiminari,*' replied Bertha, without even pausing to think.

It had always been my aim, having seen the Ashaninca in the
forests of Western Brazil, to visit them in Peru as well. In
their traditional areas they were populous: the dominant group
in many places. Yet the quiet forest life they led was in the
process of being broken up by the Shining Path's war against
the government. The jungle along the Brazilian border was a
useful place for Shining Path to operate. Like Manco Inca in the
sixteenth century, Shining Path's guerrillas had taken refuge there
and were carrying out operations against government forces. They
also tried to indoctrinate the Ashaninca who lived in the forest.

Shining Path carried out acts of deliberate terror in order to force the Ashaninca to side with them. Several hundred Ashanincas had joined Shining Path, and there was civil war in the tribe. Often Shining Path teams would move into an Ashaninca village and lure the men to come to their camps with offers of guns or knives. After that, they would be forced to carry out attacks on other Ashaninca villages, and sometimes their own, to ensure that they could never return. Groups of Ashaninca working with Shining Path had massacred villagers in Nailan and Masuriniari. When the Lima government set up self-defence groups known as 'rondos' in the countryside, the Ashaninca joined them in large numbers.

After the Nailan massacre the *rondo* which was based there had attacked the village from which the Shining Path group had come. Altogether more than a hundred people were killed. Now there was a new force in the equation: groups of Peruvian special troops, known officially as 'Delta Force' but nicknamed 'Sinchis' after a legendary Inca hero. They were based in villages which were under threat, and had been trained by the Americans, though the United States withdrew its teams when President Fujimori suspended the constitution in April 1992.

Neither Rosalind nor Cecilia would be coming with us. They were trying to set up other interviews and meetings for us in Lima. Instead, we were to go with the BBC correspondent Sally Bowen, her son Rory, and Bertha.

We put Bertha up at the Hotel Las Americas. The horrified look on the face of the hotel receptionist when we ordered a room for her was memorable. Not many tribespeople from the rainforest had stayed there before, it seemed. As for Bertha, once she had been shown how to operate the bath-taps, and the television, and the central heating, and had grasped the notion of room service, she was delighted. She stood in the middle of the room, raising and lowering her arms as though to savour the experience.

Then, having spent the night in a five-star hotel, Bertha had to face her first trip in an aircraft. Sally stayed with her as we left the airport building, and gently coaxed her on when she stopped in front of the plane, overcome with giggles. In the end Bertha climbed aboard as though she had flown many times before. We seated her behind the pilot, so she would have something to look at if she became frightened.

I watched her carefully as we rattled down the runway and soared steeply into the air, but there was nothing except a smile of interest and pleasure on her handsome face. Soon she was looking down at the ground below with great attention, laughing aloud whenever she saw a cow or a horse from the air. When we passed the Andes and began to see the forest unrolling below us, she was quieter. This was the kind of territory she understood.

Satipo was a pleasant, small forest town, relatively orderly, very green, and extremely hot by 10.15. A small air-taxi stood on the apron, and *moto-cholos* plied up and down. The soldiers who met us here were relaxed and welcoming. In Satipo they only had Shining Path to fight. There was no coca in this part of the country; accordingly, the Army had no reason to be worried about us, and nothing to hide.

Bertha was telling a group of Ashanincas about the Hotel Las Americas, making twiddling movements with her fingers and waving her arms about. The Ashanincas watched admiringly. When she spread her arms like a bird's wings to describe what it had been like on the plane, they clapped their hands together.

It felt good to be back in the forest again, with the feeling of grandeur and depth which the trees on either side of the red earth gave. We drove out of Satipo to an Army base. Here too the Army's only function was to fight the war, and they were happy to let us film. There were no stories about people being tortured or killed. The soldiers regarded the Ashanincas as their allies in the war, and their main function was to track down Shining Path bases and release the Ashaninca prisoners who were held there.

We came to a Sinchi base. It was neat and well ordered, and the officers seemed self-confident and tough. The major was slender, grey-haired and wolfish: not a man you would want to meet at the wrong end of a piece of electrical flex, perhaps, but impressive in that he and his men did not regard themselves as an occupying force surrounded by enemies, but as protectors of the local population. We filmed – with permission, for once – as the Sinchis brought out the trophies from their most recent operation: a joint attack with the police and the Ashaninca *rondos* against a village named Estrella which the Shining Path had turned into one of their model communities. There were books of poems to Chairman Gonzalo, literature condemning Western democracy, instructions on making bombs and on assembling Belgian-made rifles.

The Sinchi major warned us it was dangerous to be on the road unaccompanied, because groups of Shining Path might be about, but he didn't offer us an escort. We passed little houses which had once been neat and pleasant, but where terrible things had happened. Now they were empty and fire-blackened, with slogans painted in red on their walls. Big groves of orange trees lay beside the narrow road, but the fruit lay rotting on the ground for lack of anyone to pick it.

We stopped in the dusty, unpaved plaza of the little town of San Martin de Pongoa, with a grand blue and white church on one side and a Sinchi post on the other. A year before there had been a massacre by Shining Path here, but now it seemed relaxed. The people in the streets were indians, but not Ashanincas. They were immigrants from the overpopulated highlands, encouraged by the government to come here and settle. The women still wore the strange felt top hats of their native villages.

Our minibus would not be able to cope with the road beyond here, and we had to find something that would. Sally and I came across a man loading bananas into the back of a Hiace truck. He wore a dirty red T-shirt and his hair stuck out like something in a Struwwelpeter illustration. Sally closed the deal as serenely as if she were buying asparagus at Harrods Food Hall; then we went back to the restaurant where the others were waiting. In a heavily lavatorial atmosphere – the door to the banio in the corner was lolling open – Rory and Bertha were digging into a meal of steak and chips, The waiter was a male dwarf, tough and muscular and far brighter than the man who owned the place.

I drank some coffee and looked out of the window. Led by a town indian, an Ashaninca man who had obviously just arrived from the forest was walking past with three children, all in their brown *kushma* robes and red *urucum* paint. My heart went out to them: among the T-shirts and the tattered jeans and shoes of the town indians these four seemed like another species, gentler, more beautiful, and as bewildered as though they were wild birds newly captured. The man held his chin in his hand as he walked, as though considering what he could possibly do here in this world which was so different from anything he had ever seen or imagined in the calm, understandable forest which was all he had ever known. His children had delicate features and dark, anxious eyes. They had lost their old life for ever. Now, hand in hand, with slow, wandering steps, they made their solitary way into a different and more corrupted world.

We loaded our equipment on to the back of our Hiace while a fascinated audience watched, and set off along the broken dirt road. A good fifty people watched us go, calling out and waving, while Bertha sat beside the driver and acknowledged the plaudits of the crowd.

'Well, I think we managed to get out of there without being noticed,' said Eamonn drily. I laughed, and almost forgot the intense pain in my buttocks and hands which came from sitting on the edge of the truck and trying to keep from flying off at every bump, my feet resting on the bunches of green bananas.

We were heading for San Antonio de Sonomoro: Bertha's village. It lay alongside Nailan, where the massacre had taken place, and was divided from it by a stream.

'Like Buda from Pest,' Sally said cheerfully.

'If we're staying in Pest,' Matt said, 'I'm putting up my mosquito net tonight.'

Its position was beautiful: it lay in a gentle valley, with meadows running down to the river, and wooded hills rising up on either side. Nailan and San Antonio de Sonomoro were Ashaninca villages, but the people here were not forest indians of the kind I had seen in Brazil; they were used to vehicles, they had plenty of farming implements, and their huts were more like cottages than the open sleeping platforms of Simpatia.

As they came out to greet us, they wore their *kushmas*, but there was little trace of red on their faces. The *urucum* berry was in short supply here, and the Ashanincas of San Antonio de Sonomoro had to use it very sparingly: just a couple of thin strokes on the cheekbones at the start of the day. I thought again of the gentle figure I had seen with his children in the nearby town. He had painted his face thoroughly, feeling perhaps that since he was moving into an unknown world he must do things properly, as one of the Real People should.

Bertha had come into her own. Earlier she had been wearing a shell suit, but now she put on what Steve called 'the full Monty'. She had turned herself into an Ashaninca diva, with a *kushma* that was bright orange rather than brown, while over her shoulder she wore a collar of small beads and, in the place of parrot feathers, the entire heads and beaks of parrots. She looked a little like Mae West to me, but the Ashanincas were deeply impressed.

Soon it was dark, and we were sitting in a circle while the refugees from the massacre at Masuriniari told us what had happened to them two months earlier, when a group of Ashanincas fighting with Shining Path had attacked them. There were Shining Path people on the crest of the hill above us now: some evenings they fired down at the Sinchi post, three hundred yards away in Naira, or at San Antonio itself. A dog barked in the darkness, and everyone jumped nervously.

Masuriniari, like any other Ashaninca village, had a chief: in Peru they called him a president. Shining Path came there and took the president away with them. They kept him for a month before sending him back as an apparently converted member of Shining Path. Directly he returned to Masuriniari he recanted. When a team from Shining Path came back some months later, he told them to get out. At 6 am on the morning of 28 July 1992, two hundred Shining Path guerrillas attacked the village, bringing with them a group of Ashaninca 'converts'.

Abel, a boy of about twelve with sharp mistrustful eyes, sat close to his friend Pedro and told us what had happened. He had escaped into the undergrowth close to the village when he heard the Shining Path arrive. He watched a number of people whom he knew being killed.

They were shouting 'Death to informers!' and 'Viva Gonzalo!'
I lost my brother, who was seven years old. They killed with a
machete and cut his head off with an axe. His brains came out.
I saw it clearly.

Pedro was a little older. He had been awake when the Shining
Path guerrillas arrived. He ran out and came face to face with
another group.

I got out my bow and arrows. I shot one terrorist, and then I
went on running. I went to hide. I saw them go into our hut and
kill my father and mother, and my mother's father. They had guns
and bows and arrows and machetes. I couldn't recognise them, but
some of them were Ashanincas. There were children and women
there too, and some of them took part in the killing. I saw them
do it. The fighting went on for two hours, but they stayed for nine
hours altogether.

An old man, Miguel, showed us his forearm. In the fleshiest
part, just below the elbow, there was a large greyish lump: a
bullet had lodged in it, fired by one of the attackers.

'You must get a doctor to take it out,' I said.

'Maybe,' he answered vaguely.

Away from the camera lights a young woman sat cradling
her son, who must have been about two. She was beautiful, with
slanting eyes and a full mouth. The child was pale and wasted;
even his black hair had faded to an indeterminate brown. He slept
with his eyes half closed, his chest so fleshless as to seem skeletal. I
asked her what was wrong with him. He had been there, she said,
when Shining Path had murdered her husband, and had seen it all.
He had not eaten anything since then, and all he did was sleep like
this.

'But he'll die soon, unless he is properly looked after,' Sally said.

The woman said nothing. She merely looked down at the
child, who was stirring fitfully.

We settled down for the night in one of the huts. Sally
and Rory declined the offer of a mosquito net, but although
the rest of us put them up, there was no need; the night was
pleasant, and too cool for mosquitoes. I lay down, unable to

get the images of the night out of my head: the dying, listless child, the empty eyes of its mother, the boy who had watched his brother's brains come out, the exile in the town holding his children's hands, the gentle flute music which one of the boys had played while we filmed. Dogs barked, and glow-worms flew past the open entrance to the hut. An Ashaninca sat close by in the doorway, watching me. Undisturbed by his gentle curiosity, I fell asleep.

Puerto Bermudez

They kept the law, respected their parents and their masters, and helped one another. Having no houses or possessions, they did not make war but lived in peace.

Felipe Guaman Poma de Ayala, 1613

We woke at 4.15 to a little chorus of electronic alarms. It was a good hour before our vehicle turned up to take us back to Satipo. Bertha, more queen-motherly than ever, announced that we had promised to take her back to Lima. This was the first we had heard of it, but we agreed. She climbed in next to the driver again, while we got into the back. We lurched across the planks over the little river dividing Buda from Pest, and hooted and waved at the Sinchi post in Nailan as we passed. The soldiers turned out to wave back. I reflected again on the difference between the Sinchis, who had a proper job to do and did it with reasonable efficiency, and the Army officers we had seen in the Huallaga.

The cumulus clouds which hung over the rainforest, banking up to extraordinary heights, lost the salmon-pink of dawn and turned grey and lowering. It started to rain. As we headed up through the valley of the Sonomoro River towards Satipo we came on a small sodden Ashaninca family who had left San Antonio and were taking shelter in the fringes of the forest through which the road wound its way. They waved at us and we stopped. I recognised the man from the previous night's gathering: he had a large beaky nose, unusual among the regular-featured Ashaninca.

He and his wife and their two children climbed gratefully on board. He was carrying the barrel of a shotgun and a bundle tied up with reeds, and his wife held an iron pot in her arms: it was presumably her only possession of value. Their children were aged about two and four. The family had been among the refugees from Masuriniari, and the massacres there and in Nailan had unsettled them. Now they were leaving village life and the forest to try their luck in the town of Mazamari. The man's mother lived there, and he thought they could go and join her. It was clear he had no understanding whatever of the need for money and a job of some kind. Steve gave them a chocolate bar each, which they ate with relish. The younger child licked his slowly and appreciatively, and managed to get relatively little on his hands. Matt offered them raisins, which were closer to the kind of food they knew; they picked at them delicately. By now the rain was getting heavier. Our wheels threw up arcs of yellow-brown water as we lurched along the road between the walls of vegetation.

We arrived in San Martin de Pongoa, changed vehicles, and stopped by the café where we had loaded up the previous afternoon. The Ashaninca family mimed their thanks to us and jumped out into the pouring rain, their bare feet splashing in the puddles. They huddled into a shop doorway alongside half a dozen people in T-shirts and shoes, who were sheltering there. With their brown robes and bare legs they seemed pathetic and innocent; but they waved to us cheerfully enough and the boy, a slow eater, flourished what was left of his chocolate bar. The man raised his hand, palm towards us and fingers outspread, and when I looked round a good minute later he was still standing there, his hand raised. They had joined the exodus from the forest, and would be town indians from now on, rootless, perpetually bewildered, cut off from something they could never replace and never return to. Like the chocolate bar in the little boy's hand, their new life would be both addictive and unsatisfying.

We drove to the airfield in the drenching tropical rain. It was a depressing sight: one of the two planes we would need was unflyable, and the other could not take off until the rain and cloud lifted above the point where the hill directly in front of the runway was visible. When would that be? Maybe midday.

'I know where we should go,' said Sally.

We drove back into town and, guided by Sally, found ourselves in a street with a very steep camber, outside a questionable-looking café. The sign was, however, magnificent:

RESTAURANT 'MAZAMARI'
Carmen Burga de Pardini
THE ROSA NAUTICA OF SATIPO
offers its cordial attention to tourists, executives and
commercial travellers, with regional and
international dishes.

The Rosa Nautica was the rather grand restaurant on the pier
in Lima where we had had some of our most enjoyable meals.
In the pouring rain in Satipo it was hard to think there was any
similarity whatever; yet the place had a sleazy tropical style, all
the same.

It came from Dona Carmen Burga de Pardini herself, known
to everyone as Dona Carmela. When we arrived she was wearing
a dressing gown in red Chinese silk with a dragon embroidered
on the back; later she slipped away and changed in our honour
into vast pink silk trousers with white polka dots on them. Dona
Carmela looked like a Neapolitan, with her thick black hair striped
with grey, her heavy *jolie-laide* olive face, and her equally heavy
olive voice which sounded as though she had smoked cheroots all
her life.

We ordered fried yucca, plantains, eggs, lots of coffee and, for
everyone other than me, fish and steak. In the Rosa Nautica of
Satipo you eat in the kitchen, and we watched the slabs of beef
being sliced off and vast quantities of onions being chopped up
fine. Dona Carmela came and leant over us, the red silk dressing
gown hanging perilously open near my face, and told us about
the three well-to-do brothers who had come through the previous
week in a Landcruiser.

'They just disappeared along the road to San Ramon. The
Landcruiser was there all right, but they'd gone. I think they
were up to no good: poaching parrots and butterflies, I wouldn't
wonder. Their father came through yesterday. He was a real
gentleman. You don't get many like him nowadays.'

The silk dressing gown closed, and she moved away to say
something sharp to the cook.

Time passed. The sky was lightening, and Dona Carmela said
it would clear up by midday. We paid the bill and headed back to

the airstrip. The hills at the end of the runway were a great deal clearer now. Soon the raindrops ceased falling into the puddles on the runway, which were the colour of Dona Carmela's *cafe con leche*. The sun came out and made the whole forest steam. Someone wheeled a large plastic jerry can of fuel over to the Cessna that had been standing there, climbed a stepladder and poured it into the fuel tank. We had, meanwhile, worked out what we were going to do: Sally, Rory, Eamonn and Matt would take the Cessna to Puerto Bermudez, and Steve and I would film them taking off. Then we would wait for a light plane from San Ramon which would take us on to join them.

'You'll sleep in a bed tonight, Matt,' I said, in my capacity as a feeder of straight lines.

'Yeah,' he answered, 'me and ten thousand others.'

I hurried the pilot up: the weather was worsening again. He tried and failed to start the engine several times, until with a splutter and a nasty crack the single propellor started to turn. A donkey on the landing strip ambled indolently out of the Cessna's way. Steve and I took up a position at the far end of the runway and waited.

'I expect Eamonn's giving some last-minute instructions,' I hazarded.

'Such as strapping Matt to the undercarriage with a Video-8 [camera].' Then he added, 'And telling the pilot to lift off when he sees the whites of our eyes.'

As the Cessna took off, it passed the plane which had come from San Ramon to pick us up. Steve swung round to film it landing. It seemed to be coming in low: so low I thought it might be going to hit us. The pilot switched on his headlights to warn us to get out of the way.

'I think,' I said, more calmly than I felt, 'it's time for us to go.'

We threw ourselves to left and right of the camera tripod, and the plane's undercarriage passed over us. We were still laughing as we climbed aboard the plane five minutes later.

The forest stretched to the horizon on every side of us. There were occasional little clearings cut by the Ashaninca, whose huts on stilts we could clearly see from here. I looked at the propellor as we headed through the thick clouds of moisture which had been drawn up by the sun; if it faltered here, we would be dead men.

It didn't falter, though, and we arrived at Puerto Bermudez, another little town where the military had nothing to hide and were glad to see us, an hour or so later. We found Sally, Eamonn, Matt and Rory standing under a sign that read '*Estamos En Guerra*' – We Are At War – and headed out to see the Ashaninca *rondo* which was based in the area.

There was a hissing through the air, and arrow after arrow thumped into the cardboard box we had set up on a pole as a target. The Ashaninca archers had not been very keen on the exercise at first, but when they realised we wanted them to compete with one another they became more enthusiastic. Scarcely any of their arrows missed. In 1989, after the MRTA had killed one of their chiefs, the Ashanincas from this group attacked an MRTA camp and massacred virtually everyone they found. They forced them to run, then shot them down with their arrows. There was a ferocity about the Ashaninca which could easily be summoned up if necessary. When they did something, they took it seriously. For them, the regular forces were merely 'the Peruvian Army'. They called their own group 'the Army', just as they called themselves 'the real people'. Here in the Pichis Valley they ran everything; the Peruvian Army was merely there to see they did not get out of hand.

We bumped back to Puerto Bermudez under a crescent moon. Earthshine made the darkened bulk of the moon clearly visible, as in a drawing by Guaman Poma. The Hostal Triunfo did not have enough rooms for all of us, so Eamonn and I volunteered to move into the even less attractive Hostal Feliz Viaje next door. From the moment we went in, the Happy Journey Hostel seemed likely to provide us with an unhappy experience. A large rat ran across the landing as we went up to examine the rooms, and there was a powerful stench everywhere which showed there were bedbugs here. My room was horribly dirty, with holes in the party walls and in the worm-eaten floor, where the dirt lay encrusted in ridges.

I put up my mosquito net, and decided to sleep with all my clothes on, lying on my sleeping bag. I also burned two mosquito spirals, less because of the mosquitoes than to get rid of the smell. I put off the awful moment of lying down on the disgusting bed until the last possible moment. It is the only place where I have ever been kept awake by the smell.

Cuty Bareni

However barbarous they may have been, our ancestors had some glimmer of understanding of God... Christians have much to learn from our people's good way of life.

Felipe Guaman Poma de Ayala, 1613

In the unwholesome darkness, my radio began blaring 'Lilliburlero'. I had set the alarm for the 4 am BBC news. I thrashed around among the unfamiliar covers, taking in the fearful smell, and turned the volume down. In the rooms around and below mine I could hear noises of complaint, snoring, grunting. I located my torch while the calm voice of the BBC World Service newsreader announced what had been happening in Sarajevo and Phnom Penh. What had been happening in Puerto Bermudez was not news to anyone but me.

Through my clothes I could feel angry bumps on my chest, stomach and legs. Matt's ten thousand others had been at work. I took my clothes off, wrapped them in a plastic bag, and danced naked on the dirty floor, rubbing myself all over with Friction de Foucaud, a French colonial preparation which I buy in the Boulevard St Germain in Paris, and in whose claims to counteract all known tropical difficulties I place immense faith. In the darkness my skin felt corrugated with bites. I swore and knocked things over, and rolled up my mosquito net and my sleeping bag and put them in another, larger plastic bag. We would, with any luck, be back in Lima that evening: anything I couldn't wash I could burn. Bedbugs are nastier than fleas, and I had no desire to carry any around with me. I opened up the two plastic bags and squirted them long and viciously with insect repellent spray. After that I felt a little better, though my bites throbbed under my clean clothes.

The owner of the hotel dragged himself out of bed and charged me for my stay. I complained about the filth and the previous night's rat, and the bites. He shrugged his weary shoulders:

'*Dos soles, Senor.*'

Two soles was less than an English penny, but it was still too much. The man shrugged again: he was so dirty himself, he couldn't comprehend the notion of cleanliness.

I sat on a bench and watched the startling colours of a forest sunrise. Slowly the others made their appearance. Sally and Rory had shared a room in the slightly more acceptable hotel next door (it cost three soles, and was worth the difference). Their problem had been mosquitoes and the proximity of the communal lavatory. Apart from a slightly swollen eye from an insect bite, Sally had emerged from this dirty place looking as clean and coolly attractive as ever.

A few hours later our planes landed within a few minutes of each other at a little grass strip cut out of the forest: Cuty Bareni. Fifty or more Ashanincas stood guard on either side of us down the length of the runway, some with rifles, others with bows and arrows. The reception committee was even more exotic: a Franciscan friar, a couple of Army officers in uniform, and an Ashaninca with a feathered headdress. Each represented some aspect of the post at Cuty Bareni. It had begun as a hospital and school run by monks, but Shining Path forces had burned it down twice, in 1984 and 1989. The Army had moved in to protect it, and that had encouraged the Ashaninca from the surrounding area to move in and settle there. Now it was guarded by an Ashaninca *rondo*, with military support.

The sun was already growing hot as we laboured up the long steep path from the airstrip to the base on the bluffs above us.

'Look over there,' said the lieutenant who was guiding us. He pointed to a hilltop which emerged from the surrounding green of the forest. 'That's an observation post for Shining Path.' It was a little over a mile away.

'And there are plenty of terrorists nearer than that.'

This was not intended merely to frighten visitors, it was a statement of fact. Four days earlier a Shining Path group had crept up to the perimeter of the Cuty Bareni camp and poured rifle fire into it. I fought down the unworthy hope that something like that might happen while we were there, so that we could film it.

The military had assembled everyone for a flag-raising ceremony. A couple of hundred Ashaninca women were drawn up in lines on one side, moving around and unable to understand what it was all about. Many had babies with them, and the sun was hot. A sheep moved up and nuzzled the feet of one of them, and she giggled. The men, drawn up alongside them with rifles or bows and arrows, seemed as uncomprehending as the women. It was like a religion to which they had been forcibly converted: the rituals of faith were followed to the letter, but without the slightest notion that they might mean anything.

A junior officer, his eyes fixed fiercely ahead of him, his neck bulging his collar, goose-stepped towards the flagpole in the centre of the parade ground carrying the folded flag of Peru. Behind him, a line of little Ashaninca men armed with shotguns also goose-stepped in bare feet, their soles slapping the ground, their satchels swinging, their *kushmas* whipping up round their knees. The goose-step, which arrived in South America from eighteenth-century Prussia (where it was designed to show that soldiers were not men of flesh and blood who might feel pain or tiredness, but military automata who could put up with anything), is always mildly ludicrous; here in the depths of the primeval forest, when performed by tribesmen newly arrived from the Stone Age, it achieved a high level of absurdity.

There was something reminiscent in all this of the Requirement which the King of Spain ordered the conquistadors to read before they took possession of territory or attacked some group of indigenous inhabitants:

> I request and require you . . . to acknowledge the Church as your Mistress and as Governor of the World and the Universe, and the High priest, called the Pope, in Her name, and His Majesty in Her place, as Ruler and King. . .

If the indians ignored this, any action the conquistadors might then take was held, not only to be justified, but also to be the fault of the natives. Since the Requirement was usually read in Spanish to people who had never previously seen a European, the outcome was predictable.

The red and white Peruvian flag was run up, to the accompaniment of chanting: '¡Arriba! ¡Arriba! ¡Arriba El Peru!' Then came the national anthem of a country the Ashaninca did not know they were citizens of. The Peruvian soldiers sang it lustily, the small Ashaninca children who had been here several months sang it with a fine squeaking sound, but the older children and the adults did not sing it at all. The junior officer's eyes bulged even further in an access of patriotism.

While the others were filming, the Franciscan, Brother Jaime Paradis, showed Sally and me round his sickbay. At present it was mostly empty, though only a few weeks before they had had twenty-five deaths here from white men's diseases: smallpox, chicken pox, cholera. Between them, Brother Jaime and the Army major had established the camp on better and more hygienic lines. Too many Ashanincas were packed into it, but they could not be turned away.

I talked later to the captain, a weary, careful man in his late thirties who loved the Ashaninca and told admiring stories about their skills in the forest.

'It's the Ashanincas who do the real work,' he said. 'They know where the subversives are. Every time we go out on patrol, we bring back more Ashanincas who have been kidnapped and held prisoner in the subversives' camps. They tell us where we should go.'

He looked across the valley at the hilltop which had already been pointed out to me.

'We know there's a big base there, and a school as well. That means they're holding plenty of Ashaninca children. It'll be a big operation, when we take that. But we'll do it. They used to be stronger and better equipped than we were, but now we get a helicopter in with supplies every month. That's tipped the balance in our favour.'

A group of Ashaninca ex-prisoners was assembled for us under the shade of a group of trees by the kitchen tents: small, nervous men who looked to each other for support. They had been rescued by a patrol the day before, and told us contradictory stories about the murders of other Ashanincas which they had witnessed in the Shining Path camp where they had been held. Bertha, translating for us, was imperious:

'Ashaninca, tell us how you were captured.' 'Ashaninca, what did you see when these men were killed?'

Each man insisted that others had done the murders, and that he himself had merely watched. It was clear that all of them had been forced to take part. The Ashanincas who stood round listening understood this, but said nothing. Perhaps they did not want to dishonour their tribe in front of outsiders. The ex-prisoners were small, miserable victims, men who had lacked the courage and loyalty of the twelve-year-olds we had interviewed at San Antonio two nights earlier. They were not formally punished: it wasn't necessary. The fact that the other Ashanincas knew what they had done was enough.

We said our goodbyes and stood sweltering on the grass airstrip, waiting for the second of our two planes to come in. The insects shrilled in the grass, and flew up at every step we took. The Ashaninca were once more lined up along the edges of the runway; now we knew how close the Shining Path positions were, we understood why. The plane, like a larger insect, waggled its wings and came in fast and low. When it was still twenty feet above the ground a shot rang out from the forest. The Ashaninca peered around unsuccessfully for a target to fire back at.

Eamonn and Steve and I had a hurried consultation: given that we might well be fired on as we left, should Sally and Rory go out in the first plane or the second one? In the end we decided that the two of them, plus Matt, should travel in the first one, since the second was likely to attract more accurate fire. As we stood and watched, their plane gathered speed. It lifted off; still no sound of gunfire. Our plane followed, ten minutes later. If there was any shooting then, we didn't hear it.

Beneath lay the forest like a sea, the trees too close to allow a view of the forest floor. Sometimes we were low enough to see the parrots flying over the forest canopy, no doubt screeching nervously at us. I shifted uneasily in my seat, feeling the previous night's bites. I wanted to get back to Lima, where I could douse them in neat alcohol: the best antidote to bedbug bites, according to Bertha.

I watched her now, as she stared down at the forest where her people had come from. Her Ashaninca features, the high cheekbones, the almond eyes, the flat nose, the delicate gold skin, were indistinguishable from those of the rest of her tribe. Yet as we flew over the forest and headed gradually towards Lima, Bertha somehow seemed to lose her indian characteristics. She knew how to operate in the big city; she had made the break with the life of the forest. The others might have trouble understanding what money was, and how you got work; Bertha understood it all very well.

As for the rest of the Ashaninca, their old life was slowly being stripped away. Unthinkably vast though the forest was, the outside world had ways of penetrating it, by means of terrorism, money, guns, pollution, clearances, and the spread of little towns like San Martin de Pongoa, where I had come across the lost Ashaninca with his three children, and had said goodbye to the family we had given a lift to. I had seen the last of the Ashaninca for the time being. There was no indication when I might see them again; nor how much of their old life might have vanished in the meantime.

PART VI

HEART OF DARKNESS

A Spanish priest and a civilian attack two indians.

Villa Hermosa

The city of Lima was full of Indians who had fled from
their villages and were living on their wits... It was as if
the world were turned upside down.

Felipe Guaman Poma de Ayala, 1613

It was the most dreadful place I had ever seen; worse than
the slums of Kinshasa and the *favelas* of Brazil, worse than the
worst of Cairo or Delhi. There, at least, people had a sort of pride
and a sort of hope. Some optimist, an early settler, maybe, or a
local government official, had named this place Villa Hermosa,
the beautiful town. Its inhabitants had nothing, and no hope of
any kind. Here you felt ashamed to be human. The inhabitants
had become insensitive to suffering and ugliness, and no one cared
about them. They were stray pieces of wreckage from the social
and political disaster of Peru, which had collected in this corner
as pieces of a broken boat might collect at a bend in a river. They
had come to Villa Hermosa because they had nothing and were
nothing, and the Peruvian government cared less than nothing
about them.

We had made the hour-long journey from Lima to examine
the results of a Shining Path massacre. It had taken place two
weeks after the arrest of Guzman, and seemed to indicate that
Shining Path was still an important presence in the shantytowns.
Its violence was just another of the burdens that the people of
Villa Hermosa had to bear, as insidious and unseen as cholera,
as frightening as the criminals who preyed on people at night, as
certain as dirt and hunger and ignorance.

What had happened was simple. A teenaged boy had made
the mistake of robbing a Shining Path bagman. The next night
the organisation's enforcers had come round and murdered the

boy's parents and every male over the age of twelve in the family as an exemplary punishment. For two days the front pages of the Lima newspapers were full of it. They wanted to show how savage Shining Path still was, in the aftermath of its leader's arrest. The reports were full of words like 'tragedy' and 'pitiful victims'.

On the day of the funeral we went to the house where the murders had taken place. No one from the Lima press had bothered to turn up for it. For the newspapers, the real interest lay in its propaganda value, not in the people who had died and certainly not in those who had survived. Now the propaganda value had been thoroughly milked. We pushed our way through a crowd of noisy, excited onlookers into the hut made of plaited reeds where the Fuentes family had lived. It stank of sweat and alcohol and unwashed, musty clothes. The floor was just the sandy floor of the desert.

On the wall, a coloured picture from a magazine hung crookedly in a broken frame. It showed a little girl feeding a lamb from a baby's feeding bottle. 'El Amor', said the inscription underneath: Love. The little girl was white and slender and ethereal; the Fuentes, judging from those whom Shining Path had spared, were short, wide-shouldered, swarthy indians.

The coffins were set out, side by side, at the end of the hut: two large ones for the father and mother, two medium-sized ones for the eldest son and the teenager whose robbery had led to this massacre, and a small one for the twelve-year-old whose death had been an afterthought by the Shining Path killers. The coffins were carelessly painted white, and looked as though they might fall apart. Yet they had cost serious money for a Villa Hermosa family: they were fitted with glass panels, so you could see the bodies inside but not smell them. Their nostrils were stuffed carelessly with cotton wool, and they would not last unburied much longer.

The children's grandmother had just arrived, and was weeping noisily in the corner, her nose red and running. A little crumpled dark woman in her late fifties, she had had to pawn her coat and ring and some of her cooking implements in order to get the money for the fare from the Fuentes' village in the highlands. It was unlikely that she would ever find the money to redeem them.

Around the edges of the room people were drinking. Someone dropped a bottle, and it smashed on the hard sandy ground. There was cursing and mumbling, and the man who had dropped it staggered a little. A tear trickled down his face, the deaths and the loss of the bottle muddling together in his brain.

Two of the survivors of the massacre, a boy of six and a girl of ten, hung around their grandfather. The boy's name was William. The Shining Path enforcers had pulled him out of bed by his hair and thrown him out of the house while they murdered the others. His sister, who was called Raquel, was small for her age. She chewed at her fingers and her eyes were swollen. I knelt down to speak to William as he stood holding his grandfather's hand. Frightened by me, he burrowed his head into the old man's stomach. Noisily and unchecked, the old man snuffled and wept.

The children's mother, Gloria Canacho, was forty when Shining Path killed her: an old woman already. She washed clothes for a living. Her husband Jhon – a common misspelling in Peru – was forty-three, and earned what he could by looking after the parked cars at a hospital. They had eleven children altogether, three of whom had been murdered with them. The others were digging the mass grave at the cemetery nearby.

The cemetery was called Paradiso: another joke. When the people from the Beautiful Town died, they went to Paradise. It lay on an open hillside overlooking Villa Hermosa, with Lima some ten miles away on the horizon: as desolate a place as any on earth. A rubbish-tip further up the hill leaked down towards the cemetery like lava from a dirty volcano. There was a smell of decaying bodies from the cheap temporary vaults like filing cabinets, where space could be rented for a couple of years until the flesh had rotted and the bones could be disposed of more easily.

The graves here, mostly shaped out of cement to look like little churches, lasted longer than anything: longer than the bodies, longer than the reed huts where they lived. This was the eternity Paradise offered, an eternity which had to be protected with messages painted casually and ungrammatically on the graves: 'PROHIBID VOTAR BASURA', Do not throw rubbish; 'RESPETE EL DIFUNTO GRACIAS', Respect the dead, thank you. Down below us lay the latest offshoot from the main body of

Villa Hermosa, like a cancerous extrusion. A water-cart trundled through the streets of straw-plaited huts, blasting its horn at intervals; this area had been desert until a year or so before, and there was no other source of water. A cockerel stood on a heap of refuse and answered back gamely.

Eight grave-diggers were at work on the bare hillside. They had chosen a place a little removed from the main cemetery, within twenty feet of the closest approach of the lava stream of rubbish from higher up. We had to tread carefully: the ground was liberally covered with human shit, lying dark and neatly curled in the dusty soil. The plots must have been cheap here, and within a year no amount of appeals to respect the dead would protect the Fuentes family from disappearing under the flow. Garbage thou art, and unto garbage shalt thou return.

The professional grave-diggers were laughing drunk, and passed a bottle of red wine from hand to hand and mouth to mouth. Those who were family kept on digging, but they were incompetent and slow, and the line of mourners soon arrived by bus from Villa Hermosa, dogs and children dancing around them. The gimcrack coffins were brought up the hillside at ludicrous angles, the bodies shifting visibly behind the glass hatches, and dumped on to trestles set in the rubbish while the digging continued. Now the wooden crosses which would serve instead of headstones came bobbing up cheerfully over the heads of the crowd, marked 'Gloria Canacho Oliva', 'Jhon Fuentes Canacho', 'Omar Fuentes Canacho', 'Victor Fuentes Canacho', 'Horacio Fuentes Canacho'.

One of the grave-diggers giggled. The mourners' footsteps threw up little puffs of colourless desert dust. Nearby a man had set down a big rubbish bin of orange plastic, and was selling InkaCola and biscuits from it. Someone else was selling spring onions. People clambered on to the graves to get a better view, dropping the empty drinks cans and the wrappers from the biscuits on to the graves marked *RESPETE EL DIFUNTO*. In a place where no one respected the living, why should they respect the dead?

Now it was almost too late, the grave-diggers went to it with a will; even the drunken ones. The old grandmother who had pawned her things to get here began the ritual weeping; other members of the family were still laughing and talking. A young boy took the dead flowers from a nearby grave and used them to sweep some of the excess dust away from around the old woman's feet. The cockerel below us crowed in answer to the hooting of the water-truck, dogs rooted in the sand, a man flicked a cigarette butt away and shouted 'Mario!' at an acquaintance, a little girl kicked the pink plastic smiling head of a broken doll into a rubbish-tip. In the midst of life we are in death, and vice versa.

We looked round with some care at the faces surrounding us. We had seen our main Shining Path contact the previous night, and she had told us that someone would come up to us at the funeral and explain on camera why the Fuentes family had been murdered. Our contact had explained it to us in private already, with the beatific smile of the believer:

'I am glad they were eliminated. They were robbers from the Lumpenproletariat. The Party is the people, so robbing the Party is robbing the people.' No one made contact with us. For the time being, nothing came of any arrangement Shining Path made. Nothing, that is, except the exemplary murder of a family from the Lumpenproletariat whose members robbed to keep themselves alive.

A priest in a blue sweater and yellow shirt appeared late. He seemed to know nothing of what was going on, and kept whispering questions to someone beside him. When he came to read the burial service over the open grave he gabbled the familiar words, scarcely articulating them, and then paused before each of the names of the dead to read them off the crosses. He stumbled badly over 'Jhon' and 'Omar'. It was an obvious relief to him when he could pack away his stole and book and head off to a safer task.

A black plastic bag blew down the hillside and wrapped itself around my foot. The stink and the depression were starting to trouble us all now. The grave-diggers began with a will to fill in the jagged hole they had dug, unloading the fine light sand on to the white coffins. Someone had closed up the hatches, and the sand rattled on to them like rain on a roof. Soon clouds of it billowed up and hid it all – grave, diggers, crowd, garbage. The nephew of one of the family members came up to us at the end and told us his uncle was insisting that we had promised him a hundred soles when we interviewed him, and hadn't paid it. We had. But the boy was crying, and although I knew it was just another shakedown I handed it over all the same. What was left of the Fuentes family might be chisellers and small-time crooks, but they needed a hundred soles more than we did.

I looked back at the terrible hillside as we threaded our way between the rubbish-strewn graves. The family and associated onlookers were still gathered round the new gash in the sandy soil: I could hear an occasional high drunken laugh. The Fuentes, and tens of thousands like them in Villa Hermosa, were more alone than almost anyone else on earth. No one, not even all the members of the Fuentes family, cared whether they lived or died: not the priest, who didn't know their names; not the police, who didn't bother to patrol the shantytowns; not the press, which hadn't bothered to report their funeral; not the government, which had deliberately withdrawn from any attempt to educate, feed or administer Villa Hermosa and other places like it; certainly not Shining Path, which had nothing but contempt for the dregs of society which clustered here. Shining Path's notion that the Fuentes were just Lumpenproletariat was common to almost everyone. They thought so themselves; their ideal was the picture of the little white girl, so different from themselves in every way, who fed the lamb in the picture on their wall.

The stench of garbage, the sound of drunken laughter and hooting trucks and cockerels, the dirty taste of sand and decay, stayed with us we drove away. I couldn't get some things out of my mind: the little daughter gnawing her fingers, the ugly old woman who had pawned everything she could spare in order to be with her family. 'Am I not a man, and a brother?' I quoted to myself, for the second time since I came to Peru.

Lima

The administrator said in reply that he had no intention of altering his conduct. He was on good terms with the Viceroy... He also enjoyed the favour of the secretary to the Government, so he had nothing to fear from any quarter.

Felipe Guaman Poma de Ayala, 1613

Our time in Peru was coming to an end. It was Saturday now, and we had to leave by the night of the following Wednesday if our reports were to be edited and broadcast by the time we had planned. Eamonn and I sat and talked it over, and the best thing seemed to be for Eamonn to go back on the Monday to make the necessary arrangements in London, leaving us to get the few remaining sequences we needed. And there remained the question of Vladimiro Montesinos.

The man whom President Fujimori insisted was just another civil servant seemed to bulk larger and larger as our time in Peru passed. We had gained a considerable understanding of the links between some sections of the Peruvian Army and the drugs trade. We had seen something of the links between political power and Peruvian intelligence. It was easy to point to the apparently dubious fact that the President owed his election in 1990 to a man who had managed the acquittal of leading figures in the drugs trade, and of senior military men accused of human rights abuses. To go any farther than that was difficult. Yet we would have to go farther if we were to make a report about the real workings of politics in Peru.

One problem was the shortage of pictures of Montesinos himself. There was the famous black and white still, the only one from the past quarter-century which was known to exist, taken by a photographer from the magazine *Caretas* outside a police station in 1983. It wasn't much, but at least it meant we had an image of the man. We knew of two people who might be prepared to talk to us about him: the Vice President, Maximo San Roman, who had broken with President Fujimori when he suspended the constitution; and a leading figure in the intelligence community. And there was one other thing: we knew where Montesinos lived. We decided to start there.

A couple of hundred yards from us, the block of flats whose entire top floor Montesinos occupied dominated the skyline. We anticipated a certain amount of difficulty; things happened to people who tried to get too close to Montesinos. We had worked out a strategy: I would record a piece to camera quite openly, standing on a grassy central reservation in the middle of a large suburban avenue with the building in the background. Then we would get close to it in some way. Then ... but we hadn't yet worked out stage three.

I sat on a wall in the warm sunshine and wrote the piece to camera, getting the grammar right and checking that I hadn't said anything inaccurate or libellous. It was painfully long; standing out in the open to record it would feel like standing on the lip of a trench during the Battle of the Somme. I read it through:

> To call Vladimiro Montesinos 'shadowy' is a serious understatement. He is the invisible man of Peruvian politics. Senior figures in the government are deeply afraid of him; yet not even most Cabinet ministers have actually set eyes on him. He began his career as an Army officer, was dismissed, turned to the law and specialised in defending senior military men who were in trouble over human rights charges – and people accused of drugs trafficking. The way he won his cases is often regarded here as deeply questionable. His last big drugs case was in 1989; by the following year he'd become President Fujimori's *éminence grise*.

I checked it for the last time. It was a former minister who had told me he and others who were still in the Cabinet were deeply afraid of Montesinos, and that they'd never seen him. The history of his career was partly a matter of public record. I would have liked to go into the question of his dismissal from the Army, but the piece to camera was already too long. The legal cases in which he had appeared were well known, and I had spoken to more than a dozen people who thought the judgements in them were questionable. As for his precise role now, I skated over it by calling him President Fujimori's *éminence grise*.

It took me four attempts to record it properly. Just as we finished, a smart new black jeep drew up. Several men with guns got out, their faces hidden by balaclava helmets. They looked extremely tough, but they were not in any hurry. Those, I reflected, were the dangerous ones; the ones who get excited are easier to deal with. Steve walked towards the jeep and put the camera down on the ground. It was still running, and he stood almost, but not quite, in front of it. The resulting picture showed a certain amount of pavement, and of Steve's boot. Otherwise it was commendably clear.

'Are you in charge of this group?' asked one of the men in black. He had taken off his balaclava to speak, and his features looked Japanese. In a country where the President himself was Japanese, that was not impossible. I admitted that I was, and handed him my Peruvian press card. Then I started asking him questions; Matt had equipped me with a small radio microphone, hidden in my shirt, for just such a situation as this. The Japanese answered politely, and walked over to the vehicle with my card and talked into the jeep's radio.

'Is OK,' he said, coming back. 'The Navy know all about you.'

'But I still don't understand. Why did you stop us filming in this area? What is it about this area that makes it so special?'

'It is not possible to be here, filming.'

'But you've stopped us in our work. You might explain a little about this, because it would be interesting to us.'

No doubt; but he wouldn't say anything more.

He got back into the jeep. Steve picked up the camera and filmed as it drove off. I thought this was mildly risky, but Matt had already taken the previous video cassette out of the camera and replaced it with another, so that even if the jeep came back and we were arrested we would probably not lose our pictures. We still did not understand how the jeep's occupants had known what we were doing. I glanced round. Two gardeners on the central reservation were sitting down and watching us. They looked away quickly. Now we realised that each stretch of central reservation within half a mile of Montesinos' block of flats had a pair of gardeners who, if you looked closer, never seemed to do any gardening; and unlike most Peruvian gardeners, they were wearing wristwatches. Montesinos' guards were doing to us what General Vidal had done to Abimael Guzman.

We drove slowly past the block of flats. The drive was choked with cars, each of which had a man sitting behind the driver's seat. Steve spotted a Kentucky Fried Chicken place nearby, so we stopped there for a little and ate something. When we came out, two men were standing talking. Both of them looked to me like secret policemen. As we walked past, one of the men reached into his leather jacket, perhaps for a walkie- talkie. I turned and saw the movement. He changed it awkwardly into an effort to scratch his chest. I kept my eyes on him for a long time; he had to keep on scratching.

Across the street, meanwhile, someone got out of a taxi.

'I think,' said Steve, who a few moments earlier had felt that I was seeing secret policemen where none existed, 'that's the first time in my life I've seen a taxi drop someone at a bus stop.'

We looked across the road. The man who had got out of the taxi, and was now queuing for a bus, was keeping a careful eye on us.

Perhaps none of this should have surprised us. Vladimiro Montesinos was an important figure, who knew most of the secrets of the Fujimori presidency. It would have been disastrous for the President if the Shining Path, or the MRTA, or any other terrorist group, had kidnapped or murdered him. Even so, I could not remember seeing such a display of security before; not with Margaret Thatcher, not with Ronald Reagan after the assassination attempt on him, not with Mikhail Gorbachev. And this was not the head of a government, but a civil servant.

Montesinos came originally from the charming colonial city of Arequipa, in the south of the country. His father was one of twenty-one brothers, and although the family was moderately well-to-do Montesinos' father slipped down the social scale and was permanently embittered by the experience. It turned him into something of a Marxist, and he named his son after Vladimir Ilyich Lenin. At fourteen the young Vladimiro went to military college, and soon showed he was quick-witted and intelligent. He went on to the country's War College, and later reached the rank of captain.

When the military took over the government under General Juan Velasco Alvarado in 1968, Montesinos was made private secretary to General Mercado, who was negotiating with the Russians to buy weapons. The Velasco government was anti-American and moderately pro-Soviet, and there were plans to build a military base with Soviet money. The documents dealing with the base were taken by Montesinos. Mercado called together everyone who might have had access to the papers and told them that whoever had taken them should get up and leave the room.

Montesinos did so, but he told Mercado afterwards that he had merely gathered the papers together to familiarise himself with them. Mercado sacked him as his private secretary, but did not insist that he should be cashiered from the Army. Not long afterwards Montesinos was invited to attend a conference in the United States; as a result of the incident over the documents he was forbidden to go. There have been suggestions that even at this stage he had become a CIA 'asset', though it has never been proved. In 1976, when he returned to Lima, a military court gaoled Montesinos because he represented a potential risk to national security.

He turned even this to his advantage. In prison he studied for and obtained a law degree by correspondence course. After his release he began defending people accused of drugs offences, including a number of police officers charged as a result of the so-called Villa Coca drugs-smuggling case in 1985. He also defended Army officers charged with abuses against human rights. He won most of his cases, and his power and influence grew accordingly. When, during the 1990 election campaign, Alberto Fujimori was accused of withholding tax on the rents from thirty-two houses which he and his wife owned, he hired Montesinos to represent him. A large part of the paperwork in the case then disappeared somewhere in the Ministry of Justice, and Montesinos succeeded in converting the case from a criminal court to a civil one. It was no longer a question of whether Fujimori was innocent or guilty of tax-avoidance, but merely of how much he should pay. He did not have to withdraw from the presidential race, and went on to score his stunning victory over Mario Vargas Llosa.

He owed his success to one man, and that man started to become very powerful indeed. Montesinos was made deputy director of SIN, the national intelligence service, the day after Fujimori was elected. The following day, some fifty senior police officers were sacked. Many of them had gathered the evidence in the Villa Coca case. By March 1992 Montesinos was being publicly accused of clearing out his opponents in the Justice Ministry, the judiciary, and the armed forces, and replacing them with men loyal to himself. The new appointees had the clear impression that they owed their jobs directly to Montesinos.

When, twenty months after his inauguration, President Fujimori staged his *autogolpe* and suspended the constitution, Montesinos was the go-between who ensured the support of the armed forces. Most people in political life believed, indeed, that the whole thing had been done on his advice. He used the new powers available to him in order to weed out the files in the Justice Ministry. An enterprising photographer working for the magazine *Caretas* waited outside the Palace of Justice and got a picture of large numbers of documents being dropped from a balcony into the back of a pick-up truck.

The assumption was that anything embarrassing to Montesinos or to President Fujimori disappeared during this spring-cleaning. According to one estimate, details of ten thousand cases out of a total of thirty thousand simply vanished. A senior judge told us that the paperwork for several important drugs trials had also disappeared. The *Miami Herald* reported after the *autogolpe* that Montesinos had reinforced the position of military officers who were linked to the drugs trade, and of judges who were known to be lenient towards drugs traffickers. It seems likely that Montesinos had been in close contact with the CIA since the early

1970s, and perhaps since the incident of the missing documents in the Ministry of Energy and Mines.

We managed to obtain some pictures which would act as evidence for some of these ideas; for instance, we bought a copy of the black-and-white photograph which showed the documents being dropped from the balcony of the Palace of Justice into the pick-up truck. What we really needed, though, was interviews with people whose word would carry conviction; and there was considerable difficulty in getting them. A former government minister who had resigned because of the growing influence of Montesinos promised that he would take part in an interview; yet whenever we rang him, day after day, he was always travelling, or in meetings, or at home, and would always ring us back. He never did. In the end, with some contempt, we gave up asking.

The best prospect seemed to be the Vice President, Maximo San Roman, who had broken with Fujimori over the *autogolpe* and according to the constitution had the right to assume the powers of the presidency. San Roman had been fairly outspoken in the past, but as the protests against Fujimori declined, so had San Roman's influence. He too seemed very nervous about meeting us.

We had to wait for forty minutes at his office before his vast black official car swept through the quiet side street and up to the front door. San Roman looked like a Daumier cartoon: he was entirely pear-shaped, with the tiny feet of a truly fat man, and large pudgy hands. His hair was deep black and shiny, and he had the face of an Inca: large, broad and fleshy. He was dressed in a dark double-breasted suit and a superb silk tie.

I was annoyed that he should be so late and yet not apologise. I was further annoyed by the fact that he shook my hand without looking at me, and that he should have ignored Matt altogether. But he was a friend of Cecilia's, and she and Rosalind had put a great deal of effort into getting him to see us. Now Rosalind set out to charm him. He began by refusing to confirm that he had even said things which had been quoted in the press, but Rosalind chivvied him and lured him on, and eventually, with some grace, he agreed to talk about Montesinos. Once that barrier had been crossed, things became a great deal easier.

'Fujimori,' said San Roman, choosing his words carefully, 'is the personification, the front man, of this regime. But behind him there is a team working twenty-four hours a day. I want to denounce them, and warn my people that we are in the hands of a group of people who don't necessarily have the best interests of our country at heart, and are linked with the drug-trafficking mafia.

'Montesinos has all the power on some occasions, and I want to confirm this now, that Fujimori seems like a puppet of Montesinos. Unless a speech has been written, checked or revised by Montesinos, he doesn't make it. He doesn't move, or transfer, or change one soldier unless this has the blessing of, or is the suggestion of, Montesinos. I think everything is in his hands; which is why I have called him the shadow power.'

'We've noticed many times,' I said, 'that senior politicians, people like yourself, are actually frightened of Montesinos. Why is this?'

'I think they're right to be afraid, because many things have occurred which directly implicate this gentleman in barbaric actions.'

'Including murder?'

'Yes, of course. My country is run by a mafia tied up with drugs-trafficking.'

Courage can come in all sorts of forms, and maybe one of them is susceptibility to flattery. It was brave of him to have agreed to my statement, whatever his reasons for doing so. Soon afterwards he left, and we started packing up the gear. I was worried, however, that he might change his mind and tell us he didn't want us to use the interview after all; especially when he rang his secretary from his car-phone and told us to stand by for a message from him. Maybe, I thought, he might come back and demand the cassette from us. So while the others finished up I put the two tapes of the interview in my pockets and went for a walk in the gathering dark. After fifteen minutes of pacing up and down in the silent, unlit streets I heard the sound of Johnny's minibus. He flashed his lights at me and I climbed in.

The message that we had been asked to stand by for had never come.

The following day we had another clandestine meeting. Cecilia had many contacts in Peru's intelligence community. Her work on the Army's involvement with drugs had put her in touch with a whole range of people who had been prepared to speak to her secretly about what was going on: some from motives of revenge, others because they genuinely disapproved of the way the Army, and people like Montesinos, were behaving. Now she had tracked down perhaps her highest level contact, and persuaded him to talk to us on camera.

When he came in, he was a forbidding sight. Judging merely from his appearance, I felt it was likely that he was motivated more by a desire for revenge against Montesinos than by the altruistic desire to uncover evil. The more I listened to him, the more I felt I was right. Nevertheless his relationship with Cecilia was founded on a respect for her ability, which I liked, and he seemed to believe that she was doing the right thing by making public Montesinos's links with drug-trafficking and murder.

Our interviewee made all sorts of demands about how he was to be shown. In the end, we made triply sure by silhouetting him against net curtains, and then disguising his voice to a Mickey Mouse squeak, and blocking out his head with moving squares of colour. Yet having committed himself to doing the interview, he took no further interest in how we showed his features. He seemed to trust us completely.

I tried out on him some of the information we had received from others.

'It's been suggested,' I said, 'that Montesinos rents out a house which is used in the manufacture of coca paste.'

'Yes,' said the interviewee, 'and not only one. Montesinos has more than six houses available to him: safe houses, houses for his personal use, and an unknown number which I assume are linked to drug-trafficking. And the important and sinister link in this chain is a former classmate of Montesinos, who was put in charge of the drugs control office which has custody of the drugs seized by the police. He has pretended to burn these drugs, but in fact they have been put back into circulation. What he burns is flour. But you should not think that Montesinos has been bought by the big drugs men; on the contrary, he is the one who manipulates them.

'Montesinos is at the centre of a clearing-house for information. His men listen to two hundred telephone calls a day, and he gets the full details. Then he gives an abstract of the information to Fujimori.'

Would our phone calls be listened to?

'You can be absolutely certain your calls have been listened to.'

I turned to the question of Montesinos's supposed control over murder gangs.

'Montesinos inspires fear because he doesn't show his face. He can order an attack and you won't know where it'll come from ... Montesinos, via Army intelligence, handles a team of agents which we could call Special Operations, but which in reality take on dirty intelligence work. They make individuals disappear if they are ordered to make them disappear. The killing of people at the meeting in Barrios Altos last year was directly carried out by these agents, and was directly the work of Montesinos.'

The Barrios Altos massacre took place in 1991, at a party. Army intelligence believed that Abimael Guzman was at the party, and a group of men dressed entirely in black and armed with handguns fitted with silencers raided the house where it was taking place. They fired indiscriminately into the room for several minutes, killing fourteen people outright. Six later died in hospital. Guzman was not there.

Our interviewee was now in hiding: he knew too much, he said. Yet he remained admirably jaunty. Just before he left, he reminded us not to give any clues to his identity or his whereabouts, and he sang a little song, once popular in Peru: '¡Que no quede huella, que no, que no!': Don't leave any traces, oh no, oh no!'

He was still whistling it as he left.

Judging by the nervousness shown even by a man like this, an experienced intelligence operative with friends in high places, we were getting close to the heart of things in Peru. As we slipped out of the place where we had filmed him, and Johnny gunned up the minibus's engine, I remembered the question I had put the evening before to Maximo San Roman.

'To sum up,' I had said, speaking carefully and slowly, 'Peru is in the hands of a man who carries out murders, is a drugs trafficker, and whose control over the President is based on the President's own moral failings.' There was a long silence. Damn, I thought, I've gone too far: he's going to back away from that and I shall have wrecked everything. But San Roman was thinking, weighing up each of the things I had said. Finally he spoke. '*Efectivamente*,' he said: 'Precisely.'

Huacho

Strangers within any particular community, who feel themselves to be outcasts, abused and ill-treated by everybody,
without any living soul to whom they can turn in their
trouble. . .

Felipe Guaman Poma de Ayala, 1613

We stood on the top of a barren hillside, with nothing
except grey-brown sand and a few artificial patches of
tended green for twenty miles. It might have been Central Asia.
Across the desert of the coastal plain the wind was whistling sharp
and chilly around us. In the foreground were the ruins of a few
houses made of sun-dried brick: they looked as timeless as Inca
temples. Instead, they were the ruins of someone's life.

'Or the ruins of Peru,' Cecilia murmured.

Three months earlier, at three o'clock on the morning of 24 June
1992, three cars had made the bumpy journey up the hill in the
dark from the nearby town of Huacho. Ten men and a woman,
all of them armed and most of them in military uniform, were in
them. At the top of the hill the cars stopped and they jumped out.
Six of them went to the two houses that were now in ruins. The
rest went to the main house. A man carrying a torch beat on the
door.

'Documents,' he shouted at the bewildered woman who had
opened the door, a coat over her nightgown.

The houses all belonged to the Ventocilla family, who had
bought this barren spot twenty years earlier and used it at first
as a holiday home. The Ventocillas were of indian descent, but
they were well educated. Indeed, the women and children moved
here from the small mountain town of Oyon, in the north of the

department of Lima, because they thought the schools would be better. They were supporters of the maverick left-wing president Alan Garcia, Alberto Fujimori's predecessor. The head of the family, Rafael Ventocilla, had been mayor of Oyon for ten years, but decided to leave the town because of the threats he was receiving from Shining Path. Two of his sons were teachers. The hilltop settlement outside Huacho seemed a safe and pleasant place to bring up the family.

The men smashed their way through the houses, throwing things on the ground, kicking down cupboard doors, taking anything they thought might have resale value. They pushed the sleepy, bewildered people around but did no great damage to them. The women and children were taken into a separate room and kept there; the woman who had come with the group kept assuring them that nothing serious would happen, that it would all be over very soon, that there was nothing to cry about. When the group left, an hour or so later, they took the men with them: Rafael Ventocilla Rojas, the ex-mayor, who was 59; his younger brother, Marino Ventocilla Rojas; his three sons, Alejandro, Simon and Paulino, who were all in their thirties; and his grandson, Ruben, who was 17.

The next day the women went down to Huacho to seek the help of the police. The police said there was nothing they could do. A few days afterwards, a group of peasants discovered six bodies lying in a field, covered with quicklime. They had all been shot, and they all bore the marks of torture. The bodies were those of the men of the Ventocilla family. The women came down to identify them, and arrange for the funeral. Then they went back up to the hilltop alone, and withdrew into the biggest of the houses. Because they had nothing to live on, they had to sell things; little by little, their furniture, their jewellery, their books, their household goods were stripped away.

The wind was strong, as we approached the house. Somewhere far away a dog was barking; otherwise there was no sound but the wind, and our own footsteps. The house was like a fort, with a high fence of sticks around it to protect the little garden inside from marauding animals. A carefully tended vine grew up the walls. The windows were blocked with loose bricks.

'There's no one here,' I said.

But the lawyer from a human rights organisation in Lima who had come with us called out: 'Dona Catalina.'

There was a noise inside, and the gate of sticks was dragged to one side. An old peasant woman stood in the entrance, dressed in traditional fashion: her hair, still black, divided into two braids and joined behind; a large black skirt over several petticoats, indian-style, with blue leggings. Her full name, Dona Catalina Castilla de Leon, sounded so grand that I had expected to see a Spanish lady standing there. Instead, the disaster which had overcome her entire family had made her revert to indian ways. Dona Catalina's eyes were red, and she seemed to care nothing for who we were or why we had come. Four grandchildren held on to her skirts and looked at us round them; another was inside, looking after the sixth, a baby.

One of the little girls, bolder than the others, came forward and looked up at me.

'What's your name?'

'My name is John,' I said.

'Mine is Eugenia,' she said gravely, and turned her attention to Rosalind. Soon Eugenia was in Rosalind's arms, playing with her watch, her hair, her necklace.

'Where do you live?'

'I live in London,' Rosalind answered.

'In London. I haven't heard of London.'

A young woman came out of the house. She might have been pretty once, but now she was dirty and her shoes were broken and trodden down. She stood and looked at us. The lawyer asked Dona Catalina something; she put her knuckles to her eyes and started to cry.

'No one will help me now. I have no money. I have nothing. No one will look after my grandchildren.'

She rocked backwards and forwards. This wasn't a show, put on for our benefit in preparation for a little begging; it was a statement of the plainest fact. No government department, no private charity, would do anything to help her. At 56 Dona

Catalina was an old woman, who could expect nothing but destitution for herself and everyone around her. By comparison with this, the deaths of her husband, her sons and her grandson had been quick and easy.

The live wire, Eugenia, skipped about, as unconcerned as a flower in a cemetery. A local school had agreed to take her; none of the other Ventocilla children were being educated now. Sometimes holding my hand, sometimes Rosalind's, she led us into the house. It was desolate, and empty of almost everything now except the barest minimum required to cook a meal, wash and sleep. The rest had been sold to buy food. When that money, and whatever we gave them, was gone, they would have nothing at all.

The interview we filmed with the three women was more painful, I think, than anything else we did during our time in Peru: worse even than the interviews with the women in Tingo Maria, in the Huallaga Valley. With them, we had caught a faint glimpse of what it must be like to be a young wife and find your husband's body, or to lose your son and your husband in a massacre. It was terrible, and it would affect the whole of their future, to their very last days; yet life goes on, even if in sorrow and bitterness.

These three women, sitting side by side in front of me, dressed in black like a chorus from a Greek tragedy, had been utterly destroyed by what had happened to them. They had lost, not just the most important thing, but everything. To the women in Tingo Maria the presence of their children would be a faint recompense. To the women of this cold, barren hillside, the children were merely a further part of the intolerable burden that life had laid on them: more mouths to feed, more responsibility, greater despair about the future.

When I began to question them, they wept. It wasn't because they felt tears were fitting, or because they had suddenly been overcome by a renewed sense of their misfortune; this was the raw emotion that had never left them for a moment since the morning of 24 June. Dona Catalina described what had happened:

'They came at 3 am and took away my sons. Just as I left my room they were taking away the eldest.

'"Where are you taking my son?" I asked. I didn't see where they took him.

'I went back in and they had taken the others. They've all been killed. Now I have nothing.'

One of the daughters-in-law said, 'We hope that we will get justice. That's our hope now.'

I turned back to Dona Catalina. She had talked about the loss of all her sons, and of her grandson; what about her husband – what sort of man was he?

'A decent, good, ordinary kind of man.'

After that, I found it impossible to ask any more questions.

We decided to go down to the centre of Huacho and confront the local prosecutor, the *fiscal*, whose job it was to investigate the murders of the Ventocillas. So far he had come up with no results, and it seemed hardly likely that he would. Rosalind asked the three women if they would be prepared to come with us; they shrugged and agreed. Staying at the house or going down to the centre of town, it was all the same to them.

The children started crying when they heard; they were afraid of being left alone now. Eugenia was sent off to the house of a neighbour who was moderately friendly, to ask her to come over. The children would be calmer if they knew she would be looking after them. Dona Catalina sat on a rock and looked at the ground. Cecilia put her arms round her.

We went down to the *fiscal*'s office, in a small building painted lime green, with bars at the window. A security guard lounged in the doorway: a year before, a bomb had been planted there, and the scars were still visible around the door-frame. The human rights lawyer led the way, speaking briefly to the security man. He looked uneasily at Steve and Matt as they filmed the line of women: the two younger ones first, then Dona Catalina carrying the baby in a shawl on her back, in indian fashion. But he didn't stop us going in.

The busy clacking of elderly typewriters came to a sudden stop. The *fiscal* was sitting at a desk in the front office, the very model of a small-town bureaucrat. He was small and weak-looking, with a bushy head of grey hair, and wore an open-necked white shirt and a long-sleeved grey pullover. On the wall was a picture of Christ holding the world in his hand like an orb.

The *fiscal* must have been appalled to see us there – me, a two-man television crew, Rosalind, the lawyer, the three women. A stronger man might have ordered us out, or demanded to know what right we had to barge into his office. The *fiscal* merely took the papers which the lawyer handed him, and examined them.

'This case is now being dealt with in Lima,' he said.

'How is it possible,' I broke in angrily, 'to spend three months investigating a case where there are clear witnesses, of people who come in uniform and take away several men, and then say "We don't know who did the murders?"'

I expressed it clumsily, but the *fiscal* knew what I meant.

'We went to the barracks in this area,' he replied nervously, fingering the papers in the case, 'and we didn't find anyone who had been arrested. We didn't find anyone responsible.'

'It doesn't sound, frankly, as though very much has been done at all to help these people.'

'That's your opinion. We have acted correctly.'

Beside him, a woman clerk dressed in electric blue with long silver earrings kept her head bowed. This wasn't something a good civil servant should get mixed up in.

I might have had more sympathy with the *fiscal* if he had even gone through the motions: if he had, for instance, taken evidence from the three women as his job required him to do. He had not even done that. Plainly, he guessed who had carried out the murders, but felt it was safer to do nothing.

We went outside into the cobbled street and stood around irresolutely.

'Is that it?' Rosalind asked.

I wasn't sure; it just seemed too soon to leave. Perhaps the police or the Army would turn up. We waited in the sunshine while Steve and Matt got some more pictures. Then from the damaged doorway of his office the *fiscal* appeared. He looked from side to side, and came across the road to where Rosalind and I were standing. In the bright sunlight I could see he hadn't shaved for a couple of days. There were little clusters of pimples round his mouth.

I thought at first that he wanted to complain about the way we had behaved; but he didn't. He looked up and down the street again, then said to us that it was a very difficult case. I did not reply. I could see now that he wanted to tell us something, to explain himself a little, in an effort to persuade us not to be too hard on him. He felt ashamed and guilty. Finally he got to the point.

'The forensic evidence in this case showed that the wounds were made by revolvers, probably fitted with silencers.'

That was all. But the implication was quite clear: we had been reliably informed that the Army's death squads used revolvers fitted with silencers. The *fiscal* knew who had killed the Ventocillas; he just didn't want to do anything about it. Much easier to pass the papers on to Lima and say it was not known who was responsible for the murders. It was quite certain that Lima would take no action about it. This, after all, was a country where no one from the military had ever been found guilty of an offence against human rights.

We drove the three women back up the hill. Eugenia ran out to greet them; the other children stayed quietly behind the fence of branches and watched. Why, I asked the human rights lawyer, had the Ventocillas been murdered? To him, it seemed simple. They were all active union members. There were many large factories in the Huacho area, and the Ventocillas had spoken at a public meeting held in support of demands for better conditions.

'Round here,' he said, 'there's a close link between the big factory owners and the Army.'

'So the factory owners hired the Army to get rid of a problem for them?'

The lawyer bowed his head in agreement.

I looked at the hilltop and the houses with their sun-dried mud bricks, from which everything of the slightest value had been stripped and sold. The younger women were starting to prepare some porridge for the evening meal. The children were helping, or else taking refuge behind Dona Catalina's skirts as she said goodbye to us. Not even the money we left her seemed to make any difference. Her life was now passed in a dull dream of pain, because her sons had once spoken at a union meeting. I remembered that when we arrived I had called this hillside the ruins of someone's life; and that Cecilia had answered: 'The ruins of Peru.'

Lima Airport

If I were asked to put a price on the Peruvian... I would put the figure very high and I would draw the conclusion that he or she ought to be treated with care and kindness, in the interests of the country.

Felipe Guaman Poma de Ayala, 1613

A fter thirty-four days in Peru I was packing my suit-cases for home. There was a knock on the door. It was Rosalind, and she beckoned me out into the corridor. San Ramon had asked her to go and see him urgently.

'Montesinos has found out that we interviewed San Roman,' she said. 'His wife and children have had a pretty explicit death threat, and he's worried.'

I started to say something, but she interrupted.

'There's another thing. I was told it was possible someone would try to plant something on us – drugs, or something like that. Then they'll search us at the airport and find them. That seems to be the plan.'

'What about the documents?'

San Roman had promised us a number of documents which implicated Montesinos and the Fujimori government in cases of murder and drugs-running.

'No. He said he needed to get them together. I'll have to go back there tonight, before we leave for the airport.'

She was keeping very calm about it all, even though she had to do some of the most difficult jobs.

'I could always stay on and come home tomorrow night.' I admired her for saying that, but I couldn't allow it to happen. Once, some months before the Iraqi invasion of Kuwait, I had left Eamonn behind in Baghdad, only to find that the Iraqis would not let him go. I had a clear rule now: no one stayed behind on their own, for whatever reason.

I didn't ask her where the tip-off about the planting of drugs had come from; the fewer people who knew about that kind of thing, the better. Instead, I went back into my room and thought over what I should do. The best defence in these things is usually to be completely open about them; secrecy leaves you vulnerable. I picked up the telephone and rang Eamonn in London. I just wanted him to know, I said, speaking almost at dictation speed for the sake of the people we had been told were listening, that I was glad he had got all our sensitive tapes out of the country. If anything happened to us at the airport – if for instance someone planted something on us – then he should tell the Foreign Office at once.

Enjoying myself by now, I outlined to him in blood-curdling terms the problems the Peruvian government might have if something like this were to take place. I also told him I was seeing the British ambassador to say goodbye that afternoon. Eamonn spoke equally slowly in reply. He would make it known in the right quarters, he said.

I finished packing my bags, after going through them to find two teabags of coca tea which someone had given me. They were perfectly legal, but I flushed them down the lavatory; coca was coca, even in the harmless form of herb tea. Before I left for the British embassy to say my goodbyes, I set a roll of paper against my suitcase at a particular angle. The top of it touched the top of my case at a point which I noted carefully. Then I snipped off a quarter-inch of black thread and laid it near the lock of the case, so I could see if it had been opened. Finally I put the 'do not disturb' sign on the door, and kept my key in my pocket when I left the hotel: feeble enough precautions, but the best I could come up with.

When I got back from the embassy nothing had been touched, but there was more news. The magazine *Oiga*, much less reliable and more sensational than *Caretas*, was running a story that I had paid a million dollars for the video of Guzman's arrest. 'The Englishman did not think twice and accepted the deal,' the article said. It was a wonderful notion: BBC News and Current

Affairs had probably never paid a million dollars for anything in its history, and certainly not for a home video shot by a nervous policeman in a country which was of little interest to most people in Britain. We had acquired the full video for nothing, but we had also been negotiating separately with a nasty little freelance cameraman who had obtained a copy of part of the original, lasting only ninety seconds. He was quoted in the article: it looked as though he were trying to cover something up by making accusations against us.

I rang Sally Bowen and told her about the suggestion that we might have problems at the airport. She immediately offered to come with us, but although I was grateful I said no. She had to carry on working in Lima, and if anything did happen it would be important for her to have as little to do with us as possible. She was busy, anyhow: the sentence on Guzman had just been announced, and she had to file her reports for BBC Radio and the *Financial Times*. I wrote one last script for the BBC World Service Television about it. I added this passage:

> As for President Fujimori, it [the arrest and trial of Guzman] has totally restored his political fortunes; and he has presented the police intelligence organisation with a financial reward for capturing the man whom many newspapers here have called Peru's Public Enemy Number One. There was a distinct coolness about the ceremony, though.

There certainly had been, but I wanted to keep the full details quiet until we returned to London. Our interviewee from the intelligence community had told us that following the arrest of Guzman there had been a meeting about the allocation of a reward of a million dollars, put up by two businessmen. The businessmen themselves had been at the meeting, together with General Vidal and Vladimiro Montesinos. Vidal had refused to accept the money, saying that his work could not be bought in this way. Montesinos lost his temper with Vidal again, but at the end of the meeting a cheque was handed over to DINCOTE; though Montesinos imposed such restrictions on how the money was to be paid out that almost none of the DINCOTE detectives benefited from it.

By now it was evening. Rosalind went off for the last time to San Roman's house, to try to pick up the documents from him. Sally and Rory came round to the hotel to say goodbye. I was sorry to be leaving them: I had come to admire Sally's coolness and enterprise very much.

'Just be careful at the airport,' she said. 'And ring me if you get into any trouble.'

I promised I would.

By the time we had brought down all the gear, Johnny and Rosalind had returned. I could tell directly I saw her that she had got the documents.

'One of them is headed "Murder",' she said, barely able to suppress her excitement.

'I'll keep them in your Marks and Spencer bag,' I said. I was determined to carry the documents myself. There seemed to be rather a lot of them.

As we drove down the familiar road to the airport, past the endless factories, skirting the potholes in the road, I found myself gripping the green plastic bag tighter. I could imagine it all too clearly: the uniformed figure coming forward, the angry discussion, the move to a side office, the opening of the cases. What would happen then was impossible to forecast; but if the authorities persisted, it could be very damaging indeed. The accusation of drug smuggling would stay with me for the rest of my career, and be remembered when the circumstances had long been forgotten. I looked round at Steve, who winked at me. Maybe he guessed a little of what was going through my mind. He and I had once been virtually strip-searched when we left Rumania; we both knew what it was like.

Rosalind and the crew had gone out to choose a ring and some earrings for Cecilia, and we were also giving her the biggest and newest English-Spanish dictionary on the market. I thought about it, then wrote in my bad Spanish on the fly-leaf: 'Para la muchacha muy especial, de los muchachos de la BBC, con admiracion, respect y mucho amor.' Tears came to her eyes when she read it, and she gave me a delightful articulated silver fish, with blue stones for eyes. I put it in my pocket, so I would have it with me when we left.

We sat at a table in the airport bar, drinking pisco sours. I was dreading the moment when we would have to say goodbye almost as much as I dreaded the possibility that we might get stopped and searched. Yet it was relatively easy for us: we were going back to the safety of England, but Cecilia would have to stay. If there were any trouble as a result of our reports, she would have to face it on her own. Still, we all remained cheerful enough as we raised our pisco sour glasses and toasted our next trip to Peru.

Eventually it was time to go through to the departure lounge. Johnny, looking particularly smart in the red down jacket I had given him, waved us goodbye from the barrier. Cecilia, as a grace-note, produced her airport press card, number 0001, and started to talk her way through with us. An underling tried to stop her.

'He very huanca', Cecilia said, affronted, but the chief of airport security knew her and let her through.

We passed through a checkpoint. A uniformed official looked at us very carefully, then walked away. He pulled out a walkie-talkie and said something into it. I held the Marks and Spencer bag tighter than ever. Steve and Matt put their equipment through the X-ray machine, watched by everyone. I waited for the tap on the shoulder. A passenger at the last security point ahead of us was called out of the queue; I could see the startled look on his face. I put the green bag reluctantly on the conveyor belt, and moved round quickly to pick it up at the other end. The screen showed the outline of several dozen sheets of paper, nothing more. The security man said nothing, so I picked up the bag as it came through. The man with the walkie-talkie had wandered off. No one asked to open our luggage. No one looked at the documents about Montesinos. We were not going to be stopped. At the last security check, Cecilia had to stay. Tears were running down her face as she kissed each of us and held on to us.

'Adios, los muchachos,' said Cecilia.

AFTERWORD

Felipe Guaman Poma de Ayala answers
the questions of King Philip III.

Afterword

Some people will argue that my aim has been to discredit those in authority, but rather it has been to protect the Indians. Now, reading my own words, I begin to weep tears and to wonder how God can pardon such wrongs.

Felipe Guaman Poma de Ayala, 1613

I made a foolish mistake when I returned to London: I had to leave for another assignment, a documentary on Iranian influence in Central Asia, before the Peruvian reports into which we had put so much effort were broadcast. The result was unsatisfactory all round. The reports themselves were not as good as they would have been if I had written and recorded the script while the pictures we had brought back were being edited: if you write without seeing the pictures you miss all sorts of nuances. One consequence was that the film we had planned to make on the Ashaninca did not work with the words I had recorded, and had to be scrapped. Another was that a continuous run of five films, from Monday to Friday, proved impractical. In the end we broadcast only four, and the run was interrupted on the Thursday by some insistent piece of domestic political trivia. The documentary I made in Central Asia was not, in the end, a distinguished piece of work. And it helped to get me barred from Iran in the future.

Still, the reports on Peru attracted plenty of attention in Britain and elsewhere, and some people were very kind about them. I received a good many letters as a result, and – best indication of all – several people stopped me in the street to talk about the series. The reports stirred up a certain passion at the Peruvian embassy in London. It sent a diplomat and a rather tough-looking security man round to the House of Commons, where I was invited to talk to a group of MPs about the situation in Peru. Only one MP turned up, but the men from the embassy became very heated. The embassy was unwise enough to put out a press release in bad English, which carelessly misquoted from my reports. No one printed it; they never do. I felt a certain sympathy for the embassy, which must have got into trouble for recommending me to the authorities in Lima. Nevertheless sensible ambassadors who have to represent nasty regimes abroad know that while they have to go through the motions of complaint, they should endeavour to keep a certain balance in private. This particular ambassador behaved like a Fujimori enthusiast. He left London soon after the films went out.

In the months that followed our reports, Abimael Guzman was moved to an even safer prison than before, and constitutional moves began which would enable the government to execute him if it chose; even though the death penalty had not been on the statute books of Peru when he was arrested. Anyone at home or abroad who questioned the ethical basis of this was treated by the Fujimori government as a covert sympathiser with Shining Path. Guzman's followers continued their campaign of bombing and shooting; in the first half of 1993 Shining Path carried out 549 attacks throughout Peru, and 1,106 people died as a result of political violence. This was, nevertheless, a drop of two-thirds compared with the same period in 1992. There was little reason to think that Shining Path had the ability to rescue Guzman. The constitutional shift towards execution seemed therefore like an act of revenge by the Peruvian state for the fright which Guzman had given it; and it did nothing to change the way the outside world regarded President Fujimori's government. The American State Department seemed at first to want to improve its relations with Peru, and planted some peculiarly foolish articles in *The New York Times* and elsewhere which seemed intended to present Mr Fujimori as a regular guy who was succeeding against all the odds. Soon, though, the campaign tailed off; the effort was just too great.

The man who did the state some service by capturing Guzman was, as he had anticipated, pushed to one side. General Vidal was honoured for his work, but in January 1993 he had to leave DINCOTE and moved to the General Inspectorate of the National Police, where his duties included investigating police corruption and dealing with personnel problems. He no longer had anything to do with police operations. DINCOTE remained in the government's disfavour.

Luis Zambrano, who told us in such detail about the Army's involvement in drugs running and human rights abuses in Tocache, is still there at the time of writing. In June 1993 the drugs mafia in the town murdered the new mayor, and Zambrano clearly felt he could be the next victim. Nevertheless he rang Cecilia Valenzuela after the murder and told he was still safe.

Comandante Alfonso, on whom Zambrano gave us such clear evidence, seems to have been transferred as a result. He was shifted from Tocache, where he had made a great deal of money, and sent to the department of Aurimac, in the eastern rainforest. The Ashaninca live in this area, and will no doubt suffer as a result of his arrival. The rumour is that a large part of the drugs mafia is moving in the same direction.

Comandante Roberto, the head of the death squad in Tarapoto, was transferred from the Army base there and given a much better job with the security corps at the presidential palace in Lima. The move implies he had the full confidence of the Army's general command. In May 1993 the Peru Support Group in London organised a visit to the country, and with great courage they included Tarapoto, in the Huallaga Valley, in their itinerary. The team included the Labour MP Ann Clwyd and the Conservative MP David Ashby. Nothing seemed to have changed there, and the disappearances continued.

Ann Java, whom we accompanied to the Tarapoto Army base in the hope of finding out what had happened to her son Mauricio, still visits the place regularly. She continues to believe that her son is alive. Comandate Roberto's successor has promised a new investigation into the case, but the church in Tarapoto believes he is just playing games with her.

Cecilia herself had considerable problems after we left. A long-running legal case, in which a general whom she had named as an offender against human rights in her television programme sued her for defamation, ended with a verdict in the general's favour. Cecilia was sentenced to a year's imprisonment, but this was suspended. Soon afterwards someone delivered a package to her house. It contained a severed chicken head, and a photograph of Cecilia which had been smeared with blood. Later she received an explicit death threat on her portable phone: the purpose seemed to be to show that everything she did was known about. The day before her birthday on 1st May 1993, Gilberto invited a group of friends round to his house for a celebration drink. The doorbell rang, and a bunch of roses was delivered. The note on it said 'You are going to die, you peasant!' and ended with obscenities. It was not enough to silence Cecilia, of course; not long ago, with careful planning and great courage, she and Gilberto managed to track down Vladimiro Montesinos and obtained the first video pictures of him. At a time when Peru seems to be sinking deeper into its elected dictatorship, it was a small but definite blow for openness and civilised standards. One day, when Montesinos and the drugs industry no longer dominate the Peruvian state, those who refused to keep quiet will receive the honour they deserve.

Bibliography

A. The Incas and the Spanish Conquest

Carrillo, Francisco: *Cronistas Indios y Mestizos*, I & II (Editorial Horizonte, 1991)
——: *Literatura Quechua Clasica* (Editorial Horizonte, 1986)
de Diez Caseco, Maria Rostorowski: *Historia del Tahuantinsuyu* (Instituto de Estudios Peruanos, 1988)
Garcilaso de la Vega, Inca: *Comentarios Reales de los Incas* (ed. Carlos Aranibar, Fondo de Cultura Economica, 1991)
Greenblatt, Stephen: *Marvellous Possessions – The Wonder of the New World* (Oxford, 1992)
Guillen, Edmundo: *Vision Peruana de la Conquista* (Editorial Milla Batres, 1979)
Hemming, John: *The Conquest of the Incas* (Penguin, 1983)
Huaman Poma (sic): *Letter to a King*, tr. Christopher Dilke (George Allen & Unwin, 1978)
——: *Nueva Cronica y Buen Gobierno*, ed. Carlos Aranibar (Instituto de Apoyo Agrario & Ediciones Rikchay Peru, 1990)
Mason, J. Alden: *The Ancient Civilizations of Peru* (Penguin, 1991)
Wright, Ronald: *Stolen Continents – The Indian Story* (John Murray, 1992)

B. The Ashaninca

Anderson, Ronald Jaime and others: *Cuentos Folkloricos de los Asheninca*, 3 vols (Instituto Linguistico de Verano, 1985)
Gorriti, Gustavo: 'Terror in the Andes – The Flight of the Ashaninkas' (sic), *New York Times Magazine*, 2.12.1990
Payne, Judith: *Lecciones para el Aprendizaje del Idioma Asheninca* (Instituto Linguistico de Verano, 1988)

C. Peruvian history

The Cambridge Encyclopaedia of Latin America & the Caribbean (CUP, 1965)

Gott, Richard: *Rural Guerrillas in Latin America* (Penguin, 1973)

Harriman, Brenda: *The British in Peru* (Lima, 1984)

Keen, Benjamin & Wasserman, Mark: *A Short History of Latin America* (Houghton Mifflin, 1980)

Williamson, Edwin: *The Penguin History of Latin America* (Penguin, 1992)

D. Shining Path and Contemporary Peru

Brown, Mark Malloch: 'The Consultant', *Granta*, Summer 1991

Gonzalo, Chairman: *On the Rectification Campaign* (Central Committee of the Communist Party of Peru, 1991)

Arce, Luis & Talavera, Janet: 'Presidente Gonzalo rompe el silencio', *El Diario* (Lima), 24.7.88

Degregori, Carlos Ivan: *Sendero Luminoso* (IEP, 1989)

Degregori, Carlos Ivan: *El Surgimiento de Sendero Luminoso* (IEP, 1990)

————: *Que Dificil Es Ser Dios* (El Zorro de Abajo Ediciones, 1990)

McCormick, Gordon H.: *The Shining Path and the Future of Peru* (RAND Corporation, 1990)

Palmer, David Scott, ed.: *Shining Path of Peru* (Hurst & Co, 1992)

Poole, Deborah & Renique, Gerardo: *Peru – Time of Fear* (Latin America Bureau, 1992)

Report on the America, Vol XXIV No. 4

Shakespeare, Nicholas: 'In Pursuit of Guzman', *Granta*, Spring 1985

Strong, Simon: *Shining Path – The World's Deadliest Revolutionary Force* (HarperCollins, 1992)

Tarazona-Sevillano, Gabriela & Reuter, John B.: *Sendero Luminoso and the Threat of Narcoterrorism* (Center for Strategic & International Studies, 1990)

Vargas Llosa, Alvaro: 'The Press Officer', *Granta*, Summer 1991

Vargas Llosa, Mario: 'A Fish Out Of Water', *Granta*, Summer 1991

Index